FEVER

LITTLE WILLIE JOHN

A Fast Life, Mysterious Death and the Birth of Soul

FEVER

LITTLE WILLIE JOHN

A Fast Life, Mysterious Death and the Birth of Soul

THE AUTHORIZED BIOGRAPHY

SUSAN WHITALL

WITH KEVIN JOHN

TITAN BOOKS

Fever: Little Willie John's Fast Life, Mysterious Death and the Birth of Soul
Print edition ISBN: 9780857681379
E-book edition ISBN: 9780857687968

Published by
Titan Books
A division of Titan Publishing Group Ltd.
144 Southwark St.
London, SE1 0UP

First edition: June, 2011
1 3 5 7 9 10 8 6 4 2

Edited by Nadine Käthe Monem

Front cover © 2011, Frank Driggs Collection/Getty Images

"Blue Wing" used by permission of Hal Leonard Corporation
"Fever," "Talk To Me, Talk To Me," "Walk Slow," all used by permission of Fort Knox Music, Inc. and
Hal Leonard Corporation
"The Hucklebuck" used by permission of Bienstock Publishing Company and Hal Leonard Corporation
"Nobody Knows You When You're Down and Out," written by Jimmy Cox

Did you enjoy this book? We love to hear from our readers. Please e-mail us at:
readerfeedback@titanemail.com or write to Reader Feedback at the above address.
To receive advance information, news, competitions, and exclusive offers online, please sign
up for the Titan newsletter on our website: www.titanbooks.com

A CIP catalogue record for this title is available from the British Library.

Printed in the United States

FEVER
TABLE OF CONTENTS

"Willie John was a singer's singer. There is no deeper blues than his–and only his–"I Need Your Love So Bad," there is no rock 'n' roll quite like his "All Around the World," there is no ballad performance as simultaneously easy, swinging and erotic as his–and only his–Fever." He could kill you with a George Jones song. He sang like he owed nothing to anybody and the world might forget but he never would. His voice isn't the voice of a lot of people's hearts, I guess, but it's the voice of a few of us. We're the fortunate ones."

– Dave Marsh

I'd like to dedicate this book to the memory of my father, William Edward John, professionally known as 'Little Willie John.' Many things have been said and written about my father over the years. I believe he would be happy to see that we finally set the record straight. And also to my mother; without her consent and approval I would have not embarked on such a project. I love you, Mom!

I'd like to thank my brother, Keith and my wife, Cathy, for their special and unique contributions to this book, and my two sons, Kevin II and Keith—this is your story too, it's part of your heritage, your roots! On behalf of the entire John family, I thank Ms Susan Whitall, for her vision, professionalism and great patience. Susan, it's been a pleasure and a learning experience working closely with you. Finally, a special thanks to Mr Clarence Avant, a man who did not forget his old friend, and who continues to speak well of him more than 40 years later.

As a young man, I had four wishes regarding my father's musical legacy. Firstly, I wanted my father to be recognized and inducted into the Rock and Roll Hall of Fame. Secondly, I wanted my father's final recordings to be released and made available to those who appreciate his talent and love his music. Next, I wanted to be part of a book project that would accurately and tastefully tell the interesting and poignant story of my father's life and music. Finally, it was my hope that his story would be the subject of a motion picture. The first three of these four wishes have now come true. It is my hope that the fourth will also become a reality.

—William Kevin John

FOREWORD

BY STEVIE WONDER

My first time hearing Little Willie John, I must have been seven or eight years old, at the most maybe nine. It was amazing. I remember listening on the radio and hearing, *"If I don't love you baby, grits ain't groceries…"* They said he was a young boy from Detroit and how talented he was, that he was going to be performing at the Fox Theater. I was really excited about his voice and what he was able to do with it. He was unique—the fact that he was able to sing high, that he was able to do the riffs that he did.

There was a DJ in Detroit who would always play his music, all the time; his name was Ernie Durham and he was on a station called WJLB. Back then they would play a song, and if they liked it, they would play it over and over. Willie's songs would play, and Ernie would say *"Whoo ooo eee!"*

Growing up singing as a little boy, everybody who was a singer would try to copy or do a better riff than the next person, similar to how rappers do snapping today. Singers would sing in the backyards or wherever, there would be competition on who could do the riffs. Willie and Jackie Wilson were the ones everyone would listen to for the riffs. They'd say, "Wow, you've gotta hear this riff, LWJ did this riff!" "Well Jackie Wilson did that riff, yeah, but Little Willie John did *this riff here*!"

You can hear Little Willie John when you hear Usher. You can hear him doing those riffs sometimes, the kind that Willie would have done. What makes a singer unique and long lasting, at the end of the day, is if they are able to sing a riff to any chord progression and it makes sense. You've got to also know how to do it tastefully. Some people over-sing, you say, "OK, can you get back to the melody?" Willie had a way of singing the song, going out but coming back, similar to great jazz musicians like Miles Davis or Coltrane. There has to be a place where it's melodic enough without becoming boring.

I think the person who was most inspired by Little Willie John is his son. It is an honor that I've been blessed to have the son of such a great singer be a part of my career—my life, my group—and it's just amazing how God works that he would allow that to happen, that Keith would come into my life through someone who was a big fan of Little Willie John's, Charlie Collins. Meeting Keith and Kevin John, I saw how their appreciation for their father didn't limit them in having their own uniqueness.

You hear his influence in lots of people who sing today. It's impossible for people to talk about rhythm & blues and talk about singers and not mention the voice and talent of Little Willie John as being one of those great people.

PROLOGUE:
IN SEARCH OF LITTLE WILLIE JOHN

Every few years someone comes up with 'the last untold story' in popular music. I won't say Little Willie John's story is the last, but it is one of the more unfortunate omissions from the annals of American rhythm & blues history.

Over the decades, Willie's life and career have been boiled down to a shallow, sordid haiku: Great talent, a violent assault in Seattle, prison and then death. Sketchy details that do nothing to explain who he was, where he came from or why he sounded the way he did. I've always loved Willie's voice, from when I was a child growing up in Philadelphia and I first heard "Sleep" playing on WFIL. I had no idea who he was, or that his voice and his story would tug at me so many years later.

In my early 20s, I was on staff at Detroit's *Creem* magazine, while it was mostly riding the mid 1970s wave of rock, punk and metal. I was always drawn to rhythm & blues, the music that made rock 'n' roll possible, and was equally fascinated by how integral the Detroit scene was to it all. When I left *Creem* for the *Detroit News* in the early 1980s, I was able to dig even deeper into the city's musical history, and I had the privilege of interviewing many of the singers and musicians who helped put Detroit on the map. In talking to Joe Messina, Joe Hunter and Uriel Jones—members of Motown's studio band, the Funk Brothers— the discussion would inevitably return to their early days on the Detroit club scene, painting a fascinating picture of how the city's jazz and rhythm & blues scenes intersected and influenced one another.

Right in the middle of it all was this largely forgotten singer, the brash kid who jumped onstage with Count Basie and the big bands, became Detroit's first massively popular solo rhythm & blues star, and laid the groundwork for the singers and groups of the Motown and soul-dominated 1960s.

He died so long ago, in the spring of 1968, barely 30 years old. But in the world of rhythm & blues, Willie is like the mystical dark matter that astrophysicists search for; an essential but unknown link that seems to hold the universe together. If Willie hadn't lived for those fleeting three decades, we would have had to invent him to explain how rhythm & blues segued into soul. When I interviewed Willie's sister, Mable John, in 1995 for my book, *Women of Motown,* and she described the friendly, competitive relationship between Willie and Berry Gordy, I was even more intrigued. The diminutive rhythm & blues genius, usually laughing in those grainy black and white photographs, always eluded definition. I wanted to know more, but filed it away for "someday."

One day, out of the blue, Willie's son Kevin contacted me. He wanted to thank me for mentioning his dad briefly in a story for *The Detroit News*, but he also wanted to talk about Willie's music. A month or so later, I was at the Rock and Roll Hall of Fame in Cleveland with the Funk Brothers when I happened to run into Kevin. He asked if I was interested in writing a book about his father. Interested? I was mesmerized.

Part of the mystery with Willie is that so many of us never got to see him live, or even on tape or film. Although he appeared countless times on local Detroit television, and on *American Bandstand* three times, *The Tonight Show* (with Jack Paar), and every other regional music show there was at the time, we only have one clip of Willie in motion. He isn't singing, alas, but whacking claves, a percussion instrument, in a scene on the hip early 1960s TV series, *Route 66*. It's a tantalizingly short, but poignant clip. The way Willie nods his head while playing the claves is exactly the way his sons and grandsons move. "The John head nod," Kevin called it.

One way I did get closer to Willie was getting to know his family, especially Kevin, who provided a wealth of family stories, letters and photos and helped to set up and conduct interviews. Kevin, who gave up a career in music to raise a family in Detroit and pursue his religious interests, introduced me to his mother, Willie's widow Darlynn, as well as his brother Keith, a singer, songwriter, backup vocalist for Stevie Wonder, and producer in his own right. Darlynn once told me, if I wanted to experience what it was like to be around

Willie John, I should sit between Kevin and Keith and I'd get a stereo version. Kevin resembles his father, and both he and Keith are constantly singing, joking and generally exuding the hyperkinetic male "John" energy.

There was a lot of joy in the stories Willie's family and friends told in the time we spent together, but there was also a lot of pain. Darlynn had never spoken about much of these events outside of the family circle. It is only because her son Kevin so badly wanted for his father's story to be told did Darlynn overcome the distress of remembering Willie's final years, and open up with stories that had been buried for a lifetime. I am so grateful that she did. We don't shy away from Willie's sad final days here, but we also celebrate the tremendous talent that makes his story relevant and vital all these years later, hopefully capturing Willie in all of his multi-dimensional human complexity.

Susan Whitall
2011

Anyone with information about Willie, photographs or video, please contact Susan Whitall or Kevin John at editorial@titanemail.com

1

MAMA WAS A GENIUS

Lying in the dark of the bedroom he shared with his brothers Ernest and Raymond, Willie John would dream out loud. He would be a famous singer one day. Onstage at the mic, he was dressed in a knife-sharp, double-breasted suit, his hair plumped up in a fresh process. In those whispered dreams, he sang in front of Duke Ellington's band and partied with Sugar Ray Robinson. He drove a leaf-green Cadillac home to a sunlit, stucco house with lemon trees in the backyard.

"It all came true," said brother Raymond. "Everything he said."

The boys lived in a project in the north end of Detroit, a flimsy, one-story house thrown up for the workers during the Second World War. Seven John siblings were crammed into the tiny place with their parents, Mertis and Lillie. But they felt safe there, in a project set aside for blacks in postwar, segregated Detroit.

Mertis and Lillie John brought their children from Arkansas to Detroit in 1941, part of the second Great Migration from the South that drew blacks and Appalachian whites to the arsenal of democracy. Factories were thrumming 24 hours a day making tanks, Jeeps and bombers to vanquish the Nazis–and there was work to be had.

The first Great Migration, between 1910 and 1930, saw Detroit's population explode from 465,766 to 1.5 million in 20 years. Many of those on the human highway streaming into the city were Southern blacks seeking jobs and an escape from the hardship and dangers that loomed below the Mason–Dixon line. In 1910, Detroit's black population figured 5,741 people. By 1940, it had grown to 149,119. When America entered the Second World War, Detroit needed a lot of muscle to keep the factories in full roar, that need spurred on a second influx from the South, and by 1950 there were more than 300,500 blacks in the city. Although they were mostly doing jobs nobody else wanted to do, the pay gap between blacks and whites wasn't as large as it was in the South. Mertis John knew that, and he also knew that a dirty job in a Detroit foundry beat the Arkansas paper mill any day.

Both the Robinsons, Willie John's maternal relatives, and the Johns were originally from Louisiana. There isn't much information to be had about the Johns, but we do know that Lillie's parents, Edward and Rebecca James Robinson, were farmers in the town of Angie, about 60 miles from New Orleans. They had five children: Olivia, Eula, Lillie, Andy and Clyde. Like many Southern families, the Robinsons were a mix of black, white and Native American stock. They were a musical family, hosting Friday night fish fries in Angie, where neighbors, aunts, uncles and cousins would ride over on horseback to play music, drink homemade whiskey and sing songs together.

In later years, both Willie and his sister Mable told of how their mother, Lillie, would sneak out as a girl to sing in New Orleans' nightclubs. In Willie's telling (always the most dazzling account) Lillie sang with Louis Armstrong, no less. Whomever she was with, singing in nightclubs was forbidden, and Lillie knew it. She gave up all thought of a singing career when, in early 1930, she married Mertis John, who worked in the local paper mill steering logs into the grind.

Their first child, Mable, was born in Bastrop, Louisiana that November. When Mable was still an infant, the family moved to Arkansas, where Mertis found a job at a larger paper mill in Cullendale, doing the same thing he did in Louisiana. In 1932, Lillie gave birth to Mertis Jr, she had Haywood in the following year and Mildred a couple of years after that. On November 15th, 1937, William Edward John was born, named after each of his grandfathers. The family called him William or Edward, although after he rose to fame, they called him 'Willie' along with the rest of the world. His brothers would sometimes call him 'Fever' behind his back, but to his mother, he would always be Edward. The birth of Delores John followed a couple of years after Willie's, in 1939, and Ernest (or EJ) was the last John born in Arkansas, in 1941.

When the Johns arrived in Detroit in 1941, the sidewalks were teeming with shift workers and the sky choked with factory smoke. At night, the workers headed for the bars, and the sound of jazz and blues could be heard from every corner. The Southern blacks and whites who flocked to Detroit for work brought their music with them, making for an intriguing blend of blues and country music in adjoining neighborhoods, in the clubs and on the radio. Lillie never touched alcohol, but her husband enjoyed a drink every now and then. Both could play guitar, and Mertis Sr could imitate any instrument using pots, pans and whatever else was handy. He could also impersonate any singer around, to the delight of his children.

Prohibition started in 1917 in Michigan, two years before the Eighteenth Amendment was nationally ratified, banning the manufacture, sale and distribution of alcohol. Fortunately for some, Detroit was just a short boat ride away from Canada and its legal whiskey, so the booze was "imported" to the Motor City's nightclubs, bars, saloons and beer gardens. Most of them offered live music in order to keep patrons out longer, drinking more of the whiskey supplied by the Purple Gang—the tough Jewish gang members from Detroit's east side who manufactured and distributed bootleg hooch to much of the Midwest. After the Eighteenth Amendment was repealed in 1933 and beer, wine and liquor flowed legally again, the clubs were shorn of the lawless 'blind pig' tag (the name Detroiters still use for a club serving liquor illegally, referring to the fact that the police would often look the other way—making for a 'blind pig,' as it were). The innumerable watering holes all over metro Detroit served as the infrastructure for a thriving jazz and rhythm & blues music scene in the 1940s and 50s.

The city's exploding black population also meant a sharp growth in the number of black churches, a proving ground for singers, gospel quartets and choirs. Detroit became a major stop on the gospel circuit, and ministers like the Reverend C.L. Franklin, Aretha's father, would host visiting gospel stars like the Dixie Hummingbirds and the Soul Stirrers featuring Sam Cooke.

In 1941, Mertis John installed his family in a cramped apartment at 2120 Monroe Street near the Eastern Market, the distribution hub for Detroit's food supply. The John children liked Monroe Street, Mertis Jr remembered how truck drivers would call them across the street to pick up candy from "broken" boxes. But his parents wanted something better. Several years and several moves later, with Mertis Sr working at the Dodge Main assembly line in Hamtramck, the family moved into 14503 Dequindre, a project just south of Six Mile Road in northeast Detroit. Originally built as temporary housing for wartime factory workers, by the mid 1940s, the area was set aside for Detroit's black population.

There were painfully few housing options for families like the Johns, most were crowded into a few neighborhoods on the east side, around Hastings Street. Detroit was strictly segregated throughout the 1940s, and overcrowding fueled by the wartime boom in factory work caused simmering resentments both in the raggedy east side neighborhoods where blacks were forced to live, and on the city's west side avenues, canopied with lush Dutch elm and oak trees. There weren't enough apartments or houses for white factory workers, much less for blacks barred from those neighborhoods by restrictive covenants.

In this overheating melting pot, it was a step up for the Johns to have their own place. The project houses were basically drywall slapped up into square boxes, with walls so thin everybody called it 'Cardboard Valley.' On hot summer nights, families escaped their sweltering houses to spread blankets on the grass and sleep under the stars, undeterred by the lights and grinding noises coming from the nearby Vlasic pickle factory. Despite the cramped and sometimes crumbling conditions, the neighborhood felt safe enough for residents to leave their doors unlocked, and allow their children to run the streets, and in and out of neighbors' houses.

Daisy Stubbs and her family lived across Dequindre on the project's west side. Daisy was a frequent visitor to the Johns' kitchen, where she would drink coffee and catch up on news. Her son Levi, known as 'Lee' in the neighborhood, hit it off with Willie John, who was a year younger. It was hard not to hit it off with Willie, he was a lively, charming boy, a spinning bundle of energy with nerves always close to the surface. That nervousness was sometimes aggravated by an occasional epileptic seizure, usually brought on by fatigue or stress. The Johns didn't talk much about Willie's seizures, reflecting a common shame associated with epilepsy in the 1940s and 50s. Some of his siblings believe he was prescribed phenobarbital, but older brother Mertis Jr doesn't recall epilepsy being a major problem in Willie's childhood. It was only later, when he was a touring musician, that the seizures would become a problem, particularly if he wasn't eating well or if he was drinking too much and taking too many drugs.

Despite having to cook, clean and look after such a large brood, Lillie, known to all as 'Mother Dear,' was on top of things. Fifty years later, EJ and Raymond still talked about how their mother could drain a cheap can of butter beans, rinse the beans with water and cook them in butter, producing a kind of ambrosia the boys almost preferred to a steak dinner. "Mama was a genius," Raymond said. Years later, Willie would insist that his wife make beans the same way.

There was always something to eat in Lillie's icebox, usually beans and greens. "A lot of us was in that house, and she would look out for me just like she looked out for one of her sons," said Mack Rice, who lived in the neighborhood. A who's who of Detroit music history grew up in the north end, among them Smokey Robinson, Aretha Franklin, Bettye LaVette, Lamont Dozier and Jackie Wilson. "Everybody was your cousin," Rice said. "If you had met Jackie Wilson back in the day, you would have been his cousin, too!"

Just as her mother's house in Louisiana was immaculate, so was Lillie's house in Detroit. "You could do surgery in this woman's house," said Harry Balk, Willie's first manager. "The furniture wasn't new, but it was so clean. And here's people who lived, not in the ghetto, but close by it. If ever there was an angel on earth, it was Mother Dear."

If he wasn't sleeping or eating, Willie was outside. He often darted across busy Dequindre to visit Levi Stubbs and another friend, Stanley Lee. In the summer, the three boys would crawl through the fence just south of the project and sneak into the reservoir built by auto magnate Henry Ford for a swim. Willie was always hustling. In the 1940s, with the factories running all day and night, an energetic kid could make money all over town. Despite the long hours, Mertis Sr worked at Dodge Main, with a brood of seven (then eight, then nine) children to feed, there wasn't much money left over for luxuries. But Willie's pockets always jingled, to the amazement of younger brother EJ. A Coca-Cola cost a whole nickel, and those nickels came quickly.

Willie showed his little brother how to shine a man's shoes in the 30 seconds it took to ride the escalator to the second floor at the Woodward Avenue Sears store. Older brother Mertis Jr delivered the afternoon *Detroit News*, while Willie threw the morning *Free Press*. Even baseball was a money-making opportunity. Jackie Robinson had not yet integrated major league baseball as the first black player, and he often played at the Negro League's Dequindre Park, home of the Negro League Detroit Stars and just a short walk down the street from

Cardboard Valley. During games, Willie and his friends hovered outside the ballpark, waiting for a home run ball to come flying over the wall, so they could pick it up and sell it back to the team for a dollar.

Willie and the boys spent their nickels and dimes at the corner store on Six Mile Road. The boys would wander west on Six Mile down to Palmer Park, where they could watch the tennis players and check out the horse-drawn carriages taking leisurely rides around the park.

Both Lillie and Mertis John were devoutly religious, although Lillie was the more faithful churchgoer. In Louisiana, she grew up going to Mary's Chapel, a United Methodist church. In Detroit, the Johns attended several different Holiness churches, including the Triumph Church on South Liddesdale. Lillie sang gospel songs around the house, teaching her children the words. "But she didn't teach Willie how to sing," his brother EJ said. "Nobody did."

In the end, Willie's voice was the easiest hustle. He had a sensuous, eerily mature voice full of depth and nuance—"a blessing from God," his mother called it. It came bursting out of his skinny chest as if it was the most natural thing in the world. Willie could sing anything, even the hillbilly music he heard on the radio. "He was always singing," said EJ. Four years younger than Willie, EJ was almost exactly the same size as his big brother, but he was as quiet as Willie was gregarious.

For Willie to stand out as outgoing in the John family took some doing. Mable, as the oldest sister, was used to taking charge and issuing instructions. Petite and well-groomed, she had most things figured out, and a good few opinions that needed to be aired. Mable showed brother Mertis Jr how to slow-dance in one easy lesson, and taught him how to type as well. She managed an introduction to Mrs Bertha Gordy of the energetic, enterprising Gordy family—with business interests in printing, construction and retail. Mable could see that the Gordys were going places, and she apprenticed herself to the matriarch of the family, helping with typing, answering the phone and selling insurance door to door. When Mrs Gordy discovered Mable's interest in music, she introduced the girl to her son Berry, an aspiring songwriter.

Mertis Jr wasn't lazing around, either. In high school he worked at a car wash, then started night shifts at the Dodge Main factory where his father worked, while still going to his high school classes during the day. "I made a living," Mertis said. "I bought my books, my clothes. I bought a car in my own name.

And I was nothing but a kid."

Willie wasn't about to go into the factory. He was interested in music, sports and girls. EJ remembers even a walk with his brother would usually end up with Willie singing, and a couple of ragtag neighborhood kids following them around enjoying the tunes. Once Willie had made the connection between music and money, his path in life became clear. He entertained customers at the candy store in exchange for treats, and Mertis Jr once found his diminutive brother standing in the middle of a crowd on the sidewalk, singing his heart out as people tossed nickels and dimes his way.

It helped that Willie was a charmer, his small face set off by large, expressive eyes and powered by a ferocious bravado. One summer day in the mid 1940s, Willie, Levi Stubbs and some friends were deploying one of their favorite hustles. Willie knocked on a neighbor's door while the other boys headed to the backyard. When a woman answered, Willie flashed his most endearing smile and asked the lady of the house if she wanted to hear a song. Hearing no objection, Willie broke into a hymn, pouring his heart into every note. The neighbor went to get her purse, while out back, Levi and the boys were picking her cherry tree clean.

Willie's schooldays started with a bang. On the first day of school, when his teacher at Duffield Elementary asked him to do something he didn't want to do, Willie threatened to set his big brother, Mertis Jr, on her. In the 1940s, Detroit's public school teachers were allowed to use discipline, and that teacher wasted no time in locking Willie in a closet so he couldn't make good on this threat. Mertis Sr worked the afternoon shift, so he had to be awakened from his daytime nap to go pick up his mischievous son. A whipping followed when they got home. "An unforgettable one," according to brother Mertis.

Another time, Willie swiped a pair of glasses from a near-sighted girl in his class. He wore the glasses home, claiming that he'd failed the school eye test. Mertis continued to question his son, and wasn't buying the answers he was getting. Sure enough, that evening Duffield's principal came by the house to inquire after the missing glasses, only to find Willie wearing them. Surely now, a world-class whipping was on the horizon, his siblings thought. Instead, Mertis got a large burlap sack, put his small son into it and hung the bag from a door. There Willie would stay, his father said, until he confessed and apologized. Willie didn't cry, and he wouldn't say he was sorry either. Instead, for hours the boy prayed and asked God to bless both his mother and father. He sang every gospel song he knew, at full volume. Willie wasn't relenting, but neither was his father. Finally, two hours into the ordeal, Lillie begged her husband to take the boy down from the door and set him free.

Levi Stubbs and Willie were running the streets of the north end, both out of sight of their loving but overwhelmed mothers. Long summer days with no supervision stretched ahead of them. They both ended up in minor juvenile trouble, doing brief stints at the Moore School at the corner of Hague and Oakland, where the Detroit public school system sent its disciplinary problems. Willie was in the eighth grade at Cleveland Jr High School when he was caught in a compromising position with a girl on school property. He spent a year at Moore, between 1951 and 1952, moving on to Pershing High School once he'd done his time. Young Willie wasn't the only kid who ended up at Moore and moved onto better things; Uriel Jones (of Motown's Funk Brothers), Norman Thrasher of the Midnighters, and Lamont Dozier were just a few of the many Detroit musicians who were sentenced to a stint at Moore. Thrasher, four years older than Willie, was just getting out when Willie was coming in. "We were mischievous in regular school, acting up. Using bad language. So they sent us to Moore school, where there was zero tolerance," Thrasher said.

Fortunately for the wayward boys who later became music men, a teacher at Moore managed to get through to them with both music and discipline. "Mr Irvin," Thrasher said. "We had a glee club and we sang all over the state, under the direction of Mr Irvin. And he would talk to each one of us like a father, trying to keep us out of all difficulties when it comes to life and young girls. He had horror stories that made us not want to see *any* young girls when we came of age." Uriel Jones was only half-joking when he credited the teacher with diverting him from a life of crime.

Later, Willie told of being deputy choir director under Mr Irvin. It wasn't Willie's first experience of music instruction, of course. He was taught breath control and enunciation by his Detroit Public School music teachers, which served him well in later years when he stood in front of a swing orchestra, expected to sound like a man of the world, or when he was singing the most low-down blues, sounding like a man of experience. Willie also took private singing lessons at the Detroit Conservatory of Music on the Wayne University campus, west of Woodward. "I wanted to be more than just a singer," Willie said. He was singing classical and opera. "My earliest ambition was to be another Paul Robeson or even Caruso. When my money gave out, I gave up classical music and stopped studying it. We were poor people."

In 2006, after Levi Stubbs had suffered several strokes and retired from the Four Tops' touring schedule, Darlynn John and Willie's sons Kevin and Keith visited him at his Detroit home. Darlynn and Clineice Stubbs had maintained close ties over the years, brought together by their husbands' friendship, but also their common background as dancers married to singers.

Levi still exuded the presence and charisma of the born lead singer as he sat, immaculately dressed, in the Stubbs' serene living room overlooking a golf course fairway. He spoke haltingly, but, prompted (and translated) by his doting family, he was able to communicate and answer questions. His words were emotional and heartfelt. At times he laughed until he cried, especially when Keith John, clowning around, got down on his knees, pretending to be Willie, and sang, or when the John brothers would vocalize on a Four Tops song to tease him.

"I just loved him," Levi said of Willie. What he most admired about his vocal talent was that while improvising, off on a dazzling, horn-like solo, Willie would never get "caught up," never lose his place. "He was just a great singer. He could sing anything," Levi said. What was his favorite song of Willie's? "All of them!" he said, laughing.

When conversation turned to Willie's stint at the Moore School, Levi blurted out, "I went to Moore School! Yep…"

"But weren't you the good boy, while Willie was bad?" Kevin John said.

"That's what EJ always said." Levi just smiled.

Phil Townsend knew better, he grew up with both Levi and Willie. "We were *all* rascals."

2

NO BLUES IN THIS HOUSE

By the 1950s, jazz had become an esoteric, uptown sort of music. It was the blues that percolated through the black neighborhoods, outselling jazz records by a fair measure, much to the chagrin of record store owner Berry Gordy Jr. His 3-D Record Mart went under in the early 1950s because Gordy had overestimated the city's demand for jazz, and underestimated their love for the blues. It was a lesson the budding entrepreneur never forgot—later, at Motown, he produced pop music teenagers loved, not the jazz or blues he would have preferred.

The blues were not yet constricted by sub-genre classifications such as Chicago blues, or electric guitar rock infused with blues, or folk-blues sung by geezers in denim overalls. In the 1940s and 50s people said "the blues" when talking about rhythm & blues, jump blues—anything with a pulse. In the black community, people would dress up in their best clothes and go out to dance in the evenings, it was a vital part of life.

Lillie John loved the blues, but her mother wouldn't let her sing that way when she was growing up in Louisiana. When she became the matriarch of her own home, Lillie John enforced the same musical decorum that she knew growing up: no blues. She did make one exception, though. On the day she married Mertis John, Lillie sang him a love song. Then Lillie put the blues away for good. "She just carried it in her heart," daughter Mable said. "She loved the sound of the blues."

Growing up, Willie John heard the blues. He sang the blues. But it took B.B. King to bring the blues back into the John house. During the early 1950s, the record bus would come to Cardboard Valley from time to time. The bus was fitted out with a record player, speakers and boxes of brittle shellac 78s, driving through the neighborhoods of Detroit, broadcasting the hits of the day to entice residents to buy records. If the music peddlers were lucky, they'd get someone happy enough—and flush enough—to buy a record player, too.

The record bus was driving through the north end one day in 1953, playing B.B. King's bluesy ballad "Darlin' You Know I Love You." When Lillie John heard B.B. King crooning to his darling, "She told my father that she heard this song that identified exactly how she felt about him," Mable said. "My father, like all men, was so proud, thinking, 'My wife hears a song that identifies me to her.' So my father went out to that bus and bought that record. We didn't have anything to play it on, so he bought the Victrola too, and that was the first blues song that ever came into our home." Well, that was the first blues song that officially came into the John home, anyway. Unofficially, Willie and his siblings tuned the radio to blues, pop, jazz and country when their parents were out of earshot, and sang softly in their beds at night. Or they'd take a short bus ride to Joe's Record Shop down on Hastings, to hear the latest records blasting from the loudspeakers.

Though she was strict, Lillie didn't object to her children's passion for music. She started her brood singing at the Triumph Church in the early 1940s, gradually adding each child as they became old enough to perform. Brother Mertis describes the sequence of events: "First we started doing Bible things. We had a little thing where our pastor would ask us biblical questions. Then I began to sing, then Mable. Mable liked to talk a lot, she kept doing her talking thing. The next child came along and we were singing together. Then the next one came, she added him. The next one came, she added him. Then Willie came, she added him. We would go from church to church, singing."

In 1944, when six year-old Willie pestered his way into the family troupe, Lillie named them the United Five. It was here that Willie found his voice, singing church songs to the rumble of the Hammond organ, answered by the cries of the congregation with their paper fans fluttering in the swelter of the Detroit summertime. Willie would close his eyes and sing "Jesus Met The Woman at the Well," as the women in the front row threw hats and money at him, crying, "Sing, son!" And Willie sang, *"He said woman, woman. . .where is your husband?"* with his eyes closed, as if in a trance. At the end of the song he was still so engrossed in the music that Willie's impatient siblings would have to pinch him and yank him by the arm when it was time to leave. Singing like that, eliciting such riotous behavior in church ladies, unleashed Willie's passion for song. As Willie said, "I've been singing ever since—morning, noon and night."

The United Five didn't just sing at Lillie's home church, but at churches all over the east side. They sang on programs with the Dixie Hummingbirds, the Mighty Clouds of Joy and with Sam Cooke, when he was leading the Soul Stirrers. "And we were kids!" Mable said. "But Willie was so in tune and so addicted to music, the blues. . . and he could learn songs so fast." A church friend of Lillie's, Laura Pickens, convinced Lillie and Mertis Sr that she could open doors in the music business for their children, and she started promoting the group. Pickens took the kids to watch Sugar Chile Robinson and learn from the piano-pounding seven year-old who had a national hit with "Numbers Boogie." She also booked the United Five into Detroit's most exclusive hotel, the Book Cadillac.

"Black people could not go in that hotel, I'll tell you, but they wanted the John family in the hotel," Mertis Jr said. "So we went to sing there." Willie said that it was 1948 when his family sang at the Book Cadillac, which means he was just ten or 11 years old.

Despite the early demand for Willie's voice, gospel couldn't contain the young singer, though the spirit and intensity of church music would always be part of the primal DNA of his voice. No matter how Lillie tried, she couldn't control what her children heard on the radio, or what they were exposed to while they were running on the streets. "I heard Charlie Parker when I was eight," EJ bragged. Like his brother, Willie would have been exposed to the cool, modern sound of bebop jazz that mingled with the more popular blues in the neighborhoods.

The Paradise Theater on Woodward was where the top tier of black jazz artists played in the 1940s. The theatre was home to the Detroit Symphony and called Orchestra Hall until 1941 when the symphony moved on to a new home. The venue was repurposed and renamed after Paradise Valley, the black entertainment district east of Woodward. For years, the Paradise Theater was where black Detroiters—and music-loving whites—went to see the best in black entertainment. Duke Ellington, Dizzy Gillespie and Count Basie played week long engagements at the Paradise to packed audiences. Just as popular were the

Thursday amateur nights. "All the like-to-bes and want-to-bes, as singers and performers, they would allow them to sing," Mable recalled.

Willie knew he had to be there. He wasn't old enough, but that wasn't going to stop him. At home, his brothers would watch as Willie worked the crossword puzzle in the newspaper, then turned to the entertainment ads to see who was in town. "He'd use that to plan where he'd sneak out and go that night," said Raymond. Maybe it would be Count Basie at the Paradise Theater, or Paul Williams at the Warfield Theater on Hastings—whoever it was, Willie meant to go see them perform.

Hastings Street was Detroit's avenue of sin, with its hookers and grifters, and the smoky jazz drifting out of nightclubs like the Club Three Sixes and Sportree's. The smell of beef sizzling on the grill at Tip Top Hamburgers was as alluring as Della Reese's dusky alto crooning "In the Still of the Night" from the jukebox. It was all too tempting for Willie. Hastings Street and all it had to offer was a bit far to walk from Cardboard Valley, but Willie had already gamed that. He learned from watching a blind friend that if the conductors were convinced he was sightless, he could ride the DSR buses for free.

"All the bad people lived on the east side," Berry Gordy Jr once remarked. Good and bad lived on adjacent corners, at least. Aretha Franklin's father's church, The New Bethel Baptist Church, was in a converted bowling alley on Hastings, just steps away from the hustlers and ladies of the evening. Singer Wilson Pickett's father's house backed up on to Hastings, and Pickett remembers looking out of his father's backyard onto the strip, shivering at the thought of it decades later. "It was a dangerous place," Pickett said.

Nonsense, said Norman Thrasher. Growing up, he loved the hurly burly of Hastings Street. He was either walking down the street singing ("Everybody would say, here comes Norman!") or harmonizing on the streetcar. Before he was old enough to gain entrance, Thrasher would stand outside Sunnie Wilson's Forest Club, straining to hear balladeer Herb Lanz sing. Detroit had everything, and the north end was bursting with things to do. "Everything you could want in the entertainment business," Thrasher said. "And Hastings is where everything was. You found people on Hastings who would give you advice that you couldn't find at home. Old men would talk to youngsters to make them mind when they went back home." Mack 'Mustang Sally' Rice saw the lower element of Hastings Street as a financial opportunity. Rice would borrow his father's car, drive down to Hastings and charge the junkies for rides. "I'd follow them into these big apartment buildings to get paid, I didn't want them running off with the money they owed me."

Hastings Street was in business in all areas of the entertainment industry, even recording. At Joe's Record Shop, a regular stop for Willie, proprietor Joe Von Battle kept recording equipment in a back room that he would turn on when musicians stopped by to play. The more promising tapes would be sent down to King Records in Cincinnati. It was at Joe's that Johnnie Bassett and Joe Weaver inadvertently recorded a single for King Records one day. The teenagers were fooling around, playing in the back room. "Joe had the tape rolling one time and. . . '1540 Special' came out of that," guitarist Johnnie Bassett said. "He sold that to the King Record Company and they put it on the Deluxe label. 1540 was King Records' address."

There were nightclubs with top-notch music on every block of Hastings, but also prostitutes in every doorway plying their trade. It was that aspect of the boulevard of sin that led city fathers to bulldoze it in the name of 'urban renewal' in the late 1950s, carving a concrete canyon for the interstate highway I-75 out of the former pleasure zone.

From the age of 12 onward, Willie slipped easily out of his bedroom window and made his way out to the bright lights of Detroit's theaters and clubs. The Cardboard Valley house was only one story, so it was a short drop to the ground for the wiry youngster. Raymond begged Willie not to go, fearful of their father's belt. But his laughing brother would already have one leg out the first-floor window. "Nobody will catch me."

Phil Townsend grew up on Lawley, just around the corner from Cardboard Valley, where his friends Willie and Levi Stubbs lived. Phil was a boy soprano who idolized Clyde McPhatter of the Dominoes. Although he was a year younger than Willie, they attended Washington Elementary and Cleveland Junior High together and shared a love of singing. Phil's Aunt Gertrude loved Willie's voice, and would make the boys tuna fish sandwiches just so Willie would stick around for a song. The boys loved going to the big Arcadia Roller Rink on Woodward Avenue, although in the early 1950s the 'Cade could be a rough spot. A north end street gang, the Shakers, controlled the rink and there were often knock-down, drag-out fights. But the two tough guys who ran the Shakers, Leroy and Boo Boo, loved music even more than they liked to roller skate. There was a restaurant tucked away in part of the vast Arcadia building that served hot dogs and soda pop. Leroy and Boo Boo would set Willie on top of one table in the restaurant, put Phil on another, and make the boys have a sing-off. "Willie would do a blues number, and I would sing 'The Bells,'" said Phil, referring to his favorite, sobbing Clyde McPhatter and the Dominoes song. "Leroy liked me, but Boo Boo preferred Willie John singing the blues." Neither Phil nor Willie was in the gang, but they played along. "We would be scared to death. We wouldn't try to out-sing one another, we'd just sing so they would leave us alone."

Whether it was the roller rink or the amateur shows, Willie learned to sing whatever the restless crowd demanded, from the blues-flavored hits of the day, to big band standards or Broadway show tunes. Mack Rice remembered that both Willie and Jackie Wilson included the sentimental favorite "Danny Boy" in their repertoire. ("Danny Boy" would turn out to be Wilson's first record, as 'Sonny Wilson.') Rice describes Willie's budding stagecraft. He moved around a bit, doing what was known later as the 'Joe Tex,' a thigh-to-thigh bounce. "But he just sang so well you didn't care if he moved a lot. When he was on amateur shows he mostly would just flat foot sing. What he was doing was not that great a thing to him, he was just doing it. He was a guy who just had it."

After returning home at midnight from Dodge Main, Willie's father would make a round of bed checks. Sometimes, after a night out in the clubs, Willie barely made it home ahead of his father, leaping into bed fully clothed so he would be accounted for on his father's rounds. One night, Mertis Sr hadn't arrived home yet, but Lillie discovered that Willie's bed was empty. And she knew where to find him. Pushing her way through the zoot-suited sharpies in a Hastings Street club, Lillie collared Willie on the bandstand. "He may sound like an adult when he sings, but I can tell you he is a child," Lillie told the bandleader before frog-marching Willie out of the club. As painful as that must have been for Willie, it would have been much worse if Mertis had discovered him missing.

By the time Raymond was born in 1943 and Toronto in 1950, Mertis Sr had six sons to monitor, a lot of young male energy to tamp down in a city with temptations around every corner. Mertis was always ready with the belt—a little too ready, some reckoned. Willie's first manager, Harry Balk, explained that in the 1940s, corporal punishment was common in both black and white families. "'Spare the rod and spoil the child,' is what people said," Balk points out. But he still felt that Mertis John went too far. "Willie's father used that rod a little too hard." Norman Thrasher doesn't agree. "That was the difference between whites and blacks," said Thrasher. "Whites were always treating their children softer and kinder. They didn't go through the trials and tribulations that blacks did. Had Mertis not been strict with them, they might have turned out to be thieves and robbers, as opposed to being entertainers."

Sometimes Willie would get a whipping for sneaking out. Sometimes he'd get a whipping just for being Willie: smart, sassy and a little too quick with an excuse. One day, fed up with his father's discipline, Willie set off walking south from Cardboard Valley. Willie didn't know how far he'd walked, but the sun was still high overhead when ten year-old Valaida Tally noticed him standing outside her apartment building at John R and Montcalm, on the outskirts of downtown Detroit. Valaida was struck by the boy's appearance. "He was so cute, but also kind of sad. His story almost had me in tears. He said his father beat him and he ran away from home. It turned out to be true."

She invited the hungry boy upstairs to her apartment, where her mother fixed him lunch. (Willie's metabolism hummed along at such a ferocious rate, there were few occasions when he was not hungry. Years later, bandleader Johnny Otis wrote that the singer always seemed to show up at dinnertime. "My drummer Kansas City Bell used to call out, 'Hide the neck bones, quick! Here comes Little Willie John!'") After he finished eating, Willie offered to sing. The girl was used to hearing precocious child singers; Detroit was full of pipsqueak prodigies like Sugar Chile Robinson. Mother and daughter figured they would be entertained with some kindergarten ditty, but that wasn't what Willie John had in mind.

"That little boy started *singing*," said Valaida. "It was a church song, and you just had to listen, the sound was so beautiful. He had a high tenor, and it was so soulful for a child to sing like that. It was so moving that tears came to our eyes."

"You can come here every day, little boy," Val's mother told him.

|3|

WILLIE IS DISCOVERED... AGAIN

As recreation centers went, the Davison Rec Center was no great shakes. It had once been a library, so the center had no gym, but what it did have was a public address system, amplifiers and microphones–making it a magnet for all the harmonizing tenors, baritones and basses in Detroit's north end. On many a night, after the center had closed at eight in the evening, somebody with a key would let the neighborhood toughs and warblers in, the bottles of wine would come out and everybody would carry on, singing and celebrating the night away.

Willie's friend Phil Townsend recalls one such night in the spring of 1953 as "probably the greatest moment of my life." As luck would have it, not only was Clyde McPhatter in town playing the Fox Theatre with Billy Ward and the Dominoes, but Sam Cooke was appearing with the Soul Stirrers at the King Solomon Church on 14th Street. And that was just the out-of-towners. Local boys Jackie Wilson, Willie John and Levi Stubbs were among the Detroiters who stopped in. "Everybody came when they heard about it. We started at nine, and we sang until about five o'clock in the morning," Phil said. He was in a group of his own, the Five Sparrows, but absolutely awestruck by the company he found himself in. Sam Cooke was his idol, and then Clyde McPhatter! Singing McPhatter's "The Bells" and hitting all the high notes was Phil's speciality.

It was a time of tectonic shifts in the rhythm & blues world. McPhatter, hot off his chart success, would soon leave the Dominoes for Atlantic Records and the Drifters. Jackie Wilson was already being groomed to take McPhatter's place, but the two men were friendly. After all, McPhatter was not only giving up the lead slot in the Dominoes, he would escape the oppressive, controlled atmosphere set in place by Billy Ward's drill-sergeant rules for his singers, keeping them well-groomed, underpaid and unable to enjoy the perks of rhythm & blues stardom. That was Jackie's problem now. But on this spring night in the old recreation center, they weren't there to lament about strict bosses or group problems. There was nothing but songs and singing. Cooke sang "Touch the Hem of his Garment," starting off with his soaring wail, *"Whoaaaa there was a woman in the Bible days…"* McPhatter led on his own songs, "That's What You're Doing To Me" and "Money Honey." Willie and Levi took leads as well and everybody pitched in on harmonies. "You get wine and you feel good, and you sing," Phil said. "Nobody was doing drugs at that time."

This was the big league, the World Series of singing. It was no surprise to Cooke that Detroit's north end was fertile soil for performers; apart from Willie and Jackie, he was well acquainted with Aretha Franklin's awe-inspiring voice. The competition in the neighborhood was brutal. So much so, that with his light voice, Northern High School's Bill "Smokey" Robinson was admired as a vocal stylist and as a songwriter, but not so much as a singer. "Willie was a singer," Townsend said. "Clyde McPhatter was a singer. Lee (Levi) was *definitely* a singer! Smokey had a nice style, but they had to put two mikes on him to record him."

Harry Balk leaned against a column in the back of the Rogers Theater and mouthed a cigar. It was hard to miss Harry, all handsome six feet of him. With his long, thin sideburns and narrow moustache, he had a melting effect on the opposite sex. His friends called him Cisco, because he looked like a Spanish lover.

"Handsome stud, he could have melted anyone's butt," his friend Dave Usher said. Harry was watching as, one by one, a procession of hopefuls took the stage of the old theater on west Warren. Talent shows were still the rage in the summer of 1953, and Harry thought a good, scrappy contest between movie screenings might draw people away from the flickering blue light of those damned television sets. It seemed to be working. He surveyed the full house contentedly when a boy, short and baby-faced, strode briskly up to the microphone. He looked to be about 12, but when he stopped and grabbed the mike stand, the voice that came out sounded more like it was coming from a 32 year-old, ripe and sensuous.

Willie John.

The boy had no instrumental backup, not even a piano player, but it didn't matter. Skinny and full of energy, he sang in a tenor voice with an intense, bell-like quality, a silvery sheen that made the hair stand up on the back of your neck. He was singing "Flamingo," the 1941 Duke Ellington hit. Willie's voice sailed, high and winsome, along the romantic melody. This kid could also sing the blues, and the smooth tenor would turn husky with a potent masculinity that was beyond his years. Brimming with confidence, he danced from one side of the stage to the other, bouncing the microphone stand between his legs as he went. At the end of the stage came Willie's favorite move, a quick kick to the side that always made the girls squeal. Harry Balk still vividly recalls that first sight of Willie at the Rogers Theater 50 years later. "Nobody wanted to follow Willie John, onstage. Are you kidding? You'd have to practically hang yourself to go over," said Balk. "You couldn't follow him, he was so dynamic."

It was Daisy Stubbs who would finally let the cat out of the bag about Willie's midnight rambles. Over coffee in the Johns' kitchen, Daisy had been telling Lillie and Mertis how thrilled she was that Levi was winning wristwatches at the Paradise Theater. The Johns must be proud, she said, that Willie was winning all those first prizes as well. "Nobody here is winning any wristwatches," Mertis Sr barked. Daisy explained that Willie and Levi took turns competing each week so that each would get a chance at winning. Mertis called Willie into the kitchen. "Is someone in his house winning prizes for his singing?" Willie had no other choice but to tell all. Mertis' reaction was more mellow than might be expected. "My father said 'You know, if this is what you really want to do, we won't have a family where you sneak and steal and lie. We'll do this together,'" Mable recalled.

Not long after Willie's nighttime victories were revealed, a jazz icon came to call at Cardboard Valley. Bandleader Count Basie came to the house to ask if Mertis and Lillie would allow their son to come on the road and sing with his band. Although Lillie prepared her best meal, the Johns turned the bandleader down. "My son doesn't know those songs," Mertis Sr huffed. They also turned down Lionel Hampton, Mable John remembers. But Mertis compromised. He and Lillie would allow Willie to go out and sing locally with reputable bands, as long as it was in auditoriums or theaters and not in the nightclubs. The belt was put away.

Mertis Sr was wrong about one thing, though: Willie knew all the songs.

Chewing on his cigar, Harry Balk considered the possibilities. He had never managed anything but a theater, but he couldn't help wondering. "Do you have a manager?" Willie did not. Harry couldn't believe he was saying the words: "Kid, sign with me and I can take you places."

Harry was bluffing. At 26, he was bored with running second-rate movie houses for his uncle. With his booming voice and height, he cut an impressive figure to a kid from the projects. He had no sway with record companies like RCA, or regional labels like Chess in Chicago or King in Cincinnati that were most likely to record a blues or rhythm & blues singer. But Harry wasn't about to let this five foot four opportunity walk out of his rundown theater. Harry proved his knack for spotting talent when he later signed Del Shannon and other successful acts, but he always looked back to that first time.

"There were three guys in my life that I knew were monster talents: Little Willie John, Michael Jackson, and a kid who didn't make it, Ricky Denton. But I'll tell you," Balk said, laughing, "as unbelievable as Willie was, he was an even bigger pain in the ass."

At the time Harry made him an offer, Willie was bluffing too. Technically he didn't have a manager, but this wasn't the first time he'd been discovered. Once his parents relented in 1952 and let him enter talent contests in theaters, Willie was performing all over town, from the Paradise Theater, to the Warfield on Hastings Street.

"What got Willie over is, he didn't sound like a kid," Bassett said. "He had all the moves. This is the move that won him all the first places: He'd take the microphone, get down on his knees, then jump onto his back, take the mike and sing. The audience would go wild, to see someone doing that, a cappella, without a group! A lot of what James Brown did, he got from Willie. This guy had energy you couldn't imagine."

A year earlier, Willie was discovered by bandleader and King Records talent scout Johnny Otis, at the Paradise Theater. Otis is the kind of picturesque character who might have been created by a noir fiction writer if he hadn't already existed. A Greek-American by birth, Otis grew up in a black neighborhood in Los Angeles and lived and worked as if he were black. It's not that he was pretending to be something he wasn't. As Otis explained, he loved black music and culture and considered himself "black by persuasion."

As a songwriter, musician and producer, Otis was responsible for many hit songs, but he also loved to discover young hopefuls in talent shows across the country (he'd found Little Esther at a talent show in Los Angeles). Otis dined out on the story for years that he discovered Jackie Wilson, Little Willie John and Hank Ballard (with the Royals) on the same talent show on the same night at the Paradise Theater in Detroit. He often unspooled the yarn to illustrate how thick Detroit was with talent in the early 1950s. Taking it all in, the bandleader couldn't believe his luck, the only thing left to decide was which of these three frenetic, musical balls of fire he would recommend to King?

In 1971, Otis reminisced about his find to *Creem* magazine's John Morthland. The bandleader explained that the Paradise let him host its talent show whenever his band played Detroit. "We had talent shows in other cities, but never, other than in Los Angeles, never such a turnout of talent, of pregnant talent," Otis said. "And the ones that caught my eye that day were Jackie Wilson, Little Willie John and Hank Ballard and the Midnighters."

If this sounds too amazing to be true, Willie's childhood friend Norman Thrasher agrees: he claims it isn't true. Thrasher still lives in Detroit, overseeing several businesses and making an occasional singing appearance at the downtown casinos. Sitting at his west side clothing store one day, he cast his mind back to 1952 and the night Hank Ballard and the Royals caught Otis' eye. Although he later joined Ballard's group, on that fateful night Otis talks about, Thrasher was still in the Royal Jokers.

Otis was looking for a singer or group to record his song, "Every Beat of My Heart," Thrasher remembers. Ballard and the Royals served that purpose. "When Johnny saw the Royals, he grabbed them," said Thrasher. "We were mad, saying it was supposed to be us, because we won the contest the week before, but it was them. Jackie and Willie weren't on that show."

Ballard and the Royals won the King record company contract as well. Ballard and the group could sing and wrote their own songs, so they were a ready-made, hit-making machine. The Royals were signed to Federal, a sub-label of King Records, in 1953. (After their raunchy 1954 hit with Ballard's song "Work With Me, Annie," the group changed its name from the Royals to the Midnighters to differentiate themselves from North Carolina's '5' Royales.) Otis' claim to have discovered all three singing Detroiters on the same night may be apocryphal, but he did see Willie at the Paradise, he did tell his King Records bosses about him (they thought Willie was too young to take seriously at the time) and the two developed a friendship that continued for years.

Some of the country's biggest acts had their careers made within a few blocks of each other in 1950s Detroit. In 1951, before he lit up the jukeboxes with "Cry," an emotional early harbinger of rock 'n' roll, Johnnie Ray got his big break at the Flame Show Bar. Ray's edgy, ambiguous sexuality added sizzle to his act, but his career stumbled a few years later when he was arrested for soliciting in the men's room at the Stone Burlesk on Woodward, just a few blocks away. Jackie Wilson and Della Reese each had early success at the mob-run Flame Show Bar, as did LaVern Baker, whom Flame manager Al Green dubbed 'Little Miss Sharecropper.' In 1956, New York singer Bobby Darin played his first out-of-town gig ever at the Club Gay Haven in Dearborn–back when "gay" meant "festive."

Detroit's downtown restaurants and movie theaters never closed, operating around the clock to serve shift workers. Showbars such as the Flame and the Frolic, situated in the entertainment district just east and west of Woodward near Alexandrine, kept people out on the streets until the sweepers came out. Singer Bobby Lewis, who had a hit in 1961 with the song "Tossin' and Turnin'," got his start in Detroit when he came up from Indianapolis in 1950 to try out for Duke Ellington's orchestra. He didn't get the job, but stuck around after seeing how many clubs were booking live entertainment.

"Detroit was rolling and rocking!" Lewis said. "Every corner had a music bar or a showbar, and at the end of that corner was another music bar, then you turned left, go down to the next corner and there's another one! Across the street and there's another one. Detroit was really cooking."

There was also enough recording business in 1953 to keep one studio, United Sound, humming with bebop jazz, along with the advertising jingle sessions that paid most of the bills.

Jazz promoter and producer Dave Usher was busy enough that he didn't have to spend much time at his family's toxic waste cleanup business. (Toxic waste is a day job he still maintains today, in his 80s. As the ever-bohemian Dave puts it, "Everybody needs a gig. Gotta have a gig, otherwise how can you make your scene?") Although Dizzy Gillespie was based in New York, when Dave wasn't promoting jazz shows, he ran Dizzy's record company Dee Gee Records, out of Detroit.

Harry Balk and Dave knew each other from the music scene: "Nice guy,

Dave was a good friend of mine," Harry said. Dave was also the first producer to record Jackie Wilson (under the name of 'Sonny Wilson,' on a 78 of "Danny Boy"), so Harry went to work on him to record Willie John. Dave shrugged him off the first four or five times, but he wasn't against the idea, he was just mulling Harry's pitch over. They already had a minor national pop hit with Gillespie's "Ooh Shooby Dooby," but Dizzy and Dave weren't jazz snobs, they would record everything from novelty records to pop and comedy. Gillespie was already high on Willie, so Dave agreed to go see the boy sing.

By then Harry had a partner in his budding music managing career, Frank Glussman, who owned a jewelry store in the Metropolitan Building downtown. "Harry and Frank conned me into going," Dave said. "They kept saying 'Davie, Davie, this guy is really something! We can make money!'" Harry and Frank were hustlers, Dave says, not thugs, but certainly persuasive rascals. "These were guys who would sell you your own watch three times over," Dave said. "I didn't mind it! They were soft, they weren't hard guys."

So Dave met Harry and Frank at the Rogers Theater. After the movie ended– *Titanic* featuring Clifton Webb, as it happens–the talent show began, and out spun Willie, fresh as a new dime. "Man, the house went down," said Dave. "They just went crazy. And he did this every time. Every time this kid came out, he won every talent show they put him on."

Harry and Dave put the full-court press on with Lillie and Mertis, trying to convince Willie's parents to sign a management contract for their teenaged son, making several trips out to Cardboard Valley. In the course of these outings, Harry got to know the Johns, and developed a lifelong fondness for Willie's mother. Dave remembers the Johns' small house well. "A one-story pre-fab," he described it. Toronto, the baby of the John family at three years old, was playing in the living room as the two managers talked to Willie's parents. It took more than one attempt, but Harry and Dave finally cinched the deal, and Willie John had a management contract.

4

A SURPRISINGLY WELL-POISED BOY

Willie was still 15 in the early fall of 1953, and he was still doing talent shows, often with the backing of guitarist Johnnie Bassett. Harry Balk managed both boys, and he was booking them into nightclubs they weren't legally supposed to set foot in, including Basin Street and downriver clubs south of Detroit, like Chappy's and the Downriver Lounge.

Willie was used to hanging around in nightclubs and roaming the streets of Detroit. But the promo photos his managers distributed painted a different picture, showing a boy who looks younger than his years, grinning sweetly in a pristine white v-necked sweater. They also had Willie, by now in the ninth grade at Pershing High School, photographed surrounded by the school's all-white cheerleading squad, all a-giggle over their classmate's success.

Willie's management team now numbered four. Harry, Frank and Dave had a new partner in their talent-managing scheme, another middle class Jewish boy: Ed Bierman. It was Ed's task to drive Willie around to his various gigs, often stopping at Frank's jewelry store downtown, where Willie would try on watches "for my mama." Often Ed would take a quick detour to his mother's house in the Russell Woods neighborhood, a comfortable, west side enclave of well-kept brick homes that was to loom large in Willie's imagination.

Russell Woods was about as far from Cardboard Valley as the moon, with solid brick Georgian Colonials and early American foursquares tucked into beds of hydrangea and roses. The Biermans' kitchen was often fragrant with cloves and cinnamon from the hermit cookies Ed's mother would have cooling on a rack. Every time Bierman picked Willie up, no matter where they were headed, the boy begged to go by Russell Woods so he could have some of those cookies. It became a dream vision of home for the boy from the projects. With his love of cookies, fun and games, Willie could often appear childlike, but there was another, more impudent side to him. "Willie would come in and sit down next to you, and you'd say 'Isn't that a nice little boy!'" Dave said. "Let me tell you, this little boy would kick your ass in a second. If you were a girl, he'd try to make it with you."

After they saw him tear it up at the Rogers Theater, Willie's handlers knew that they were onto something. But what to do with a 15 year-old who looked ten, but sounded like a grown man? Harry kept hammering away at Dave throughout the fall to record Willie. Dave pushed back with an arsenal of excuses. It was October, a crazy time to cut a record. The distributors had their holiday releases all ready to ship, Willie's record would get lost in the shuffle, the list went on and on.

"Let's do it, let's do it," said Harry. "Can't you think of something he can do?" Dave could not. A few weeks later, he was at a music convention in Minneapolis when he heard a pop group demonstrating a new holiday song, "Mommy, What Happened to our Christmas Tree?" Pure hokum, but this was 1953, the year a grown woman pretending to be a little boy had a hit record lisping the song "I Saw Mommy Kissing Santa Claus."

The Christmas tree song hit Dave like a rock. Sung by an innocent kid, it could be dynamite. The lyrics were simple: A child wakes up a few days after Christmas and is perplexed to find that the tree is gone, taken down secretly by his parents during the night. The child sadly describes the tree all shining with candles, and wonders whether angels, or Santa himself, took it. Dave made the call. "Harry, I've got the song. We can record Willie. But you have to do exactly what I tell you." "Sure, anything," Harry said.

The men booked a session at United Sound, a dowdy-looking two-story white frame house on Second Avenue, just south of General Motors' New Center headquarters. Transformed from a two-family house into a studio in 1933, United Sound was Detroit's premier recording venue, churning out sessions for Chess Records and other labels in between advertising gigs.

In 1953, United Sound owner Jimmy Siracuse was using the front living room as the recording studio, working the controls from the dining room. Just five years earlier, John Lee Hooker sang of Hastings Street in that front room, moaning and chopping his guitar on "Boogie, Chillen" as he name-checked Henry's Swing Club and other clubs young Willie John had already explored. Berry Gordy Jr was a frequent guest at the studio, a short, friendly young man who liked to lean in the doorway of the mixing room, watching Dave work the controls on a jazz session. Having failed with his 3-D Record Mart, Gordy was writing songs and trying to break into the music business from a new angle. He often smiled, so Dave figured he was digging the rhythm.

When the day finally came for Willie's recording session in November, near to his 16th birthday, Harry and Frank collected their artist from the front steps of Pershing High School. He had carefully dressed in a polka dot shirt, his pants held up by suspenders. Waiting for them at the studio was a band and a group of professional background singers, Three Lads and a Lass. On an average day Willie was vibrating at a higher, faster frequency than most people, which is how he could eat so much and stay whippet-thin, at the time, 90 pounds of churning, chaotic energy. But Dave was stern, and once the recording light snapped on, Willie settled down and took direction. That was fortunate for all concerned, because in 1953, recording technology dictated that he had to sing the whole song perfectly, start to finish, with backup singers and musicians chugging along on the same track. The tools to splice a good note over a bad one were still several years away, so one mistake meant they would have to stop the session, put a new plate on, and start all over again. Once it was finished, the hot wax record was cut with a lathe and driven up the old two-lane highway from Detroit to a plant in Owosso, in mid-Michigan, where it was pressed into hard shellac 78s. The record was released by a new label called Prize, under the umbrella of the Gillespie–Usher venture, Dee Gee Records, with the artist billed as "Willie John and the Three Lads and a Lass."

When the needle hit the groove on "Mommy," a sparkling vibes intro evokes bells, then a big, boyish voice with a lush vibrato erupts. *"Mommy what happened to our Christmas tree, last night it was so big and bright. Tinsel and holly and bells one two three, and candles made such a nice light. . ."* On the flip side Willie sings a jazzed up "Jingle Bells" confidently, with Three Lads and a Lass providing a bohemian counterpoint to his boyish lead. Only once does he seem to hesitate, deciding how to hit a note.

Vocally, Willie was caught on a high wire between boyhood and manhood. Entertainment writers struggled to describe his voice. It only added to the confusion that Willie's four managers were telling everybody that the boy was 14, when in fact he had just turned 16. "Willie sings in a strange voice that is a cross between a soprano and a high tenor," reported the *Detroit Times*. According to the *Detroit News*, Willie sang in "deep, soulful tones."

No matter how his voice was described, Detroiters loved the record. It went into heavy rotation on Ed McKenzie's popular *Jack the Bellboy* radio show on WJBK, and 'Rockin' Robin Seymour played it frequently on WKMH (which later became WKNR). Things really started to percolate after Willie was invited to sing on Don McLeod's television show *TV Bandstand* on WJBK-TV, a program that imitated the pre-Dick Clark *Philadelphia Bandstand*.

Willie wasn't shy with reporters. He loved talking about his dreams. "I can only hope we make money, so I can get my family out of that project into a home of our own," Willie told the *Detroit Times*. "One thing is for sure—*we'll* have a Christmas tree." A month later, he told the *Detroit News*, "I'm going to save all my royalties, and buy a new house for my mother."

In a somewhat patronizing aside, the *Times* described the 16 year-old as a "surprisingly well-poised boy of above average intelligence," who earned all As and Bs at Pershing High School. There's no indication in the story why Willie's appearance and academic achievement were surprising.

The big score for Willie's managers was when they managed to get an item about him in Dorothy Kilgallen's powerful, nationally syndicated show business column on December 8th, 1953. "Sudden stardom seems to be in the cards for a 14 year-old Negro lad named Willie John, all because of his first record, a jivey little Christmas novelty titled 'Mommy What Happened to Our Christmas Tree'?" Kilgallen wrote. She added that the disc sold "close to 5,000 copies," that both Duke Ellington and Stan Kenton wanted the youngster to tour with them and that he had been offered an exclusive contract with Capitol Records, "but his sensible mother is keeping him in her own Detroit backyard so he can finish school."

Harry and Dave, flush with the success of the single, had decided to storm New York with their prodigy. There the men could call on record companies, booking agents and the network television shows to shop their young singer around. It was just days before Christmas when the two managers and their charge arrived at Grand Central Station. As they rode in a cab to the Hotel Victoria at 7th and 51st Street, Willie was quiet for once, awestruck by the holiday lights.

The trio got settled at the hotel into adjoining rooms, but Willie was jumpy. He was finally in New York, and nothing was happening. Desperate to hit the streets, he made a run for the elevators, but Dave collared him and brought him back. As his managers lounged on their beds and watched television, Willie continued to fidget. The men were watching a live charity telethon featuring a number of top entertainers. When the Count Basie Band came on, Willie came flying into the room to watch. He knew Basie; if he could get to the theater, surely the bandleader would let him sing. Willie begged his managers to get him on the show. "No, Willie," Harry thundered. "It's too late, forget about it." Dejected, the boy walked out of the room.

A few minutes later, Dave sat up abruptly. "Where's Willie?" The adjoining room was empty. "The little bastard ran out on us!" Dave and Harry ran up and down the hall, but the boy was gone. A half hour or so later, they heard it. A shimmering, confident, oddly familiar voice was coming out of the television set. Dave darted over to look. A skinny teenager was dancing in front of Count Basie's bandstand. It was Willie, and he was singing with the Count Basie Band.

"That. . . son of a bitch!" Harry roared, settling in to watch.

An hour later Willie found his way back to the hotel. Once everybody had calmed down, he explained that he'd slipped downstairs and got directions to the theater from a bellman. Dave and Harry were dumbfounded, but they weren't angry, how could they be? "That's *chutzpah,*" said Dave. "That's the kind of strength Willie had to go where he was going. That's why he made it."

In the next few days, Dave and Harry toted Willie around to record companies, New York DJs and television shows, and they managed to get him on a five-hour midnight benefit at the Apollo Theater, sponsored by the *New York Amsterdam News.* The line-up included Duke Ellington, Ruth Brown, Nat 'King' Cole, the Drifters, comics Pigmeat Markham and Nipsey Russell, and several talented juveniles, including Leslie Uggams and Willie. But none of those spots seemed as impressive as the television appearance Willie managed to get for himself on that first night in New York City.

When they got back to Detroit, his managers updated Willie's resume: "Television appearances in Detroit *and New York.*"

5

THE DIRTY BOOGIE

Harry, Dave and Willie had returned from New York in December to discover that Willie was still hot from his Christmas song, so they booked him on a brief tour of cities where the record was making the biggest splash; first Baltimore, then Philadelphia. After those dates, Willie returned to Detroit to play a big variety show at the Michigan State Fairgrounds. By now they were billing him as 'Little Willie John'. There was a long tradition in the blues world of naming artists 'Little' or 'Big'–Little Esther, Big Mama Thornton, Big Joe Turner, Little Walter. And the managers were still touting Willie as younger than his actual age, so for the pint-sized tenor, it seemed a natural fit. Unlike some 'Littles,' Willie never outgrew the description. Little Richard reminisced in later years, "it was Little Esther, Little Willie Littlefield, Little Walter, Little Willie John, and I came out as Little Richard. Most of them when they got grown, like Stevie Wonder, changed it. I didn't change it." Nor was Little Richard ever very little, even when he was young.

Dave Usher laughed about what he got out of helping to launch Little Willie John on his recording career. "They conned me," he said of Harry and Frank. "I don't think I even got paid. Wait, I did get paid–I got married!" Frank Glussman had set Dave up on a date with an airline stewardess, Althea. The date was a success by Dave's reckoning–he and Althea were married for 23 years and had three children. "So I guess I'm even," Dave concluded.

Willie was dreaming again, bigger dreams of Cadillacs the color of a flamingo's wing, of tailor-made suits and young girls swooning when he sang. On Hastings Street, where the air was thick with the smell of the fry baskets in Etta's Shrimp

Shack, Willie heard dozens of new records every week booming from the big jukebox speakers. "Sexy Ways" by Hank Ballard and the Royals, "Sincerely" by the Moonglows, "Honey Love" by the Drifters, they just kept coming. Savoy Records, King Records, Chess Records, every week there were new 78s, and more and more were on the new 45 rpm format. Every kid on Hastings Street wanted to cut a record of their own, Willie more than anybody. The streets were buzzing with music of all kinds. In the early evenings, just before the streetlights flickered on, Levi Stubbs and the Four Aims could be heard singing at Hastings and Hancock, while Norman Thrasher and the Royal Jokers harmonized across the street on a patch of sidewalk near Etta's.

Willie was doing well academically, as usual, earning all As and Bs on his winter report card of 1953 and 54, but he didn't want to waste another minute as a high school boy. His life was ticking away. Willie argued to his father that he was going to be a singer, and he knew what he needed to know. Mertis Sr argued back, and for a time, he won. At Pershing, Willie tried to distract himself. He loved dressing up in his high school ROTC (Reserve Officers Training Corps) uniform, standing tall in his first pair of elevator shoes.

During the early 1950s, there were so many record company and band manager offices on Detroit's Alexandrine Street at Woodward that it came to be known as 'Record Row.' The neighborhood also had showbars such as the Flame, the Frolic and the Village Club, but it was sliding into the realm of seediness, with several fading taxi dance halls, and the infamous Stone Burlesk strip joint ("We Know What Men Want!" the marquee boasted) out on Woodward. Some record companies, such as Chess and King, had local branch offices, so it was possible for a hot young singer to be discovered and signed out of Detroit. But Willie couldn't stop thinking about New York, still the center of the recording industry in 1954.

Mertis Jr arrived home that winter from Korea after two years serving in the Army as a medic. The Johns had moved to a house on Waterloo Street on Detroit's lower east side, down the way from Miller High School and near the Elmwood Cemetery. All of the Johns were at home to welcome Mertis except Mable, who was living in an apartment with her husband, and Willie, who couldn't stay in one place for more than a minute. When Mertis finally caught up with his little brother, he noticed that 17 year-old Willie's voice had changed, it was deeper and more mature than when he last saw him. Just in time, too, because Willie's adult life was about to begin.

According to Mertis Jr, bandleader Paul Williams came to the house to ask if Willie could go out on the road with him and this time, Mertis Sr and Lillie agreed to let their son go. Mable remembers it differently. She insists that nobody asked, Willie just took off on the road with Williams and his band, ending his high school days forever. "I was the one who had to go tell my parents he was gone," Mable said. However it happened, Mertis Sr and Lillie were so careworn and busy with their younger children that they resigned themselves to the departure of their most impatient child. EJ remembered Willie's parting vow: "You have to make it somewhere else before you come back here. I won't come back to Detroit until I have my own record."

Baritone saxophone player Paul Williams was a popular attraction both in Detroit and on the road in 1954. In 1949, he'd scored one of the biggest dance hits of the century with "The Hucklebuck," a song with risqué lyrics and frolicsome dance moves, the 'dirty boogie,' it came to be called. In 1954 it was still a popular song, and a year later, on a memorable episode of *The Honeymooners*, Ed Norton (Art Carney) showed Ralph Kramden (Jackie Gleason) the moves.

You push your partner out,
Then you hunch your back,
Start a little movement in your sacroiliac,
You wiggle like an eel, you waddle like a duck,
That's the way you do it when you do the Hucklebuck.

Ironically, in 1949 "The Hucklebuck" knocked another Detroiter, John Lee Hooker, off the top of the rhythm & blues charts (Hooker had scored with "Boogie, Chillen"). It was a long way from singing church songs with the United Five, but if the dirty boogie could get Willie to New York, he'd sing "The Hucklebuck" every night of the week.

When he called long-distance, that familiar, silvery voice chattering excitedly down the line, Willie told the family that he'd made a record in New York with bandleader Williams. The song was "Ring a Ling," and was recorded for George Goldner's Rama label in early 1955. To his family, it appeared that Willie was on track, he was making all of those waking childhood dreams come true. "I wasn't making much money," Willie told a reporter, of his days on the road with Williams. "But I was having a lot of fun singing and traveling all over the country, and meeting some of the big names in the business."

The fun would soon end. Willie was acting up, hanging out with a rough element and taking part in gambling parties. Paul Williams refused to be a babysitter, and he dropped Willie from the orchestra when they were in New York during June of 1955. For Willie, the timing was perfect. He was as grown up as he'd ever be, and flush with talent. All he had to do was hustle himself into a meeting with a producer who would harness his raw talent into a hit record.

The Johns didn't protest when their teenaged son called to say he would be staying in New York, and that he would be bunking with with the boxer Sugar Ray Robinson. Besides, he had an audition with King Records to look forward to. Like Willie, Sugar Ray Robinson was from Detroit, slight of stature and had endured a tough childhood, running with a gang for a time. The boxer had his own nightclub in Harlem, Sugar Ray's, and was always trailed by a flashy entourage. Sugar Ray picked up all the tabs, and an impressed Willie watched and absorbed it all.

It's not surprising to the boxer's son, Ray Robinson II, that his father would allow the teenaged Willie John to join his retinue and stay at his house. Brash and unstoppable, Willie probably sought Sugar Ray out at his nightclub in Harlem. It was no big deal that Willie was making friends in nightclubs. "You've got to remember, in those days the law wasn't watching out whether a person was of age as much as they do now," said Ray II, who was six at the time. "People weren't worrying about below-age drinkers at the bar, or children."

Sugar Ray's wife Edna had taken an interest in Willie. Sophisticated and artistic, the former Cotton Club and Duke Ellington dancer surrounded herself with a salon of young athletes and entertainers. Edna loved Willie. "He was a jewel, a wonderful spark of light," said Ray II. "He was a favorite of everybody I knew in New York, an affable, likable young man. Everyone thought he was going to go far. We thought he was going to be as big as Nat King Cole."

Willie admired Sugar Ray Robinson's urbane, polished way of speaking, his effortless cool. Ray II explains: "We had just gotten out of farm animal days, in the view of white society, and here was this man who was a boxer, flying around and meeting with heads of state and doing things that African American boxers, that athletes, just didn't do." Willie already knew about Sugar Ray's famous pink flamingo-colored Cadillac convertible, he had been dreaming about it for years, and now he was seeing it in living chrome and steel.

Willie's fateful meeting with King Records producer and A&R man Henry Glover took place in late June at King's New York offices, in a building on West 54th Street. In 1955 King, via its subsidiary labels Deluxe and Federal, was home to Billy Ward and the Dominoes ("Sixty-Minute Man,"1951), Hank Ballard and the Midnighters ("Work With Me, Annie," 1954) and Otis Williams and the Charms ("Hearts of Stone,"1954). For a black teenager from Cardboard Valley, King Records meant success.

Years before Berry Gordy Jr and Clarence Avant made their mark, Henry Glover was a pioneer as a black record company executive, hired by King in the early 1940s. A trumpet player by trade, Glover was an educated man, earning a degree from Alabama Agricultural and Mechanical University in 1943. He'd done considerable work toward a master's degree from Wayne University (now Wayne State) in Detroit when he quit his studies in the mid 1940s to go out on the road with Tiny Bradshaw's orchestra. By then he was an accomplished arranger, comfortable writing music for any part of the orchestra.

It was while performing in Cincinnati with Lucky Millinder's orchestra that Glover came to the attention of King Records boss Syd Nathan. Short, asthmatic, with a stubby cigar dangling from his mouth, Syd was a hard-boiled, mid-century record man who rarely spoke below the level of a raspy shout. He was especially loud when exploding with fury at musicians during sessions at King's studio in Cincinnati. Most of his artists and musicians didn't take offense, but admired his uncanny nose for a hit. "If we made a mistake, he'd say 'Leave it there, leave it there,'" said Billy Davis, guitarist for Hank Ballard and the Midnighters from 1959 to 1960. "We did a song called 'Sugaree,' and I hit one wrong note at the end. I said, 'Oh, let me do that again.' Syd said 'No no no! Leave it alone! Go to the next song.'" Syd wasn't just being cheap, he truly believed that the occasional mistake gave a record an added dimension, an interesting texture for the listener. "He said if you make a record too perfect, it wouldn't sell," Davis recalled.

Like many successful businessmen, Syd drove several ventures into the ground before hitting his stride as a record company boss. He'd been selling used records out of a storefront in Cincinnati but couldn't find enough product, so he resolved to make his own. In the process, almost by accident, Syd became the owner of one of the most important regional record companies in America. His genius—or his good luck—was in recording music for what he termed "the little man," tapping the rich vein of hillbilly and black music being played and enjoyed in the three states—southern Ohio, Kentucky and West Virginia—around the Queen City. The New York-based record companies had temporarily lost interest in roots music during the 1940s, leaving the field open for regional labels like King to expand beyond their local following.

Hiring Henry Glover as a King producer and A&R man was another genius move on Syd's part. Glover became one of King's top producers, writing, arranging and producing not only rhythm & blues, but also many of King's hillbilly sessions for artists such as Moon Mullican, Grandpa Jones and Cowboy Copas. Because Syd held the copyright to many King hits, he wanted his country artists to record rhythm & blues songs, and his rhythm & blues artists to cover 'hillbilly' songs. This musical cross-pollination may have been driven by Syd's desire to make a buck, but the result was creatively explosive. When raw country players like the Delmore Brothers sang "Blues Stay Away From Me," and blues shouters like Bull Moose Jackson covered hillbilly tunes, you can almost hear the music's racial barriers melting away. It all played into creating the mixed-up, hybrid stew called rock 'n' roll.

After several years in Cincinnati, and after King's recording studio and pressing plant were launched, Syd let Glover go to New York and run King's office from a building on 45th Street. It was there that Willie met with Glover at five pm on June 27, 1955. King executive Hal Neely claimed he was present as well. In fact, Neely insisted that it was he who arranged for Willie to come to King, and delivered the singer into Glover's hands. One way or another, Willie got there, and once he started singing, Glover was knocked back on his heels. This was a man who had heard a lot of singers in his day, but it was Willie he called "the artist of all artists."

"He was a really, truly great singer. . . The blues came so natural to him that he was just a master at that and no one living in that day could touch him," Glover said in an interview with Steve Tracy. Glover particularly admired Willie's control over his voice, his ability to perform "some of the greatest blues gymnastics and voice gyration that you could ever dream of a person having." Glover wasted no time, he summoned some of New York's top players for a session at the Beltone recording studio that night. He had a shortlist of players he liked to use. Guitarist Mickey 'Guitar' Baker was his first call. Baker had become New York's top rhythm & blues guitarist after a major career re-boot. He was playing a jazz gig in a club in California in the late 1940s when he heard guitarist Pee Wee Crayton play a song called "Blues After Hours." "I said, 'You mean to tell me you can make money playing that shit?'" Baker recalled, laughing. "I never paid any attention to blues music at all, because I spent my whole life in New York City. The blues didn't mean a thing in New York. We had Count Basie, Duke Ellington, Benny Goodman, Lionel Hampton, all these people like that, but the blues we didn't pay attention to." But money was money. So Baker woodshedded, got his chops together, and when he left California, "I was a blues guitar player." Because he was willing to play blues, Baker became the king of New York session guitarists, on call for most Atlantic, Savoy and King sessions, and particularly tight with Henry Glover.

Glover also called tenor player Willis 'Gatortail' Jackson, a frenetic showman known for dropping to his knees in the middle of a set, as well as for being singer Ruth Brown's boyfriend. Playing piano was the able veteran boogie woogie player 'Champion' Jack Dupree; Ivan Rolle was on bass and the drummer was Calvin 'Eagle Eye' Shields. The veteran musicians gathered at the studio on West 31 Street, just off Fifth Avenue, to play behind this wonder boy who'd walked in off the street.

Most of these musicians were 15 or 20 years older than Willie. "He was funny as a kid, he was very young when I knew him," Baker recalled. The sophisticated New Yorkers thought his clothes were a fright. "Willie had borrowed a suit from someone who was bigger than he was, the cuffs were rolled up because the pants and arms were too long, it was funny," Baker said. "We laughed at him! But he didn't care."

Three hours after Willie set foot in his office, he was standing in a booth at Beltone opposite the orchestra stand, singing a song that had just been released that day, Titus Turner's boasting blues, "All Around the World." Turner had written and recorded the song a month earlier for Wing, Mercury's jazz and blues sub-label. When Glover played the record for Willie, he bragged, "I can do better than that." Glover worked up a different arrangement and Willie made good on his boast, making each word his own. He sang the line, *"If I don't love you, grits ain't groceries, eggs ain't poultry and Mona Lisa was a man,"* with such grown-up male fervor that within weeks of the record's release in July, those lyrics became imprinted in the hearts of a generation of African Americans.

The song was classic street corner swagger; the singer lists all the things that couldn't be true if it weren't true that he loved his baby, and the feats he would perform to prove that he did: be a fly so he could lie on his girl, staying with her "till I die," use a toothpick to dig a ten-foot ditch or run through the jungle fighting lions with a switch. The musicians are having a ball behind the energetic 17 year-old, playing a rollicking, stop-start backup. Guitarist Baker rips off fat blues chords, Dupree plays a hot boogie-woogie piano and Jackson takes over the break with a wild sax breakdown.

Two days later Glover brought Willie back into the studio to record "Are You Ever Coming Back" with the same players. Everything in Willie's life had been in preparation for this moment, and to flip his first time in a recording studio into one of the mid 1950s' most memorable rhythm & blues hits right out of the box was almost too much to take in. But from the moment he took direction from Glover and stood in the isolation booth, surrounded by the best players in the business, Willie had found his place in the world.

Finally, Willie had his own record as an adult artist in his hands. The platter hit two cities like a bomb: his home town of Detroit and New Orleans, the ancestral home of the Robinsons and Johns. All spring Willie had been advising his family back in Detroit that he wasn't coming back until he had a record out under his own name. A month after Willie recorded the song, it soared up to No. 5 on *Billboard*'s rhythm & blues chart. EJ remembers his brother's excited call home. "He said, 'Y'all turn the radio on. I have a record out. It's called 'All Around the World.'"

"And they started playing it," EJ said. "And that's all you could hear, all summer. All summer! 'All Around the World.'"

WALK SLOW

When Willie banged out of the house as a child, his mother would holler out to him: "Walk slow, Edward, don't run." But Willie never walked slow. When he was a slick, teenaged band singer on and off the road with Paul Williams, Lillie John would say the same thing, to little effect. "Willie was in a hurry, an anxious dude," said the singer Jimmy Scott. Jimmy met Willie in 1954 in Cleveland, when Paul Williams' orchestra came to town for a gig. Jimmy was one of the few singers Willie encountered who was even smaller than he was, with an even higher, more ethereal range. Jimmy was also prone to self-destructive behavior. He sensed a kindred spirit.

"People around him were trying to say, 'you don't get it in a hurry, it takes time,'" Jimmy said. But it was almost as if Willie sensed he didn't have a lot of time. Although he didn't seem to be listening to his mother's words, they eventually took shape in his mind in the form of a song that became "Walk Slow," a lush pop ballad he recorded in 1960. He's singing about a romance, but some of the lyrics echoed what Lillie John was trying to tell him.

Walk slow, don't run, every earthly power has ways of having fun/So when the race is won, walk slow. . . and don't forget to remember to take my love wherever you go. . .

In the middle of September in 1955, before he headed out on tour, Willie reported to the studio in New York for his third recording session for King under Henry Glover's supervision. He was still two months shy of his 18th birthday, but Willie infused "Need Your Love So Bad" with a smoky, late night sadness, as if he'd been loving and losing women for decades. Hearing it today, we take the gut-wrenching soul emotion of the vocal for granted, the way it takes the listener into the back rows of the black church, out the back door and to the juke joint in the woods. But in 1955, they weren't calling this sound soul, not yet. In terms of pop music it was still underground, a unique amalgam of gospel, blues and rhythm & blues bubbling up from the mysterious, unexplored depths of black culture.

Mertis Jr wrote much of the song in Korea, and brought it to Willie, who worked on it and eventually finished it off. Clearly, Willie's indelible stamp is on that tune, and Mertis restored Willie's name as co-writer in 2008. Much of the ace team that backed the teenager up on "All Around the World" was reassembled to record the new song. Mickey Baker plays the scorching blues lick that anchors the track, which Peter Green riffed on so memorably in Fleetwood Mac's 1968 remake. Baker laughed when he recalled seeing Willie in the fall of 1955. The teenager was no longer the ragamuffin whose sleeves and pants were flapping loose on his limbs. "He was really well dressed, beautiful suit and driving a Thunderbird," Baker said. "I said, 'Boy, that's a big change in six months. You're a big star now.'"

B.B. King didn't know when he heard "Need Your Love So Bad" that he helped bring the blues to Willie's Cardboard Valley house, he just knew that he loved Willie's voice, and that he loved that song. King loved "Need Your Love" so much that he recorded it several times, including a version in 1968 and another one in 1980. In 2005 he recorded it again as a duet with Sheryl Crow. On a midsummer day in 2006, as King's tour bus crossed over from Indiana into Michigan, he was listening to Willie sing "Need Your Love So Bad" on his CD player. Having reached his mid-80s, King likes to reflect back on his favorite music from his younger years, and he confessed that he listens to Willie almost every day. "He was a singer's singer," said King. "God, he had a voice that was beyond most people I'd heard at that time. And it still stands out, (when) you hear him years after his death. He had that identifying voice on him." All singers of "Need Your Love" over the years follow the template of Willie's 1955 vocal, but no one can match the depth of feeling and lush texture of the original.

In the studio along with Willie and guitarist Baker for the "Need Your Love" session were Willis 'Gator Tail' Jackson and David Van Dyke on tenor saxophone (joined by Reuben Phillips on baritone sax), with Calvin 'Eagle Eye' Shields on drums. Bubber Johnson played a funky piano, and future jazz great

Milt Hinton played bass. "Need Your Love So Bad" was released by King in November 1955, while Willie was in the middle of the Lucky Seven Blues tour. *Billboard*'s review on November 5th applauded Willie's "warm sincerity" and "easy showmanship," as well as the song's "authentic blues sound."

After he finished recording, and before heading out on the road, Willie returned to Detroit to visit his mother and the family. It was a blue and gold fall day when Billy Davis found himself gazing out the window of Miller High School on Detroit's lower east side. He could see this flash car all the way down the street. It was the ultimate big shot ride of 1955, the stuff of dreams for every man and boy in Detroit, the one Chuck Berry saw Maybellene sitting in at the top of a hill. There it was, a long and sleek 1955 Cadillac Coupe de Ville, with the brazen, two-bullet front rack and creamy, buxom lines of a Vegas showgirl. Davis recalled the colors dreamily: "It was kind of a yellowish green, the top was a little bit darker."

The Coupe de Ville was parked in front of the John's battered two-story house on Waterloo, so Davis had an inkling who it belonged to, but he had to find out for sure. He knew Delores John, that she was Willie's sister. She looked a lot like her brother, with the slender John build and that baby-faced smile. After class, he tracked her down and asked about the Cadillac. "That's my brother Willie's car," Delores said. Willie had bought it as an 18th birthday present to himself. "Oh man, I was really excited," Davis said. "I said 'Will you introduce me to him?' Willie was the greatest singer I ever heard in my life. He was hot with 'All Around the World,' and I said 'Oh my God, I get a chance to meet him!' Delores took me over, but he didn't have that much to say to me."

Only a year younger than Willie, Davis might as well have been ten years the singer's junior. Here was a gawky high school boy and Willie was a man of the world, with a hit song under his belt and an impressive nickname already, 'the prince of the blues.' Willie was too busy showing off his two-tone Cadillac and his fine self to the family and neighborhood to pay much attention to this high school boy. It wasn't until a few years later, when their paths crossed as professionals and Davis was playing guitar with Hank Ballard and the Midnighters, that Willie treated him like a peer.

There was just enough time to visit with the family, spruce up his wardrobe and get his automobiles in order, Willie was hot and in demand, and having started a lifelong association with Universal Attractions, which did not believe in days off for its touring artists, he was officially a creature of the road. His dates were booked by Ben Bart, and later, he was road-managed by Ben's son Jack. When Willie wasn't touring, King Records had a contractual hold on him for sessions.

Willie was top of the bill for a week at the Apollo Theater starting on September 23rd, with 'Champion' Jack Dupree, the piano player from "All Around the World," and King labelmates Otis Williams and the Charms. Just a month later, October 28th, he would be back at the Apollo for the kickoff date of the Lucky Seven Blues tour, which also featured Earl King, Little George, Marie Knight and Hal 'Cornbread' Singer. The Lucky Seven was a typical mid 1950s rhythm & blues tour, a grueling run of one-nighters by bus: Pittsburgh, Cleveland, Detroit, Indiana and Iowa, then back to Saginaw, Michigan, swinging down to Toledo and Cincinnati in Ohio, then on to the South: Tennessee, Georgia, Alabama and Florida. Without a day's rest, the tour headed up the eastern seaboard, to North Carolina and Virginia.

There was a bit of a break when they played a whole week in one city at the Howard Theater in Washington, DC, but just as soon as they were settling in, Willie and the troupe were on the road again, headed for the West Coast.

Willie had been preparing for this for much of his 18 years. He was tight and clean, barbered up and tour-ready for the chitlin circuit. The rolled-up cuffs and sleeves that made the musicians at the "All Around the World" session laugh were a thing of the past, he stocked up on suits at Hot Sam's, a Detroit haberdashery that specialized in discount, off-the-rack clothing. He could spend two hundred dollars and get ten or 15 suits from the boys' department to do him for the run. But Willie wouldn't be buying off the rack for long.

Laying out cash for suits that fit paid off. In late October, Joe 'Ziggy' Johnson wrote in the *Chicago Defender*: "Little Willie John came to town looking like a little man, and just to think just a year or so ago, he was singing 'Mommy, where is my Christmas tree?'" What Johnson and the fans heard on "All Around the World" was the fulfillment of what Harry Balk and others had sensed when Willie was 14; an intriguing, unsettling combination of youth and worldliness.

Joe Hunter, later of the original Funk Brothers, played piano on the road for Hank Ballard and the Midnighters in the mid 1950s. He would do double duty on those tours, playing behind Willie as well. Hunter saw Willie as a natural, someone whose voice swooped effortlessly up to high notes that other tenors sang as falsetto. Years later, Willie's sons Kevin and Keith would laugh about how there were high notes, and then there were "dad's high notes," which, as an adult, Keith could reach after a lot of sweat and grit, but as he says "not in my natural voice!" As Joe Hunter pointed out, "When you don't use falsetto, and you can reach those notes with real tonation, you're a natural. Willie did. He had the control to do what he wanted with the note." Some believe it's because Willie's natural range is so high, that his vocals have that extra edge of excitement, an intensity that helped make his voice so unique, and so hard to deconstruct. "He had an original tone of voice that you could not emulate," said singer Andre 'Bacon Fat' Williams. "He had a really different sound."

Joe Hunter particularly loved it when Willie sang the down and out blues song, "Nobody Knows You When You're Down and Out." "He would sing, *'Once I lived the life of a millionaire, spent all my money, just didn't care…'*" Hunter crooned. "He put emotion into it. The tears would be rolling out of his eyes." Willie didn't know it at the time, but he was singing his future.

…Took all my friends out for a good time,
Bought bootleg whisky, champagne and wine.

Then I began to fall so low,
Lost all my good friends, I didn't have nowhere to go.
I get my hands on a dollar again,
I'm gonna hang on to it till that eagle grins.

'Cause no, no, nobody knows you
When you're down and out.
In your pocket, not one penny,
As for friends, you don't have any.

At 18, Willie's voice sizzled with the muscular, assured macho of a seasoned man of the world. But he could also tilt his head, dreamy-eyed, and let you hear the cry in his voice, the keening whine, coming at the notes in different ways depending on the lyric. Willie could color a tune with hope or eagerness, or summon pain from some hidden place. On the stages of the chitlin circuit, Willie was discovering how a man with a sob in his voice could send the sisters into orbit, and like clockwork, the purses, stockings and lacy unmentionables would start hurtling their way toward the stage.

The emotional catch in his voice, that texture of longing, impressed other singers too. Singer Bobby Taylor was touring with his brothers as the Pharoahs when they scored an opening gig for Willie at the Royal Peacock Club in Atlanta. When they heard they were going to be onstage with Little Willie John, the Pharoahs jumped in their car and drove through the night from Columbus, Ohio to the venue. When he got to know Willie, Bobby tried to crack the code on that irresistible, girl-pleasing, pleading tone in Willie's voice. "I'd ask him, how did you get this?" Bobby said, singing through his nose: "'*Taaaalk to meeee...*' Are you singing through your nose?" Willie insisted that he was not. "That's the way it comes out," Willie said. Taylor speculated that Willie had a sinus problem, "and that's why it sounded that way. It was so emotional, it was like he was crying." There was no sinus problem, Willie's brother Raymond snorted. "That was his voice."

Despite the hit status of "All Around the World," Willie wasn't raking in much money from record sales. But he learned early on that Syd Nathan was willing to buy Cadillacs for his artists in lieu of a proper pay packet. Norman Thrasher explained how it worked. "Syd would say, 'I don't have no money, what you all want?' We'd say, 'OK, we need two cars.' He'd call the Cadillac dealer on Moross Avenue (in Detroit), tell him we were on the way up there. We'd go up and pick out two Cadillacs from the show window. Turn in the ones we had. Drive off."

It was in Thrasher's suite at the Gotham Hotel in Detroit that Willie and Jackie Wilson had one of their increasingly frequent, alpha male bust-ups. Despite his years in the group, Jackie was on his way out of Billy Ward and the Dominoes, because it had been little better than indentured servitude—he barely came out even. Willie started later than Jackie did, but as a solo star with no boss, he was dressed in fine clothes, had a hit under his own name, and—Scotch on the rocks in hand—Willie was bragging about his new Cadillac Fleetwood. Silver-gray. Air-conditioning. Power seats. The works. "Jackie told Willie, 'Next time you see me, I'm gonna have the same thing.' At that time Jackie was getting with Berry (Gordy Jr), so then he recorded his first hit, he came out and finally had him a Fleetwood too," Thrasher said.

With a Cadillac, fine clothes but not a lot of money coming in, live appearances

(Clockwise from top) Willie poses with his parents, Lillie and Mertis Sr in 1951–52 (aged 14), when he first started getting press attention. *Courtesy John Family.* Willie was popular with his classmates at Pershing, especially once he had a record out. *Courtesy Ed Bierman.* Willie's report card from Pershing High School, 1953. *Courtesy John Family.*

(**Clockwise from top**) Bandleader Johnny Otis, pictured here with Willie sometime in 1955. *Courtesy Johnny Otis Productions.* Promotional shot of Willie, 1955–56. *Courtesy Universal Attractions.* Willie promotes his single "Mommy What Happened to My Christmas Tree" on the set of a local Detroit television show. *Courtesy Ed Bierman.* Willie goes over a song with an arranger at King's stuidio in Cincinnati, circa 1955–56. *Courtesy John Family.*

Willie having promotional shots taken at a studio during 1952–53. *Courtesy Ed Bierman.*

(**Clockwise from top**) King released Willie's first long-playing album in 1956, titling it *Fever* after his big hit that year. *Courtesy Bob Kelly*. Despite Willie's dislike for the song "Fever," Henry Glover was adamant that he record the song, and Willie came through. *Courtesy Bob Kelly*. Promotional shot of Willie, circa 1956. *Courtesy Universal Attractions*.

(**Clockwise from top**) Willie (center) acting up onstage with the dancers at the Siesta Room at the Club Paradise in the black resort town of Idlewild, Michigan in 1956. From left, Val Benson (then Tally), Clifford Fears (to the left of Willie) and second from right, Clineice Stubbs (then Townsend). *Courtesy Clineice Stubbs.* The marquee of the Apollo during one of Willie's engagements; the Chantels were also on the bill, 1958. *Courtesy John Family.* Willie on stage at the Apollo Theatre in Harlem, his home away from home, 1958. *Courtesy John Family.*

(**Clockwise from top left**) Willie no doubt rocked Wichita, Kansas to its core on March 23rd, 1957 when he played the Mambo Club with Hank Ballard and the Midnighters. *Courtesy Bob Kelly.* For two dollars on October 5th, 1957, you could see Willie and other acts besides at the Kiel Opera House. *Courtesy Bob Kelly.* Willie onstage, causing a stir among the female fans, circa 1958. *Courtesy* Sepia *magazine archive.*

(**Top left**) Willie performing onstage in a tuxedo, circa 1958. *Courtesy John Family*. (**Other images**) Willie, seen here in outtakes from several of the photo shoots for his King Records album covers, circa 1958–61. *Courtesy Stephen Hawkins, King/Gusto Records*.

Willie, seen here in rare candid moments between takes for his King Records album covers, circa 1958–61. *Courtesy Stephen Hawkins, King/Gusto Records.*

kept the cash flowing. "When (Willie) started recording, they only got a penny and a half a side," EJ recalled. "But if you were popular, you could work every day, and you got paid every day." In cash.

When Willie was in New York, he stayed at the Hotel Theresa, the "Waldorf-Astoria of Harlem." The tall, faux Renaissance castle perched on Seventh Avenue and 125th Street attracted the elite of traveling black celebrities in the mid 1950s, with the coffee shop a particular magnet for musicians. Here was where Willie could have a late breakfast, teasing and bragging with friends like Jimmy Scott and Solomon Burke. Willie and Jimmy loved to meet up and talk about who was doing what, to and with whom. Jimmy loved Willie's voice, and Willie returned the favor. Joe Hunter, who played keyboard on the road behind Hank Ballard and the Midnighters, remembers one night when Willie was having a drink (or two), listening to Jimmy's record "When Did You Leave Heaven," with tears rolling down his face. "This guy can beat me singing," he cried to Joe. But you've got a bigger hit, Joe argued. "I know, but he can beat me singing" Willie lamented.

Solomon Burke was another like-minded soul. "Willie John. . . I have to smile when I say his name," said Burke. A Philadelphia native, boy preacher-turned-gospel singer-turned rhythm & blues crooner, Burke was even younger (by two and a half years) than Willie, another unfettered adolescent on the loose on the chitlin circuit. "Willie was a character. Along with myself," the singer said. "Back in those days we were all characters, always something crazy to do or say because we lived in an atmosphere of prejudice, segregation, mood swings and changes." Burke was deeply religious, but at the same time, a canny businessman. While everybody else was partying or sleeping the party off, Burke would be fixing chicken sandwiches and Kool-Aid to sell backstage at the Apollo, on the bus or in the hotel. He was more inclined than Willie to keep hold of a dollar in his pocket, but he did admire Willie's talent, if not his prudence. "What a singer," Burke said. "What a performer. Always well put together, well dressed. He always had something going on." He enjoyed the buzz around Willie, the sense that anything could happen. "Willie had an appetite for creating excitement. He wasn't afraid of anybody, so he would jump on the biggest guy he could find, know that he couldn't win, get everybody involved in his fight and walk away. . . saying, 'What are they fighting for, I'm over here!'"

One night Burke watched as an angry Jackie Wilson chased his wiry hometown nemesis for blocks down the street behind the Apollo, enraged by some bit of mischief Willie had pulled. In a world of big personalities, Willie cut a wide swath through the Theresa. Sometimes the spirit would move him to run through the halls of the hotel at three in the morning, knock on all the doors and yell, "The bus is leaving, everybody get up!" Burke was there to watch as the entertainers spilled out of their rooms–often not the rooms they were supposed to be in–hastily pulling on clothes and dragging bags into the hall. That was a big laugh for Willie. "I just wanted somebody to wake up, because I'm awake," he said. Everybody saw Willie's playful side, but close friends also saw the sensitivity, a passing moodiness that would descend over him, perhaps connected to his occasional epileptic seizures.

Willie kept such problems as much to himself as he could, although occasionally an episode would alarm his fellow partiers. There was the time at the Hotel Theresa when Willie was partying with two female friends and he had a sudden seizure, frightening the girls. At the time they thought he was having a drug overdose. Certainly illicit substances couldn't have helped, but it was undoubtedly a direct result of his condition.

Etta James noticed the melancholy side of Willie. She was just 16 when she recorded "The Wallflower (Roll With Me, Henry)" but was, if possible, even more streetwise and trouble-prone than Willie. The two met when Willie was singing with Paul Williams. On road trips they would cut up on the bus and tease the older musicians, throwing rubber band-powered spitballs at their elders and sneaking off to smoke weed. In her autobiography *A Rage to Survive*, Etta James recalls that Willie was a Scorpio, "moody and deep, just like his crazy daddy. He sang with the pain and real-life experience of an adult. . . He sounded like a Jewish rabbi, wailing with a thousand years of pain. He was deep. Willie had the musical emotions of a grandfather without ever becoming an adult himself. He played from the time he woke up until he fell asleep. . ."

Sometime in late 1955, Willie's father quit Dodge Main to go out as a road manager for his son. Willie was still technically underage, although that didn't slow him down much. It was a nice break from the grind of factory work, but Mertis also wanted to keep a closer eye on his son. Over the next few years, Mertis Sr, Mertis Jr, Mable and EJ would all go out on the road with Willie from time to time. Mable even spent several years as part of Willie's act, singing a duet with him on the record "Dinner Date." Various Johns would accompany

Willie to Cincinnati for recording sessions, which led King drummer Calvin 'Eagle Eye' Shields to marvel to an interviewer in 2002, "that family was like the Jacksons!"

Mertis John Sr already knew what Willie's managers all came to find out– nobody could keep track of Willie, let alone control him. Mertis would often ask the older musicians for help. He once asked Joe Hunter to intervene. "This guy had given Willie a little liquor, and after the show, Willie was going to go shoot dice," Hunter said. "His dad said to me, 'Make sure my son goes back to the hotel after the show.'" Hunter laughed. "Saying that was like saying, 'Tell President Bush to stop the war in Iraq.'"

Willie's father also asked singer Bobby Lewis to help. Lewis and Willie knew each other from the Detroit club scene. "His father said, 'Bobby, do me a favor, say something to Willie. I can't handle him, I can't talk to him, he won't talk to me.'" Lewis protested that he didn't want to interfere, but Mertis insisted. "You're part of the family!" Lewis told Mertis Sr that he would have a word with Willie, but had no intention of doing so. "I didn't want to get caught up in a family thing," he said.

Keeping track of Willie would fry the nerves of family members and a good few managers over the years. He had an insatiable appetite for gambling in low and high places, in catching the nightclub acts of his friends, squiring women of all sorts and having more than his share of Scotch on the rocks. "Wherever he was, Willie set up the bar," said brother EJ. Friends in New York, Miami, Los Angeles and all points in between knew that, and would appear out of the woodwork wherever Willie was staying. There would be minor scrapes involving disputes over a hotel bill, running off temporarily with the Midnighters' tour money, and "misplacing" Jackie Wilson's gun (Willie tried to sell it to the hotel receptionist in New Orleans, "for her protection"). Andre Williams grins when he remembers those times, and puts it in context. "At that time all of us had a little gangster in us," the Fortune Records star said. "It wasn't as easy back then as it is now. We had to do a little hustling, we called it." Harry Balk still remembered the sense of dread he felt when he was awakened by the telephone late at night. A phone ringing after midnight usually meant that Willie was in a jam.

To Henry Glover, Willie was "the artist of artists," out of all the singers he worked with over all of his 50 years in the business. But, ever the sophisticated jazzman, Glover could also sound condescending. He described Willie as "a typical rhythm & blues artist, egotistical. . . Willie John was a headache." Willie presented himself as an adult from the age of 16, and sang with the heartache and worldly self-assurance of an ancient soul. But the childhood that was seemingly cut short actually never quite ended.

Joe Hunter saw a direct line from Willie John—the energy, the soul, the dance moves—to James Brown and later, Michael Jackson. The similarities didn't end there, Willie and Michael were also both teenagers caught up in a seductive show business world that presented them as polished, seasoned, adult performers while they were still children. Joe wasn't the only person to draw the parallel. Lattimore Brown, whose band often backed up Willie on the road, laid it out. "When you're a kid, you're dressed up in a suit of clothes like a grown man, 'cause you had to look like a star. You didn't get a chance to have that childhood play. So you become a grown man with childhood ways about you, because you didn't live out your childhood." Lattimore observed Willie's entourage at the Apollo Theater. "He got to have two bodyguards, security to walk with him. He would walk out on 125th Street and look at the red light like a little child of four or five years old. That's what happened to Michael Jackson. Just a little bitty kid, turned into a man before he got a chance."

Despite the challenges of dealing with Willie, he beguiled just about everybody that he drove crazy. "The best, kindest guy I ever met in my life," said Clarence Avant, Willie's road manager during the late 1950s. "He was a sweetheart, he loved everybody," said Bobby Lewis. "He was easy to get along with. If he knew something that would help you, he would tell you about it. It was one exciting thing after another with him." And the excitement was only set to increase—to a fever pitch.

7

FEVER

Willie reserved his most eloquent charms for women. From when he was a young child, he loved to smooth talk and flirt, and as his music rose in popularity, he was delighted at how many women were receptive to his attention. But his wasn't merely the prurient interest of the touring musician; Willie also seemed to feel genuinely protective over women and girls in his company, as he was with his mother and sisters.

Lithofayne 'Faye' Pridgon was 16, fresh off the bus from Dirty Spoon, Georgia, when she met Willie in Harlem in 1955. He was the first musician she went with, but hanging out with Etta James and other fast movers on the scene, Faye got up to speed quickly, A few years later she became Sam Cooke's girlfriend and then, the consort of guitarist Jimmy James, later known as Jimi Hendrix. Decades later, Faye has had time to assess her high-flying years in and around the music business. She dismisses a lot of the stories about Willie as hype, knowing that the reality of the man was vivid enough. Willie loved to have wild fun backstage and on every floor of the Hotel Theresa and he didn't take any guff from anybody, but she insists that he was grossly misunderstood. "This was a guy who would be sitting in the corner with his hands together in front of his face in a very pensive mood, many times with nothing to say and nothing to do," Faye said. "He was thinking, 'Oh, I got to go past that' because somebody had said something that would stick with him. He was sensitive. He was remorseful about things, or wished people wouldn't feel a certain way. He was a good person."

The days were gone where Willie had to jump out of a window to escape, but every so often he still felt the need to get lost—to run, and keep on running. "He could get away from people better than people can do today," said Faye. "He would often go a route that nobody would think, to not be available to people he didn't want. He could get off the beaten path. Sometimes he just didn't want to be bothered with people. Even though you like to do what you like to do, there were times when you need to get away."

When he needed some time to himself, Willie was drawn to Florida. It was still half-wild in parts during the 1950s, or at least rustic—not yet malled and chain-restauranted into a giant suburb of Atlanta. He loved the warm weather, the bougainvillea, and especially Miami, the high-living, tropical Eden that drew the Rat Pack and Jackie Gleason to party in mid-century modern hotels.

But Willie often eschewed the glitz and glamour of those nightspots for wilder places. "I remember when he was, not a flower child. . . *vagabond,* we used to call it," Thrasher said. "He used to go down to Miami. Ben Bart, who owned Universal Attractions, owned some orange groves down there. Willie would go stay down there for a long time." He was always writing, scribbling poems and lyrics down on notebook paper. He once gave keyboard player Joe Hunter a notebook full of these works. "'See if you can make anything out of this,' he said. I gave Mertis (Jr) the little scratches that Willie wrote. Poems. I don't know if Mertis did anything with them," Hunter recalls.

Despite his periodic need to escape the turmoil of the music business, Willie still felt his career wasn't moving fast enough. Even Mable couldn't slow him down. "His sister tried to cool him down, tell him he didn't have to rush," said Jimmy Scott. Scott suffered terribly as a result of his medical condition. He was born with Kallman's Syndrome, which froze the singer in pre-puberty and suspended his beautiful voice in a netherworld, not exactly childlike, but not quite adult either. Like Willie, he sometimes over-compensated for his small size with aggression, carrying a gun for a time. This wasn't an entirely disproportionate measure; with the perils of the road being what they were, stick-up artists sometimes jumped entertainers, and promoters often needed the persuasion of a pistol before they would pay. Many musicians packed guns.

Singer Johnny 'Pledging My Love' Ace was so fond of playing with his gun, it wasn't considered a big deal when he pointed it at his manager in jest. Unfortunately, playing Russian Roulette with his gun backstage one day in 1954, his luck ran out and Ace shot himself in the head, and died from his injuries.

Guns were easy to come by in America during the 1950s, particularly in the South. As Billy Davis of the Midnighters tells it, all you had to do was walk into a gun store or pawn shop, show some identification, then the clerk would log the purchase in a book and you would walk out with a gun. Davis remembered that routine, and that a .38 cost about 30 or 35 dollars. "I had a collection at one time of about 25 guns," Davis said. Not just for protection or wage collection. "I just wanted to have it, it was so easy to get."

Willie was no gunslinger. More often than not, he used a gun for show, or as part of one of his pranks. Once in Denver, the promoter invited the whole package show, including Willie, Sam Cooke, Jackie Wilson and early Motown singer Marv Johnson out to a club after their performance. Willie and Johnson got into a beef over a girl they both liked. Willie suggested to the tall, husky and very irate Johnson that they go outside and settle things. Johnson agreed, and took his jacket off. Davis tried to talk Willie out of it, but Willie insisted, "I'm gonna do this, I'm gonna do this." Willie and Johnson squared off, when suddenly Willie reached into his pocket, pulled a gun out and shot it into the air. "Marv stopped in his tracks and just froze," Davis said. "Willie put his gun in his pocket and just fell out laughing. Because he didn't intend to do nothing to him, he was just a practical joker. As dark as Marv was, he went from black to gray."

As 1955 turned into 1956, Willie had barely finished the Lucky Seven tour when Universal Attractions had him booked on other dates. In February, he performed at Irving Granz's Second Annual Rock 'n' Roll Jamboree at the Shrine Auditorium in Los Angeles. Blues man B.B. King was headlining; he had a hot record on the rhythm & blues charts with "You Upset Me, Baby." King noticed the effect that Willie had on women. They either wanted to cuddle him and sit him on their lap, or slip their room key into his pocket. When the young singer was on stage, the stockings, panties and purses would rain down. King had a string of rhythm & blues hits under his belt, but insists that it didn't bring him that level of feminine attention. "Girls was crazy about him because he could sing so, and he had that something about him," King said. "So a lot of us wanted to be near him so we could get the girls! Not that I know him dating any of them, but they always would come to him. Some women would say "little and cute." But oh God, could he sing. He didn't have to jump up like Jackie Wilson and James Brown and all of them and do all of the many things to excite people by moving. He could stand—we use the word 'flat foot'—and just sing, and his voice did the rest of it. I'm a man, and I could sit there and listen to it!"

Willie was second on the bill under King; then came Smiley Lewis, Jack Dupree, Shirley Gunter, the Turks, Otis Williams and the Charms, Earl King and Richard Berry. To cater to the new market of music-crazy teenagers in 1955 and 56, there was an explosion of rock and rhythm & blues caravan shows crisscrossing America. Promoters didn't believe that rock acts on their own would draw enough of an audience, thus six, seven or more acts would be featured for a dollar fifty, or two dollars in advance, packing thousands of teenagers into large civic auditoriums. Willie spent much of March traveling with the Rhythm & Blues Revue around Texas and the Southwest. On the road with him were the '5' Royales, Camille Howard, Roy Brown, Percy Mayfield, Joe Tex, Linda Hopkins, and the Jimmy Coe Band.

Later that month, Willie was booked on a one-off, "Jazz vs Rock 'n' Roll" show in Detroit at the Graystone Ballroom on Woodward. The Graystone had been one of Detroit's premier venues for jazz since the 1920s. Benny Goodman once drove all night to see Bix Beiderbecke, who was part of the Graystone orchestra. But rock 'n' roll (which at the time still included rhythm & blues) was increasingly coming to dominate the bookings by the time the 1950s rolled around. In fact, rock 'n' roll was quickly becoming the topic of the day, with newspaper pundits weighing in on its evils. The music didn't suddenly spring, fully-formed, from the head of Alan Freed or even Ike Turner in the early 1950s. It had been marinating for years in the bottom of a muddy barrel of country, jump blues and jazz in a swamp town at the back of beyond. But in 1956, rock 'n' roll became notorious, and it was publicly named and shamed as defining a worrying new teenage culture. That year, parents, teachers and ministers were moved to denounce the "new" sound for sending the nation's youth straight to hell against a soundtrack of freakish saxophone honking and flailing guitars. There seemed to be a collective amnesia about how swing music was thought to lead millions astray in the 1930s, and jazz and gin incited youth to mischief and all sorts of peril in the 1920s.

The Detroit "Jazz vs Rock 'n' Roll" concert was meant to exploit this controversy. Willie, his career kicking into overdrive, was placed on the rock side of the concert bill, along with T-Bone Walker and the Clovers. Thelonius Monk and Miles Davis represented the jazz side, but sadly no evidence remains as to whether the beboppers or the rockers prevailed. One thing is for certain, rock 'n' roll was white-hot in the first quarter of 1956. Elvis Presley swiveled through the gate in January with his first No. 1 record, "Heartbreak Hotel," and that same month, shook his greasy locks in his first national television appearance on *The Dorsey Brothers Stage Show*, undermining the morals of a whole generation. Musical barriers exploded into dust as Carl Perkins' "Blue Suede Shoes" soared up both the country and rhythm & blues charts in *Billboard*. Things were indeed hot, and they were about to get hotter as winter melted into spring. Willie John was about to record "Fever."

Details of the recording of "Fever" differ from person to person. Some of the accounts shed light on what happened, others only add to the mystery. The passage of years doesn't help, clouding memories and leading to conjecture. According to Michel Ruppli in *The King Discography*, compiled (with Bill Daniels) in the late 1970s with the help of musician interviews and session notes from King company files, "Fever" was recorded in Cincinnati on April 1st, 1956 with Jon Thomas on piano, Bill Jennings on guitar, Edwyn Conley on bass, Edison Gore on drums and Ray Felder and Rufus Gore on tenor saxophone. Felder confirmed in an interview that he played tenor on "Fever" in Cincinnati.

Intriguingly, guitarist Mickey Baker and drummer Calvin 'Eagle Eye' Shields also claim that they played on "Fever," and that it was recorded, like "All Around the World" and "Need Your Love so Bad," in New York. Baker was always based in New York; Shields, like several other Cincinnati-based King players, went back and forth, depending on where Henry Glover needed him. Baker is more certain that he played on "Fever" than he is that he played on "All Around the World," which is considered beyond doubt.

Baker is credited on "All Around the World," in Ruppli's discography, but what the guitarist remembers is playing on Titus Turner's earlier version, rather than Willie's. In fact, he describes proudly the chord played on "Fever" that recurs through the song and chimes at the end. It was a chord that was popular in jazz circles at the time, giving a sort of fresh, slightly dissonant sound that was uncommon on a rhythm & blues or rock 'n' roll record. "The chord that I play on 'Fever,' a special chord that I play there, is a minor 9/13 chord," Baker said. "You hear the chord through the song. I used it on lots of things. It had nothing to do with rhythm & blues. I put it into rhythm & blues." Baker often had leeway to improvise on sessions for Henry Glover. Glover would sometimes write out a detailed arrangement, but just as often he merely provided lead sheets with marks where the breaks were to come in, expecting the musicians to plug the gaps with their imagination. "He didn't know what the hell you were going to play, he just knew the right musicians to do this would be so and so, and so and so," Baker said. "We were always very adept musicians. The guy would say, 'You Mickey, you do this, put some noodle around in there.' Then you'd start playing guitar and he'd say, 'Yeah that's it, that's it.'" Though Baker seems certain, it may be the case that he and Shields remember playing on an early dub of "Fever" recorded in New York so the songwriters could take it around as a demo, or for Henry Glover to use as a guide for the finished track.

Willie's brother Mertis says firmly that "Fever" was recorded in Cincinnati. "I know, because it was a scheduled session, we were told to go to Cincinnati, and when we got there ("Fever") was the first thing they had for him to do," Mertis said emphatically. "Willie wanted to do some other things, some things that I had written, but he was told, 'You're not going to do anything until you do 'Fever.'" Mertis also has a strong visual memory of the guitarist on the "Fever" session–Bill Jennings–being left-handed. Baker is right-handed.

Even more than the musician credits, the issue of who *wrote* "Fever" was clouded for years by the fact that Otis Blackwell used the pseudonym of 'John Davenport' on the song because he was under contract with another company under his own name. There was a persistent rumor in some corners that 'John Davenport' was in fact Willie John's real name, and that he wrote the song. Some web databases still credit Willie as a co-writer of "Fever," and he may have put enough of his mark on the final song to warrant that attribution. Years later, Blackwell told musician Tom Russell that he wrote "Fever" with Willie. Over the years, Blackwell said that Eddie Cooley brought him the rough basis of the song, and that he worked on it and finished the tune. He then brought it along with a batch of other songs on a routine visit to pitch Henry Glover, and Glover chose "Fever" right away.

Singer Joe Tex had a particularly colorful claim. In the mid 1950s, ten years before his "Skinny Legs and All" fame, Tex was a struggling singer specializing in rhythm & blues ballads, often on the bottom of the bill of shows featuring Little Willie John. Years after "Fever" was recorded, Tex claimed he wrote the song for rent money when he was down and out. His story fluctuates a bit from time to time, in 1977 he told one writer that he was struggling in New York for money and sold the song for three hundred dollars to Otis Blackwell. That same year he told a journalist with Britain's *New Musical Express* (now *NME*) that he sold it directly to Henry Glover for three hundred dollars. He claimed that the lyrics reflected Tex's nostalgic memories of a smoking-hot Texas girlfriend, and instructed Glover to put the words to the tune of Tennesse Ernie Ford's "16 Tons," a hit over the previous winter, "and let me pay my rent." One thing everybody agrees on is that Willie took an instant dislike to "Fever." Before the session started, he greeted Henry Glover with a sassy, "Whatcha got for me?" "Got something good for you," Glover replied. He ran down the changes and lyrics for "Fever."

"Never know how much I love you. . ." snapping his finger. "Willie didn't like it, I could tell he didn't," said brother Mertis, who had accompanied Willie to the session. Willie asked his brother if he liked the song, and Mertis confessed that he did not. But, he reminded his brother that there was no choice, Willie was going to have to do it. Why such a strong reaction? Like many songs pitched to producers, "Fever" had been recorded as a songwriter's dub, with no polished arrangement. "The dub sounded really crazy," Mertis said. "But Henry say, 'That's the dub. You're gonna sing it.' Willie began to sing the song the way Henry wanted. But it was still a problem," said Mertis. The song was dead and cold for Willie. That held no water for Henry Glover, however; he was used to forcefully dealing with wayward musicians and opinionated singers. It didn't matter that Willie had a hit song in the stores with "Need Your Love So Bad," Glover laid down the law with the John brothers. "Henry say, 'I tell you what, if he don't do this song, he's doing *nothing*,'" Mertis recalled. "He said 'Mert, take it to the hotel, make sure he learns it.' So I went to the hotel and we started going over the song." Blackwell knew that Willie didn't like his song. "That's what Henry Glover tells me," Blackwell said in a 1970 interview. "It wasn't the type of thing Willie was doing at the time, he didn't like the finger snapping."

It took an all-night session with the tune for Willie to find his way in. Somehow, in the tangle of notes and words on the dub, he found something to tap into, bringing out a sensual reading that was as hot as rock 'n' roll, but as cool as jazz. By morning, he had nailed it. "Willie hit the groove," Mertis said. He called Glover, who set up a time to go to the studio that night. "We went over it and that night, we recorded it."

Still four months shy of his 19th birthday, Willie sings with a voice taut with melancholy, and an almost ecstatic lovesickness. Just as in "All Around the

World," his voice catches at one point, as if overwhelmed by the exquisite pain of love. According to Mertis, King's staff arranger, Andy Lipson, sketched out the arrangement with heavy input from Glover. The arrangement gave the two minute and 44 second pop song the complexity and pleasing ambiguity of jazz, perfect for a tune that celebrated both romantic longing and fulfillment. While the song is in a minor key, the combination of blues and jazz licks gives it an uptown, urbane feel. Willie, the veteran of so many Count Basie gigs, swings effortlessly with his voice, echoed by a bluesy backup chorus. Even the finger-snapping ends up adding to the charm, giving the recording a cool, late-night vibe.

What makes the song is the guitar. The guitarist is in the unusual position for a 1950s pop session of adding color and mood, instead of just playing rhythm or fills. A key element is the change-up at the break, when it's just Willie singing. The saxophones continue their ominous, scolding line while the guitarist chimes in with another intriguing blend of jazz and blues chords. The song ends with Willie humming sensually, as if his emotions have taken over and finally, words have failed him.

Backed with "Letter From My Darling," "Fever" (King 4935) was released in late April, 1956, amidst a batch of singles put out by the Cincinnati company that included a rough-hewn single on the Federal subsidiary, "Please Please, Please" by James Brown. King boss Syd Nathan was so used to Willie's soaring vocal abilities by then, that he flew into a rage when he heard Brown howl, scream and plead on "Please, Please, Please." This, Syd insisted, was not singing. It was, of course, rhythmic genius in nascent form. "He's just singing the same damn word over and over!" Syd yelled. Thankfully Hal Neely, by then running day-to-day operations at King, prevailed upon Syd to release the song anyway. But the godfather of soul was still years behind Little Willie John. His time would come though, and soon.

In the "This Week's Best Buys" column in May 12th, 1956 *Billboard*, the reviewer wrote, "Of the singers developed in the last year, hardly any have shown the consistency of Little Willie John. This time at bat he is certainly wasting no time making his way to home plate. 'Fever' is already on the Detroit territorial chart, and is becoming well established in Cincinnati, Cleveland, St Louis, Nashville and Chicago." The song landed on the No. 1 spot on *Billboard*'s rhythm & blues charts by July 21st and stayed there for three weeks. Willie finally invaded the pop charts as well. "Fever" rose to No. 22 on The Cashbox Top Singles chart where it sat for several weeks in July. In *Billboard*, it peaked at No. 24 on the pop charts.

One statistic is particularly telling: "Fever" was the No. 6 most played jukebox song of 1956, according to *Billboard*. What other song would you play if you were sipping a cocktail and wanting to impress the slinky dish down the bar? Or, if you were that dish and wanted to sway around in your red dress, getting the local boys all excited, what song would handle your business? The people spoke—with innumerable nickels plugged into jukeboxes all across America.

SUCCESS

"Little Willie John did not know how to sing wrong, know what I mean?"– Dion DiMucci

In 1956, the pop charts were an uneasy mix of the rough and the tame. Insurgent rock 'n' roll numbers by Little Richard, Frankie Lymon, the Elvis tidal wave and Little Willie John shared space on the Top 100 with a raft of frothy pop by Mitch Miller, Patti Page and Pat Boone. Rock 'n' roll was on the prowl, but in the summer of 1956 the lush, nostalgic movie theme "Moonglow/Theme From Picnic" was still the song dominating sales and radio play. Since January, Elvis had been getting all the press with his loose hips and smoldering sexuality, but "Fever," with the frank eroticism of Willie's voice, was just as subversive. Nestled in next to Gogi Grant's sobbing "The Wayward Wind" and Nelson Riddle's crisp "Lisbon Antigua," "Fever" sounded uptown and jazzy, but the subtext was unfettered sexuality.

Jerry Butler explains it by singing the lyrics: *"'When you put your arms around me, I get a feeling that's so hard to bear, you give me fever, in the morning, fever when you hold me tight...'* Today that would be considered a very tame lyric, but in those days that was hot, torchy music... You couldn't do that on public radio and not at all on television, singing that particular song. He could get away with 'Talk to Me' or 'Heartbreak' maybe."

"Fever" had grown on Willie, considerably. "He liked it even more after it was released, when it took off," Mertis Jr said, laughing. "Myself, and my sisters and brothers, we even started saying they ought to stop playing that 24 hours a day."

Thankfully, they didn't.

With "Fever" tearing up the charts, even a brand new Cadillac wasn't payment enough; Syd Nathan had to fork over some cash. Willie stopped buying boys' suits off the rack at Hot Sam's and discovered Harry Kosins' shop in downtown Detroit, where he had suits and sports clothes custom-made to fit his short, muscular frame. For Willie, there was little division between his stage clothing and his street ensembles. A decade before Marvin Gaye and the Temptations cut a memorable style in mohair suits, Willie was a male peacock, groomed to within an inch of his life. He preferred either a sleek, urban presentation in featherweight silk or mohair, or a tweedy, English look that brought to mind the offstage turnout of Hollywood icons Bing Crosby and crooner Frank Sinatra.

Willie had a system of circulating suits between his road wardrobe and the John home in Detroit. Brother EJ was in charge of the haberdashery, picking up the new threads that Willie had ordered from Kosins' store, and rotating suits so his brother always had a fresh look for the stage. "He'd call up and say, 'You know that brown suit I left? Send that along to me,'" EJ remembers. Leaving the clothing in his younger brother's care was also a kindness, because Willie knew that, being roughly the same size, EJ would enjoy sporting such fine threads in the neighborhood.

With "Fever" still gathering steam in late summer, Henry Glover called Willie to New York for a session. He had a song, "My Nerves," that he wanted Willie to record. Dressed in a light gray silk summer suit, white shirt, silver-gray tie, black moccasins and flashing a four-diamond ring on his pinky finger, Willie was a sight for sore eyes. Harry Balk was still his manager, the last man standing of his four Detroit-based handlers, and he was in the studio that day keeping Willie company. The two old friends conferred as Glover ran over the tune with the band for what would become King catalog number 8779.

Willie was buoyant, singing the first verse with verve for the run-through, then bursting out of the vocal booth to dance during the instrumental break. A reporter from *Rhythm & Blues Stars 1956* was in the studio too, observing the electricity of Willie's performance. How did Willie like success? "I like it," Willie said. "It's good, but you can't quit. You can't slow down. You got to keep givin'."

Hy Grill, King's director of A&R, was also present, and it was Grill who sat in the control room and gave Willie his final instructions via the talkback mic, while Glover gave the downbeat to the band. "Willie, I want you sitting on that mic. I want you sitting on my lap!" Grill said. Glover gave the band a whispered countdown to a downbeat, while Grill called out "8-7-7-9 cut one!" and they were off. The technology still dictated that Willie and the band sing and play each note together, so when a tenor saxophonist hit a clam, everybody had to stop, and it was on to take two. That take felt too fast, which led to take three, and so it went on, with Willie singing all out for each take. To the writer observing in the studio, it appeared that Willie was feeling some strain. "This is nothing," Harry Balk growled. "They took six hours making 'Fever.'"

Willie told a writer, an uncredited scribe for the one-off music mag, that his next move would be to send his mother house-shopping. "When I was a kid, we didn't live in no palace," Willie said. "I always used to say to my mom, someday I'm gonna get you a real house to live in. I'm buyin' her that house— this week!" "You couldn't do anything nicer than that with your money," the writer replied. To which Willie added, "An' I'm getting a Cadillac. Pink an' black." Yes, another one.

In 1957 Willie found himself booked into Henry Wynne's Royal Peacock Club in Atlanta with a like-minded, diminutive singer, Bobby Taylor. Bobby was just back from the service in Korea, playing in a band called the Pharoahs with his brothers. The Pharoahs were booked for four dates at the Royal Peacock, opening the show for Willie. That wasn't four days, Bobby hastens to say, but four engagements of ten days each. At 23, Bobby was three years older than Willie, and as a pair of pocket-sized tenors, they formed a close bond.

Henry Wynne was one of the South's busiest promoters of caravan tours of rock and rhythm & blues. It was at the Royal Peacock that Bobby and Willie struggled to match hard-living bluesman Jimmy Reed drink for drink. They spent a good deal of their time drunk, Bobby admits. To make things worse, comedian Redd Fox mentored the two young men. This was in the years before he was known as the crotchety Fred Sanford on television's *Sanford and Son*, and Fox was notorious for his X-rated routines, with most of his albums being sold under the counter at the record shops, the ones that dared to stock them at all. Fox's most memorable advice to Bobby and Willie was: "I better not catch you suckers with any ugly women."

At the Royal Peacock, Fox shared the bill with rock 'n' roll singers and down-home blues musicians. One crooner, Tommy Brown, would weep and cry while singing his set. In the middle of a song, Tommy would walk into the audience, go over to a window and jump out. After defenestrating himself, Tommy would make his way back up the stairs and into the club, still crying and singing. "This was his act!" marveled Bobby.

Bobby and the Pharoahs didn't have a record out yet, but that didn't prevent their youthful high spirits from showing through with a bit of bravado aimed at the other performers on the bill, bragging that they'd "eat them up" onstage. It wasn't easy to eat up Willie John. Taylor remembered women giddily throwing lacy underthings at the headliner, including garter belts with metal hooks that could smart when pelted with the right amount of frenzied force. "They didn't have no stockings that stayed up on you all day," Bobby said, referring to one-piece pantyhose. "Those stockings were first class. Real silk. One touch on it and it'll run." The hotel where the entertainers stayed had communal bathrooms, which meant dismal, shared showers and "creepy-crawlies" everywhere. But Bobby sighed, recalling the "delicious" 50 cent dinners of soul food at the hotel restaurant, fried up in good old-fashioned lard. Without a lot of artificial ingredients, it was better for you, he insists. "You wouldn't believe it, but those were great days," Bobby said.

There was change in the air in 1956, and the turmoil wasn't confined to the *Billboard* charts. A push for desegregation of schools, restaurants and other public places was causing social unrest in the South on a scale not seen for decades. The big caravan tours played separate shows to black and white audiences, but some white teenagers would infiltrate the livelier black shows, raising the ire of a few dangerous people. "White Citizens Councils" had sprung up across the South to fight desegregation in response to the Supreme Court's decision in Brown vs Board of Education (1954) that ruled separate schools unequal. Rock 'n' roll and rhythm & blues were clearly turning up the gas on an already heated situation. Those decadent rhythms teenagers danced to were dissolving the color line, and the White Citizens Councils meant to stop them.

Willie embarked upon yet another caravan tour that spring, the Big Rhythm and Blues Show of 1956, with Fats Domino, the Clovers, Ruth Brown, the Cadillacs, Little Richard, the Turbans, Ann Cole, and the Choker Campbell Band. After a few dates in the north, the caravan was heading south. Then in Birmingham, Alabama, on April 12th, several men knocked Nat 'King' Cole off his piano bench and dragged him toward the edge of the stage as he prepared to sing for an all-white audience. Cole's attackers were subdued by police, arrested, and found to be members of the White Citizens Council of Birmingham. After recovering his composure, the singer reemerged to a standing ovation, but he didn't complete the show. He did, however, play for a black audience later that evening. Racial anger and fear continued to ripple through the South as the Big Rhythm and Blues Show headed toward the heart of Dixie. On the tour's May 4th stop, a mini-riot erupted in Roanoke, Virginia when white teenagers streamed through the doors and joined black teens enjoying the concert. The next day, the plug was pulled on the tour, and everybody went home.

Back in Michigan, Willie started to get bookings in a place as far away from the brutally segregated South as possible: Idlewild, Michigan. A beguiling lake town south of Ludington, near the Lake Michigan shore, Idlewild was a sort of black Shangri-La. Here was a place that not only welcomed black guests at a time when most resorts were off limits, but its hotel, motels, nightclubs and stores were largely owned or controlled by black people. There was also a string of high-end nightclubs that attracted the top black acts traveling the circuit, showcasing performers like Billy Eckstine, Dinah Washington, Della Reese and the pre-Motown Four Tops. The caliber of talent that made Idlewild a regular stop between Chicago and Detroit also drew white fans down from northern Michigan cities like Petoskey and Traverse City.

In June, LaVern Baker had the gang at Phil Giles' Flamingo Room mambo-ing to her hit song "Tweedle Dee," while Willie sang "Fever" for the shooters in the Siesta Room at the Club Paradise. The Paradise was run by Arthur Braggs, a numbers man out of Saginaw, and owned by Lila Wilson, who'd built half of Idlewild during the 1910s. Syndicated columnist and choreographer Ziggy Johnson emceed the shows at the Paradise and directed its troupe of dancers, "Arthur Braggs' Braggetts." Every summer Ziggy Johnson would start a dance craze at the Club Paradise: one year it was the Satin Doll, another time he unveiled the Chickaboo. Woe to the chorine who couldn't match Ziggy step for step.

Among the hoofers were three Detroit girls, Valaida Tally (the little girl a runaway Willie charmed with his voice), Clineice Townsend and Inez Clinstables. Sitting in the audience one night watching the Four Tops sing, the girls divvied up band members Obie Benson, Levi Stubbs and Duke Fakir, respectively, later marrying the men they picked that night.

At two in the morning, after the last floor show, Willie and the other entertainers would hang out at the after-hours El Morocco Club. During the day Willie would swim, go fishing and relax a little after the breakneck pace of the last two years' touring schedule. College boy William Colden was keeping a close eye on all the action, he was staying at his parents' cottage during his summer off from Hillsdale College. "It was a ball!" Colden said. "Idlewild at that time was packed, jammed with people, because black folks couldn't go anywhere else. They came from Chicago, from Indianapolis, from Kansas City. Idlewild was probably the largest black resort in the country." Ironically, Idlewild started to fade after Frank Sinatra and the Rat Pack helped to end segregation in Las Vegas. The entertainers insisted that blacks be allowed to see their shows and stay in the hotels, spelling demise for Idlewild. "Why go way up in the woods, when you could go anywhere?" Colden said.

But in the 1950s, Idlewild was at its peak, a seductive blend of glamorous nightlife and rustic, lakeside charm. It was the most fun that teenagers and adults could have without breaking the law. Well, without breaking *most* laws. At 19, Willie was closer in age to Colden and his running buddy Joe Brown than most of the show folk, and the boys hit it off immediately. "I wasn't part of the entertainment, but I knew the showgirls and the Four Tops, and I ran around with them during the day when they didn't have matinees," Colden said. "You know how college kids are, kind of wild and rowdy. It was fun for us to hang out with the show people. We did all sorts of nefarious things with them. We'd go out in the woods, smoke weed, drink and have a good time."

Colden recalls Willie as short and "just a regular, nice guy. Most of the people he ran with were older, I guess that's where he picked up his worldliness," he mused. Where Willie picked up his infinitely cool, practiced stagecraft, Colden couldn't begin to say. "He was very good," Colden said. "Very good! And intense." Unlike Billy Eckstine, Willie would do steps onstage, and was once caught by a photographer twirling around on the dance floor with the chorus girls.

Willie's then-frequent Apollo Theater dates in New York were another welcome respite from the endless, brutal Southern tours. The Apollo was as close to a performing home as Willie had, with the Hotel Theresa close by up 125th Street, and as much club-hopping in between as a nightowl such as Willie could ask for.

Bobby Schiffman, son of Apollo owner Frank Schiffman, saw a lot of acts in his three decades managing the theater, but famously rated Willie as number one. "Willie John was the best singer I ever heard," Schiffman told writer Ted Fox. "He used to send chills up and down my spine, and I never met a singer who had that kind of emotion and feeling in his songs. Willie would appear at the theater and do 31 shows, and I would stand in the wings and watch every one. He was incredible." Schiffman also saw how Willie could empty his pockets within days and then plead and moan to borrow more from his employers. No dice, not with the Schiffmans. They loved him, but they were tough.

Sometime in 1956, thunderclouds raced across the upper Great Lakes, wolves howled and a future music legend made his way from the Iron Range of upper Minnesota down to Detroit. Fifteen year-old Robert Zimmerman was accompanying a friend on a visit to some relatives in Motor City. After crossing Lake Superior, the boys made their way through the piney north woods of Michigan's Upper Peninsula, across the straits of Mackinac and down the long two-lane highways to Detroit. The boys arrived in a rundown neighborhood in a city crackling with rhythm, as different a place from Minnesota's austere Iron Range as there could be in North America.

Zimmerman, better known as Bob Dylan, told the story of his early exposure to Detroit rhythm & blues onstage in 1980, speaking to an audience in San Francisco. "I can't remember how it happened but I found myself in a bingo parlor, there were people coming to eat all day and they played bingo all night and there was a dance band in the back," Dylan said. "And that was the first time. . . see, where I'm from I'd only hear mostly country music, you know, Hank Williams, Hank Snow, Hank Penny, all kinda Hanks. But anyway so this was my first time face to face with the rhythm & blues, it was in Detroit. . . There was a man there that was singing this song here, I don't think I'll do it as good as he did it but I'm going to try it anyway." And then, Bob Dylan sang "Fever."

Dylan said he was "about 12" at the time, which can't be right because he was 12 in 1953, and "Fever" wasn't released until 1956. Either he saw Willie sing another song, or it's possible that Dylan was story-telling, talking about what should have been or what he wished he'd seen. Then again, he was only three years off. If Dylan saw Little Willie John at full power and velocity in Detroit during the 1950s, it's possible the intensity of the experience might have obscured some of the minor details.

That fall, Willie found himself in the crosshairs of one of rhythm & blue's most explosive showmen. Between 1948 and 1955, Wynonie 'Good Rockin' Tonight' Harris was one of the most exciting singers in the world, a living, human link between jump blues and the incipient, vibrant mess that was rock 'n' roll. If any one person could be credited with "inventing" this new sound, it was 'Mr Blues,' who'd been honing his craft since the 1930s. DJ Alan Freed is still widely credited with naming the new sound rock 'n' roll, but Wynonie was singing about it back when Freed still had hair. *"Have you heard the news? There's good rockin' tonight,"* Wynonie howled back in 1947. Two years later he was singing: *"All she wants to do is rock and roll all night."* A skirt-chasing, hard-drinking rabble rouser whose off-the-mic life was as torrid as his songs. Wynonie disappeared from the music scene in 1954 to take care of "pressing personal business." When he returned in 1956 to ink a deal with Atlantic Records, he was outraged to find three upstarts had taken his place. "I'm king of the rock and rollers," Wynonie proclaimed, "not Elvis, Little Willie John and Pat Boone."

But by then, it was too late.

|9|

TALK TO ME

At 19, Willie had enjoyed more than his share of girlfriends, the sort of backstage hook-ups that added spice to the downtime between shows. Faye Pridgon, a self-described party girl and free spirit, wasn't one to linger sentimentally with a boyfriend. She jumped from Willie to Sam Cooke after he grabbed her hand at a party and the electric rush of a new love propelled her from one relationship into another. "I got it with Willie, and that's what I liked about every relationship," Faye said. "When that died off, I got my knees with the breeze. (Cooke) was nowhere near the person that Willie was, but it was very serious."

In the spring of 1957, Willie had a leggy new distraction. At the Apollo Theater, he liked to watch the showgirls and stagehands play a card game called Tonk in between acts. Tonk was well suited for killing time backstage, because each hand was over with in a few minutes. The players bet with nickels and dimes, and it would soon add up. Willie hadn't even introduced himself to dancer Darlynn Bonner when she discovered that he had been quietly paying her Tonk debts behind her back.

Darlynn insists that she wasn't all that great as a dancer. "*Willie* was a better dancer than I was," she said, laughing. He was a whiz at ballroom dancing, particularly. Darlynn added, softly, "He could have had anybody." But it was the slim, shy Philadelphian with the long ponytail that Willie wanted. He watched her from the wings as Darlynn kicked and twirled across the worn Apollo Theater boards with her fellow Hortense Allen dancers. Darlynn was taller than Willie by a hair–who wasn't?–and at 23, she was four years older than him, although she didn't know that yet. He kept his teenaged status quiet. Older woman or not, Darlynn was no match for Willie John's intense focus and attention.

One day the Allen dancers were onstage doing a routine when Darlynn noticed Willie standing in the wings, staring. "You sure are pretty," he said, smiling. That night he asked her out to dinner. A week later he proposed. A few days after that, he called Mother Dear in Detroit to tell her he was getting married. Darlynn was the last to know. "The next thing I knew, *Jet* magazine had that we were engaged," Darlynn said. Weren't they? "No!" she said, laughing. "But he was very sweet. He sent me flowers, candy, everything." She sighed. "He was so alive, such a jovial person. I never saw him angry, I never saw that."

Self-deprecating and quiet, Darlynn Bonner was convinced she had gotten her slot with the Philadelphia-based Hortense Allen Dancers because of her fresh looks, not for her dancing ability. She had attracted the notice of powerful men before, dating top Philadelphia DJ Georgie Woods, who also emceed shows at the Uptown Theater. The Bonners' neighborhood was a mix of hard-working blue collar and middle class residents, although, along with the rest of north Philly, it was starting to get a little rough around the edges by the early 1950s. Darlynn graduated from Simon Gratz High School in 1951. One of her best friends was Esther Hawthorne, whom she'd met in 1945 at Vaux Junior High School. They were, in Esther's words, "just a bunch of silly little teenagers." Darlynn was quiet, but like Esther and all the girls in their clique, she enjoyed the glitter and glam of dressing up.

"We were kind of standoffish," Esther remembered. "With the hairdos and the jewelry, I guess we thought we were special. We were into the glamorous-type life." The girls went to parties after school at different friends' houses, where they'd dance the bop in the basement to DJ Randy Dixon's *Ebony Hall of Fame* radio show. Darlynn did some modeling, and caught the eye of choreographer Allen when she accompanied a friend to rehearsal at her dance studio one day. Allen liked her look, and asked to see what Darlynn could do. Darlynn was invited to join Allen's troupe, as was Esther, although only Darlynn ended up traveling with the group.

By the time she turned up on Willie John's radar, Darlynn was a stylish 23 year-old whose reserved, ladylike manner stood out amid the raunch and floozies of the backstage whirl. That demure exterior masked some pain.

Born in North Carolina, Darlynn had come to Philadelphia as a child when her parents Willie and Margaret Bonner sought work there. They settled in North Philadelphia, where Willie Bonner secured a job in a box factory. It was a difficult childhood. Her family wasn't the type to express love and affection, and Darlynn envied her friend Esther's loving, stable family.

Willie's warmth, his effusive nature, was a revelation to Darlynn. She had never experienced such lavish displays of affection and protectiveness. "He was so kind and thoughtful," Darlynn said. Willie was never shy about public displays of emotion toward his girlfriend. "He was a wonderful person," she said. "He loved me. And he would kiss you or hug you in Times Square! I never knew anybody like that at home."

The engagement item in *Jet* was no accident. Willie was already savvy in the ways of the entertainment press, and he knew who to call or who to pay to get his name in the columns. The subterfuge was right out of the 1957 Burt Lancaster–Tony Curtis film *Sweet Smell of Success*, with press agents paying to get items into the paper, and columnists openly acting as double agents. One syndicated columnist who wrote about Willie often was Masco Young. Young's double life as both press agent and columnist was revealed when he sued Willie, James Brown and Hank Ballard in 1962 for "unpaid publicity fees and expenses," complaining in the suit that he was "totally disgusted at the irresponsible, reckless, adolescent shenanigans of rock 'n' roll artists who gladly boast of earning 100,000 dollars or more a year, but who still can't handle a publicity bill of 200 or 500 dollars."

In the case of Willie and Darlynn's engagement, the item in *Jet* may not have been true at the time it was printed, but it soon came to be true enough. Their whirlwind engagement spun forward to a quick conclusion when Willie made arrangements for Darlynn to visit Detroit. He flew her in–her first time on an airplane–and booked her a room at the Gotham Hotel, a 200-room monolith at John R and Orchestra Place, in one of Detroit's entertainment districts. The Gotham was the height of chic in the black entertainment world, the classiest place for stars like Duke Ellington or Sammy Davis Jr to stay, with ornate mahogany suites freshened daily with lush bouquets of flowers. Willie showered Darlynn with attention, gifts and food for a week, while secretly making arrangements for their nuptials.

"I didn't even know we were getting married. He didn't tell me," Darlynn said. "He'd gone down to get the marriage license, and filled it all out." When she saw the marriage license, Darlynn realized that her self-assured groom was just 19, four years younger than she. There was no time to wonder if it mattered. Willie and Darlynn were married at the John home on Leslie Street on May 25th, 1957. The ceremony was conducted by Reverend Clinton Levert of the Triumph Church.

Were the Johns startled by the marriage? It wasn't the first time Willie had been impetuous. He said he was going to become a professional entertainer, and he did it. He predicted that he would go to New York and cut a hit record, and he came back with "All Around the World." If his family were suspicious of the sophisticated, well-dressed model and dancer he brought home as his bride-to-be, maybe it was the fear that the Johns' 19 year-old breadwinner would now be a married man, with a wife and family of his own to support.

Surrounded by the large John family, all noisy, outgoing and physically affectionate, Darlynn was over the moon. "I thought, finally, I'm in a place where people show love," Darlynn said. "I guess I should have realized that I wouldn't be accepted with open arms.

She sensed some ruffled feathers, if not outright resentment, from some of her in-laws. Mable in particular was close to Willie, liked going on the road with him and didn't care to share her brother with an outsider. "I mean, they were all very nice to me. But I guess it's natural they may have thought I was out for money." That pained her. "I thought it was wonderful that he bought his mother a home," she said. "I didn't want to take that away." For just as he was marrying Darlynn and starting his own family, Willie made good on the promise he'd made as a 14 year-old. He'd bought his mother a house on Leslie Street, a substantial two-story place in Russell Woods, near the Dexter–Davidson neighborhood. Lillie had chosen the house on her own, although Willie had often shared his dream about Russell Woods and Ed Bierman's leafy street with those famous hermit cookies cooling on the rack in the kitchen.

At 19, Willie was still a minor, but he was also the alpha male of the John family. A warranty deed confirms that the house at 3260 Leslie was "conveyed to the estate of William E. John, a minor," from a couple, Alan J. and Lee Stone. Willie said later that he paid 20,000 dollars for the place. The Johns now owned a solid, middle-class home in Russell Woods. "It was like Hollywood!" EJ marveled, still glowing with the memory of it. In 1957, Russell Woods, with its broad streets, stately homes and well-kept lawns, was still an aspirational neighborhood for most Detroiters.

Just as Willie was generous with his family, he showered his wife and later, his children with gifts. "I never asked him for money," Darlynn insisted. "He would see what we needed, and give it to me." He loved bringing her presents back from the road, especially clothing and more often than not, high heels. "Oh, the high heels that he bought me! They were so high. Now I'm paying for it," she said with a laugh. If Willie felt torn between his bride and his family, he didn't mention it to anybody, there was simply another name added to his protected list. Darlynn would laugh at how she wouldn't be allowed to do certain things when he was home from the road, like walking down to the corner store by herself. "What did he think I did when he was gone?" she said, laughing.

That sort of male protectiveness left older sister Mable bemused, and often annoyed. On tour with her baby brother in the late 1950s, the sophisticated Mable found herself locked into her hotel room, under orders by Willie not to join the late night parties he himself had every intention of attending.

"Willie was very protective, so you'd have to go along with it," said brother Mertis. "There was one way, his way. 'I do what I want to do. But you stay out of trouble.' That was Willie." It was partly a result of the dominance of males in the John family, Mertis believes. "There were only three girls in my family," Mertis said of his siblings. "Boys dominated." During a 2006 visit with his nephew Kevin, Willie's son, Mertis barked: "How many boys do you have, Kevin?"

"Two."

"How many girls?"

"None."

"That's the way it goes in this family," Mertis said, chuckling to himself.

Love and loyalty persist with the Johns, despite the conflict and loss that has occurred over the years. But as in most large families, the individual siblings often have differing views of internal family dynamics. Mable felt that she wasn't appreciated as an entertainer by her brothers and sisters, except for perhaps Mertis. By 1957, Mable had graduated from selling insurance door to door for Berry's mother, Bertha Gordy, to the more glamorous duties of assisting Berry with his rapidly expanding musical interests. The would-be mogul didn't have a car, so Mable would drive him all over town. In return, he was grooming Mable as a singer, accompanying her on piano at local clubs. Because his sisters worked the photo concession at the Flame Show Bar, Gordy was able to secure Mable a slot opening for Billie Holiday. It was an early professional triumph for both the budding record executive, and the singer. Mable would go on to record for Motown, but her grown-up, sexy blues sound was suited more to Stax Records, where she had a hit in 1966 with "Your Good Thing (Is About to Come To An End)." Four years later she joined Ray Charles' troupe as his head Raelette.

Despite her own success in the music business, as far as Mable understood, it was clear who brother EJ was referring to when he said, "There is but one singer in the John family." He'd talk about the United Five and about Raymond's later singing career, but EJ always maintained, "There is but one singer." Mable's siblings also sometimes bristled at her authority. "Mable was always throwing it in our faces—'I'm the oldest!' So what? Everything has to begin," Mertis said. "It means nothing. I'm the oldest boy, so what? Named after my father, so what? Everybody can't be born at the same time." For her part, Darlynn believed that Willie's father, Mertis Sr, was harder on some of his offspring, notably EJ and Mildred, than on others.

The John siblings may have squabbled within the family unit, but they presented a formidable, united front to the outside world. Mable described how John family unity worked when everything was going well. "If you do have a tight-knit family, the family can get together and fund you, and cushion you until you're able to go on to the next plateau. That's what the Johns did. We all started writing songs, traveling and working with each other, and that's the thing that strengthened us, and we were able to grow."

Darlynn felt no resentment from her brother-in-law EJ, and the two remained close over the years. "Ernest was real," Darlynn said. Hobnobbing with Willie's show business contacts over time made her appreciate that "realness" all the more. She came to prefer the company of workaday people who held down regular jobs, and were there for her when the glamour of Willie's career had faded. "Ernest never had any schemes," Darlynn said of her straight-talking brother-in-law.

The rebellious Willie, having borne the brunt of his father's discipline for so long, was now the golden child, the son who supported everybody. He was also the son whom Mertis Sr could no longer control. Everyone depended on Willie financially, and after Mertis Sr gave up his job in the factory to join his son on the road, he did too. Willie got used to being in the position of power. So much so that he gave Mable some grief when she started spending more and more time working with Berry Gordy. Willie was the big shot in Detroit, the "No. 1 jukebox sensation in the nation," so who was this Gordy upstart? "Willie started first, and he was becoming successful very fast," Mable said. "He and Berry would talk, but there was this thing with my brother, he would become a little jealous sometimes because I spent so much time with Berry. I think that was one of the reasons it was so easy for my brother to take me on the road with him, because he thought he was taking me away from Berry. He would always tell me, 'I'd like you to go on the road with me and do so-and-so.' I'd say, 'No, I have to do this with Berry.' Then he'd say, 'But I'm your brother.'"

EJ remembers Berry Gordy submitting songs to Willie, just as he did with Jackie Wilson. Willie never bit, but Jackie took the songs. Was there some alpha dog competition between Willie and Berry? Mable believes that it was a complex mix of competition and admiration. "I think in their hearts, they would have loved to have done something together," Mable said. She wanted to burst with pride when Willie flew to Detroit for her gig with Billie Holiday at the Flame Show Bar. "Willie flew in so he could be with me on closing night," Mable said. "That was the highlight of the week, along with working with Billie."

After they were married at the John house, the newlyweds enjoyed a brief honeymoon before Willie had to head back to the one-nighters and caravan tours. Darlynn stayed in Detroit with his family.

The third week of October 1957 was stunning for the array of blockbuster single releases. "Lonely Teardrops" by Jackie Wilson, "Sweet Little Rock and Roller" by Chuck Berry, "Stagger Lee" by Lloyd Price and "Heartbeat" by Buddy Holly all came out in that one week. At the same time, King released "All My Love Belongs to You" by Willie. It wasn't a hit, those were few and far between for him in 1957, but it had been a lucky year for Willie in other ways.

Twelve year-old Marty Schein of Westchester, New York was lucky too, in his case to have a hip young dad who was willing to take Marty and his ten year-old sister on the half-hour train ride from Westchester to Harlem's 125th Street Station to catch a show at the Apollo. Sometime in the late fall of 1957, Marty was supposed to go to the Apollo to see two of his favorite bands, the Jesters and the Paragons, but he fell sick and was put straight to bed. By the time Marty was well enough to make the trip, Willie John was the Apollo's headliner. At the time, Marty admits, he would have preferred to see the Jesters. But realizes now that he lucked out. "I got to see an icon in rhythm & blues, Little Willie John."

The Scheins went for a bite to eat on 125th street, then they headed down to the Apollo for the five pm show (often called the 'maid's show' because domestic workers would stop in on their way home from work to see a show for 99 cents). Schein remembers that Willie was dressed in a lavender tuxedo jacket and black pants, and that he glided across the stage as if he had no bones, as if he was walking on satin. Willie sang "Fever," the only song of his that Schein knew. He was struck by Willie's voice, hearing a distinct difference in tone from the usual blues balladeer. "His voice was very special, it had almost an angst to it. There was a little bit of pain in it, the way he sang."

The Chantels opened for Willie on one of those 1957 Apollo Theater shows. Group member Lois Harris Powell remembers hearing the screams from the audience all the way backstage when Willie was singing. "The consummate performer," Powell says of Willie. "They loved him. He had a very unusual voice. He and Little Jimmy Scott had voices that were similar. But Willie had. . . there was a sweetness to his voice. The timbre of his voice was heavier than Jimmy Scott's." Between shows, Powell and the Chantels were routinely locked in their dressing room, away from Willie, Jackie Wilson and the other rhythm & blues wolves, but in her fleeting encounters with Willie he was kindly, signing a photograph to the girls and giving them show business advice.

In January 1958, Willie was called down to Cincinnati for a recording session. Among the songs chosen for him to perform that day was the Joe Seneca-penned "Talk to Me, Talk to Me." Willie's session that day finally captured his ability to melt female hearts with emotional warmth, that sweetness that Lois Powell describes. Even the white-bread backing singers somehow added an extra layer of feeling, giving the soulful record a pop sheen that helped it cross over, never a guarantee for the 'prince of the blues'. After achieving No. 5 on the rhythm & blues charts in *Billboard*, "Talk to Me" hit the pop charts and ran up to No. 20. At last, Willie had the ultimate killer ballad for the middle of his show, the song that would provoke missiles of silk and lace lingerie to come hurtling out of the dark as he knelt and pleaded to a frenzied female audience.

"Talk to me, talk to me, ooh I love the things you say," Willie sang, as—clunk—the purses hit the stage. Seneca's lyrics were romantic yet worldly and wise, the .

sentiments of a man who, like Willie, had already loved many times before succumbing again. "The many ways you speak of love I've heard before, but it sounds so good every time." The swooning would start in earnest as Willie drew out the words, then ended in a swooping sob: *"Pleeeeaase say the part I love, just once more, darling I'm so glad you're mine."*

He pulled other ballads out of his trick bag, not only his own, but pop standards like the Platters' "My Prayer." Singer Bobby Lewis saw Willie slay the girls with that one. Lewis crooned, imitating Willie: *"My prayerrrr is to linger with youuuu* (sings). Oh, he would sing the hell out of that." Worked up, wrung out women would run down to the stage and give Willie a dollar or two after a particularly heartfelt ballad. One girl raced down to the stage and handed up five dollars. "The house," Lewis reported, "went wild."

Few singers could match Willie's intensity onstage, but as a solo performer he was dependent on the whims of a different backing band in every theater. That would soon change, with an infusion of almost nuclear energy from a band almost as wild as he was.

10

A VALUABLE SCIENCE

L ittle Richard was on a ferry when the meltdown began. Yanking the heavy rings off each of his fingers, he threw them out the window and into the Bay of Sydney, ignoring the shrieks of his band. No more rock 'n' roll! No more sin, only salvation, the gospel and the Lord!

'Little' Richard Penniman had been on a hot streak since the release of "Tutti Frutti" in 1955, when he was 23. Seven No. 1 singles and several movies, including *The Girl Can't Help It* followed in quick succession. His banshee howl– *wap bap a doo wap a lap bam boom*–that towering quiff of greasy, teased hair and campy, black kohl-rimmed eyes enraged parents as much as it intrigued their children. He'd been walking on the wild side in his personal life too, and guilt over that contributed to his emotional turmoil. Richard had grown up immersed in the speaking in tongues and gospel fervor of the Pentecostal church, but when he went onstage he put all that aside and poured his frenetic energy into his music. As his star rose, Richard felt increasingly torn about the wild lifestyle that came with success.

The crisis came in the fall of 1957. He acknowledges that, but Richard denies tossing the bling into the drink. "I heard all of that too, that's not true. People just love to make up stuff and see how it sounds," he said, laughing. "I would like them to throw some rings in my lap right now!" But two surviving members of his band, the Upsetters, saw it happen. "We were in Australia, south Australia, going to a town on a ferry. He threw them out the window," said tenor saxophonist Grady Gaines. Drummer Charles Connor agrees. "That's right, he threw his rings. It wasn't a river, it was a canal, like. It was about 25,000 dollars worth of rings." The Upsetters howled and moaned as they watched the glitter disappear into the depths as Richard renounced all. And he was as good as his word. Tickets were sold out for a big November 3rd show at New Orleans' Masonic Auditorium, but when he returned from Australia, he canceled. Richard went back home to Georgia, where he refused to let his brothers and sisters play any rock 'n' roll records. He enrolled in the seminary in Huntsville, Alabama and the Upsetters were officially on their own.

The band lost more than just an employer. Richard was their biggest fan. He loved that they were showboats, doing wild steps of their own, with Gaines walking the bar while honking his sax. Whatever it took to get over, the Upsetters were up for the job. Drummer Connor's ferocious attack, a combination of steady 4/4 time on the bass drum while he ghosted eighth notes on the snare drum and closed sock cymbal, gave their sound an "exciting and highballing, freight train-like backbeat," as he described. After Connor and the Upsetters backed James Brown, Connor's proto-funk style inspired Brown to alter pop music forever with his own rhythmic experiments.

Little Richard had long been an advocate for the Upsetters, arguing with Specialty Records owner Art Rupe that only his band could convey the excitement of his live show when the producer wanted to use studio musicians on the records, but Rupe usually won that argument.

The Upsetters were, at their core, a New Orleans band. Richard found drummer Connor and saxophonist and pianist Wilbert 'Lee Diamond' Smith in the Crescent City in the early 1950s, where the underpaid and underfed musicians were backing up the duo Shirley and Lee. Richard bought them breakfast, got Connor's drums out of hock and made them an offer. Along with tenor saxophonists Gaines and Clifford Burk, tenor and baritone saxophonist Sammy Parker, guitarist Duncan Connally and bassist Olsie Robertson, they became the Upsetters, named for their ability to get audiences hopped up and upset. Though there would be personnel changes over the years—Milton Hopkins replaced Connally on guitar, and Connor came and went several times—they always maintained the same high level of energy.

Richard's 1957 spiritual crisis left the Upsetters with a slew of dates to fill and no lead singer to fill them with. Lee Diamond could sing, but they needed a bigger name to front the band. For a time, they brought in singer Dee Clark, who had a hit with "Raindrops" and could get by singing "Tutti Frutti." That took care of the remaining Little Richard and the Upsetters West Coast dates, but Clark on his own wasn't the electrifying showman they were used to, not even close. The bookings dwindled.

It was most likely Universal Attractions' Ben Bart who put Willie together with the Upsetters. Willie had been a solo act since he left the United Five. Johnnie Bassett and his band were often pressed into service to back Willie at Detroit's Warfield Theater, and he used Johnnie and the group around town. But after the hits started coming, Willie was most used to being the featured attraction, the singer leaning on a stool waiting for his turn at the mike. More recently he was one element of several different package shows, singing in front of whatever musicians Bart or the promoter put together for him.

When Willie and the Upsetters became a team and hit the road, Richard insists there were no hard feelings. He was proud that the Upsetters, at one time or another, backed up the heaviest hitters in rhythm & blues. "Sam Cooke also had them for a while and Sam Cooke's brother L.C. as well," Richard recalled. "Little Willie John and James Brown traveled with my band as me, once I was famous." The Godfather of Soul screaming *"Wop bop a doo wop..."*– it's not such a stretch. "We had some dates booked and my managers wanted to fulfill the dates, so they had James go out and be me," Richard explained.

Sam Moore, who wasn't yet hooked up with Dave Prater as Sam & Dave, doesn't buy that Richard was okay with all of this. "If that's the way Richard wants to describe it," Sam snorted. "No, Willie stole his band!"

Certainly, when Richard and Willie were on the same bill they were known to practically self-immolate onstage in their attempts to outdo the other. "He didn't stand no foolishness," Richard said of Willie. "He wasn't the kind of guy you play with. But he had a good heart. He was a good guy and a great entertainer." Willie's brother remembers strife and male posturing when Willie and Richard shared a stage. "Richard would say, 'I'm the star!'" Mertis said. "Well, he just wanted to be a star. He was never a singer. There are some people who can perform but not sing, some who can sing but not perform. Willie could do anything he wanted to!"

Drummer Connor remembered first meeting Willie on The Top Ten caravan show in 1956 that included Fats Domino and Little Richard. Even next to a foghorn like Little Richard (his siblings called their brother 'War Eagle') Willie impressed Connor with his sheer vocal power. One trick of Willie's was to start singing from behind the curtain before he came out, without the benefit of a microphone. "Then he had that dance," Connor said. "James Brown and Michael Jackson did it later, Jackie Wilson too, but Willie John used to dance like that first." Remembering those long-ago days, guitarist Milton Hopkins unleashed a big, gruff laugh. "It was exciting most of the time. You never knew what the next moment was going to bring. Willie was like that." By then the Upsetters included Gaines and Clifford Burks playing tenor, Olsie Robinson on bass, either Connor or Emil Russell on drums, Milton Hopkins on guitar and Wilbert 'Lee Diamond' Smith doubling on piano and saxophone. Willie and the Upsetters immediately launched into a one week residency at the Howard Theater in Washington, DC. Pairing Willie with the Upsetters seemed to be the answer to everybody's prayers.

Match, meet fuse.

If you were lucky enough to be alive in 1958 and plunked down the two dollars and fifty cents to see Little Willie John and the Upsetters, you were in for several hours of high-voltage entertainment. First the Upsetters came stepping out, dressed in identical glittering jackets. Lee Diamond would sing two numbers to get the audience warmed up. Then, out of nowhere, from the ether, came a voice with an unmistakable, jewel-like tone, its raw power causing the stage curtains to flutter. Before anybody could take a breath, Willie burst through the curtains and onstage, burning on all cylinders from the jump.

Willie wouldn't be dressed like the band, but turned out in a tuxedo jacket tailored to his compact frame. He never started with a slow song, his first number would usually be "All Around the World," although later he would start with "Heartbreak." "He came on with a blast, and came off with a blast," guitarist Hopkins recalled. "He did all his ballads and sad stuff in between. He was onstage between 45 minutes and an hour."

In the middle of the show, Willie would pull the immaculately folded handkerchief out of his pocket to wipe away his sweat and tears. He'd cry and moan for the girls, even drop to one knee while singing a lovesick tune. A few songs later, he was rocking, coolly whipping the audience into a frenzy with "Fever." Connor marveled at how neat Willie was, and utterly silken in his movements. "The way he would move his body, he had a professional 'scene' about him. He had a beautiful smile and he was a neat guy, his clothes were tailor-made. Silk suits and patent leather shoes, and he kept his process up real neat."

Processed, or straightened hair, the "black man's bouffant," was a vital part of the rhythm & blues star's look in the 1950s. The process, or "conk," required male dreamboats like Willie to endure hours at the barbershop as the hair was straightened, and then cemented into structured waves atop the head. Willie's quiff was always fairly short and neat, compared to the high-sheen towers rocked by James Brown or Little Richard. By the late 1950s, his process was very short, and he segued soon after that into a tight haircut with no treatment, similar to Sam Cooke's. Willie's face was smooth. "I don't know if he shaved or not, but he had a face like a baby, like a little boy," Connor said. His silk suits weren't just for dress-up occasions, Willie even wore a tie and jacket when driving his father and brother in his gold (or green, or pink and black) Cadillac from city to city. Blue jeans were for field hands. Khaki pants were for somebody else, but not William Edward John.

As the Upsetters did their steps, Willie would often fall in and mirror their dance during instrumental breaks. When he was in the throes of a ballad, Willie confined himself to small, economical moves, expressing himself with his hands. On the rockers, he was energized. "He moved around quite a bit, if you were doing a certain tempo," Grady Gaines said. "When we were doing the slow stuff, he'd do the flat foot and sing. He'd sing you out of the building!"

Willie wasn't doing the sort of gymnastics he used to dazzle Detroit audiences with at the talent shows. "He didn't need that, Willie wasn't that type of act," Gaines said. "He would move around, and give people a good show, but it was more like Frank Sinatra or Sammy Davis, a kind of classy thing."

With the Upsetters, Hopkins played behind a lot of live wires–James Brown, Jackie Wilson, Joe Tex, even Roy Head, the spinning, splits-executing 'white James Brown.' But Willie still stands out as one of those guys who could do it all. "Willie could dance! Wasn't too many routines that you would get by him. He had a lot of energy, a lot of spark in him." Apart from Willie's "hellfire voice," Connor was also intrigued by the age span of his female fans. There were older women, but then, Willie's youthful looks also drew a sea of pre-pubescent girls, who no doubt thought he was their age– and they probably weren't far off.

With Willie and the Upsetters, there was always a lot of mischief on the bandstand. While saxophonists Gaines and Burks were honking away, deep into a solo, Willie liked to sneak up and tug on one or the other's ear. "You couldn't get mad with him, because you know that was part of the show, that was Little Willie John's personality," Connor said. Willie delighted in pinching the bass player on the leg or moving the guitarist's amp where he couldn't reach it. The teasing was worse offstage. He pulled on Connor's coat, ruffled up his process, even unbuttoned the top button of the drummer's shirt before Connor knew what was happening. If he got close enough, Willie would slip Connor's wallet out of his pocket, provoking a foot chase. . . But it was the teasing Connor had to endure when he was trying to sweet-talk girls that finally drove him to work out a "system" to deal with his lead singer's provocations. Willie wanted the same kind of attention off the bandstand as he wanted on it, Connor said. "He wanted to be number one in everything... and he was a smart guy. But, I said... I gotta figure out something, because it was embarrassing. I mean, I'm taller than the guy, he's a little bitty short guy." The next time Willie interfered with Connor while he was talking to a girl, the drummer grabbed him by the neck, digging his thumb and fingers in. "The people I was talking to, they don't know I'm actually hurtin' the dude, but I was hurting him. And so, he quit messing with me."

There were no bad feelings. Like Little Richard, Willie was a great fan of the Upsetters. When they were playing in between his sets, instead of repairing to the dressing room, Willie stood at the side of the stage, clapping and cheering them on. "John looked like the Upsetters had been playing with him for the last 15 or 20 years. Which, it hadn't been that long, but you could see that confidence on the bandstand, he just had it," Connor said. "You could just see that certain encouragement he had, and he just felt good with the Upsetters playing behind him." Willie had reason to be cocky. With Little Richard off preaching the gospel, he was one of the four most powerful black male entertainers in the business, along with Jackie Wilson, Sam Cooke and James Brown. "You could see that confidence in his eyes," Connor said, "Like, 'Hey, this is my band man, the Upsetters!' and he was proud of every one of us."

Off the bandstand, Willie loved to discourse on a variety of topics. Connor believes he was over-compensating for his stature. "He couldn't do it with his size, so he did it with his knowledge and wisdom about certain things," Connor said. On the road, Willie would find a cocktail lounge with a television set, set up drinks for the band and watch the game, it didn't really matter which kind of game it was, as long as he could share his thoughts about it. He admits that Willie's rapidfire banter was usually correct. "You might be talking about football or baseball, he'd jump right in, and he'd really know what he's talking about. . . basketball, hockey, golf, anything man, John would know about all these things. He was an interesting little guy, he knew about everything, not only sports, he knew about carpentry, I mean as far as laying a carpet down on the floor, shampooing a carpet, painting a house, I mean, just anything. He had all the information."

Pay for Willie and the Upsetters was kept separate; Universal Attractions set it up that way–to the band's relief. Willie was known for either spending all his cash as soon as it was in his hands, or sending it home to Detroit. "Willie was a very young man and he had very young ideas," Milton Hopkins said. "Sometimes in very serious business situations, that's a bad combination." But he was generous with the Upsetters in other ways. If he wasn't setting up a bar in his hotel room, he was shelling out for drinks or dinner for them after the show. If you wanted a nice steak, Willie was your man. Why not? He was the boss, the lead singer. Just like the silk clothing and the Cadillacs, it went with the territory.

"Here's a guy walking around, 20 (years old) or just out of his teens with two or three thousand dollars in his pocket," guitarist Hopkins said. "No guidance, no nothing, just loose. So he blew away a lot of his money, on nothing... He didn't keep money very long." Hopkins sighs, thinking back on his rambunctious lead singer. "Willie's biggest enemy was youth, that he was young and there was nobody to guide him and keep him going. His dad was his chaperone when I first went on the road with the Upsetters, because Willie was so young, but he couldn't do a whole lot with him. Willie was a strong little fella. Once he got his nose pointed north, that's the way it was going, don't give a damn what anyone thought!"

Guitarist Hopkins was older than Willie by some years, but he considered it a learning experience to play behind him. "He was a perfect singer. He sang like a horn player would play. I used to like that. The years that we worked with Willie, I learned a whole lot as a guitar player, about phrasing, not leading the singer but following the singer. I learned all that stuff playing behind Willie John." Hopkins was particularly blown away when Willie mimicked a tenor saxophone solo by Bill Doggett, using only his voice, putting words to Doggett's song "Hold It."

With the Upsetters behind him, Willie could not be stopped. Jerry 'the Iceman' Butler witnessed the act many times. With his group, the Impressions, he had already been on the bottom of several bills under Willie. Butler was in awe of him, although he was only two years younger. "We had grown up listening to Little Willie John as a star," Butler said. "So to work with him, wow! That's Little Willie John! It was kind of the relationship the rookie has to the star quarterback. Here we are, five guys out of Chicago, Illinois, never been anywhere in particular, all of a sudden we're sharing a stage with one of our idols, one of the guys that we grew up listening to." Butler watched and learned. "He was a little guy, but he was a big guy, in the sense that he was small physically but his stature, in terms of the industry and in terms of command of the stage and knowing how to perform, he was a giant."

Butler remembers the legendary showdown between Willie and Jackie Wilson at the Rockland Palace in Harlem. Jerry Butler and the Impressions were on the bill. Butler remembers it as 1959, but it was probably later if Willie did indeed sing "Heartbreak," as the story goes. The old dance hall was teeming with 1,500 eager fans who, for less than two dollars, were going to see the two top dogs of rhythm & blues go toe to toe. Willie and Jackie immediately started squabbling over who was going to go on last. The audience generally didn't care, but the performers did. It became a battle royale between the two pint-sized Detroiters.

"Jackie Wilson was getting started as a solo artist," Butler said. "Little Willie John had seniority. But it wasn't even about that, it was about this ego thing between these two guys who were both from Detroit, both tremendous performers. 'I want to be the star tonight,' kind of thing."

The opening acts had all performed and left the stage, only Willie and Jackie were still to go on. After some additional haranguing back and forth, the promoter stepped in and insisted that somebody had to go out there and play. The audience was getting even drunker and rowdier than usual. Butler observed Willie change gears. He instantly calmed down and oozed a mischievous confidence. Sure, he'd go onstage before Jackie, he said. "Let Jackie Wilson follow me if he can."

The Upsetters hit the stage and Willie came out on fire, his luminous voice filling up every corner of the old hall with the cry, *"Heartbreak, it's hurting me."* "These cats had a groove going," Butler marveled, describing the Upsetters. "Their attitude, and Willie's, was, 'I'm going to make that stage so hot that Jackie won't be able to get on.' So that's what he did. He went out there and he heartached them, he sang 'Talk to Me' and fell down to his knees and was looking into ladies' eyes, holding and caressing them, and the big-bosomed ladies ran up there and want to cuddle him, he was so little and cute. Well! The show was over. It was time to go home!" After Willie walked off, the stage looked as if there'd been a fight in a lingerie store. Stockings, purses and even panties lay in piles, thrown up by women driven out of their minds by the sound of a male voice expressing such romantic fervor. Jackie came out and sang, but it just didn't matter anymore, nobody was really listening. To Butler, Willie was a combination of natural ability and a ferocious work ethic. "Willie was par excellence, he was studied. It wasn't by accident that he did what he did. He practiced and rehearsed it and got it down to a valuable science."

And it wasn't personal. EJ saw the warmth between Willie and Jackie, who both grew up running to and from trouble in Detroit's north end. Neither were gang-bangers, but both had to learn to handle themselves, and maneuver in and around bad guys. "There's a lot of things that people say, but he and Jackie were great friends," EJ said. As long as Willie wasn't teasing him, Jackie liked the fact that, as compact as he was, Willie was even smaller. The two were once overheard at the Gotham Hotel in Detroit comparing notes about the best shoes with "lifts." But onstage? That was war. Even family relationships were put aside, as Mable John found out. When she opened a show for Willie, he expected his sister to go out and kill, or pack up and go home. It was showtime, let the best man or woman win.

Willie and Jackie had a memorable tangle once in Detroit, at the Graystone Ballroom. Jackie won the battle that time, but not the war. A teenaged Aretha Franklin was in the audience watching with her sisters Erma and Carolyn. EJ remembered Willie courteously helping the Franklin sisters, his north end neighbors, into a car after the show. Jackie was still hot off with "Lonely Teardrops" and Willie was suffering a brief drought, so Willie agreed to go on first. But trickster Willie hit the Graystone stage in a white tie and tails, loaded for bear. "He came out, tore the joint up," EJ said. "When it came time for Jackie to come out, Jackie came out, started coughing and said he was sick, and didn't go on. So Willie came out and did another show!" Jackie was down, but not out. "Two weeks later Jackie came back, played the Graystone and tore it up. Tore it up!" EJ said. "But he wasn't going on after Willie."

"Jackie was good, he did what he did well," Faye Pridgon mused. "But nobody was any match for Willie. There was something magical about him."

11

THE PRINCE OF THE BLUES

Willie liked to take Darlynn out on the road to show her off. They made a cute, compact couple, Willie dressed to kill in silk suits and Darlynn swathed in glittering sheaths, topped off with a fur no matter what the temperature. No alpha dog rhythm & blues singer's wife left the house without a mink stole or coat, and Darlynn had three or four in her wardrobe.

Jerry Butler has a special reason for remembering those furs, as well as Willie and Darlynn's kindness to his wife. Butler had known Willie since the mid 1950s, when he and the Impressions had been on the same shows together. Butler was still the struggling singer on the underside of the bill, but he and Willie had become fast friends. "We were going out for the evening one time, and Willie wanted to know where my wife's fur was. She didn't have one," Butler said. "So he said, 'Darlynn, go get her one of your coats.'" It wasn't a loan. Willie figured Darlynn had plenty to spare. "If you met him, he loved you, because that's the kind of guy he was," Butler said.

Darlynn was the first of her Philadelphia circle to marry, and her girlfriends also came to benefit from Willie's largesse. He invited four of her friends to come up from Philadelphia to New York, to catch his show at the Apollo. The friends were broke, as usual, so Willie sent them the train fare to ride the Reading up to New York, then comped them admission to the venue.

"We were so proud, sitting in the first row, hearing them holler at Willie. Well, we were somebody!" Esther said. On one visit to New York, Darlynn's girlfriends came face to face with one of Willie's most formidable showbiz friends: Dinah Washington. Just as Willie was the 'prince of the blues,' the salty Washington had graduated from being hailed as the 'queen of the jukeboxes' to the more regal 'queen of the blues.' She was still living in New York, although she would soon move to Detroit, after her marriage to football player Dick 'Night Train' Lane of the Detroit Lions. Dinah was normally outgoing and friendly, but she also cussed like a sailor and things could turn ugly at a second's notice. 'The queen' once cleared a nightclub table of glasses and cutlery with her arm when another girl dared to sing one of her songs. This was a woman who knew what she wanted, she married seven (but not all) of her boyfriends.

After one show at the Apollo, Willie had brought Darlynn and her Philadelphia girlfriends up to Dinah's luxe apartment for an after-party. Dinah had dubbed Darlynn 'little one,' and scolded anyone who used profanity when she was around. But when she opened the door that night to find a mob of starstruck Philadelphia girls, she wasn't feeling kindly toward either 'little one' or Willie. Dinah snapped, "What are you doing here with all these people?" "A nasty woman," the friends agreed later. As for Willie, he was clearly smitten with his bride. "He'd look at Darlynn and just smile," Esther said.

As 1957 wore on, Darlynn was almost as busy as Willie. She had big news: she was expecting a baby, due the following February. Willie decided that his wife should be in more familiar surroundings, back home in Philadelphia, as she prepared for the birth. He helped her set up an apartment on Oxford Street, in the same building as her parents. Darlynn continued to dance in the early stages of her pregnancy. But as the wife of a major rhythm & blues star, she found that her business was public. Art Peters wrote in his "Off the Main Stem" column in the *Philadelphia Tribune*, in late September: "The long kissance wires burn up when Darlene (sic) Bonner, one of the Hortense Allen Dancers at the Bandstand Nightclub gets her daily call from her husband, Willie John, of 'Fever' fame. Their lovemaking via telephone is sizzling."

William Kevin John was born at 11:34 am on February 3rd, 1958 at the Pennsylvania Hospital on 8th and Spruce Street in Philadelphia. *Jet* magazine published the story, even if they got his gender wrong, in its March issue, reporting that "the stork" delivered a girl to Willie and Darlynn.

Now Willie had another John to protect. Grady Gaines of the Upsetters remembers Willie bringing Darlynn and Kevin out onstage at the Apollo Theater in March, when he and the Upsetters headlined with Bill 'Honky Tonk' Doggett and the Pastels. Willie asked the audience if they wanted to see his newborn baby and wife. "And then he'd bring Darlynn and Kevin out there on the stage," Gaines said. "And they would just go wild... excited! He did that on quite a few dates we did."

Willie loved to sing to the baby. "Sometimes when he's crying, I pick him up and sing to him," he said. "He coos right along with me. If the record player is on, he is content, and when the record stops playing, he starts crying. He knows music!"

With another John to feed, Willie didn't take any time off. He was out crooning "Talk to Me, Talk to Me" with the Rhythm and Blues Cavalcade that spring, playing St Louis, Tucson and points west. By May 5th, the song was No. 10 on *Billboard*'s "R&B Best Sellers" chart, after just four weeks. On May 6th, 1958 Willie traveled to Philadelphia to perform on Dick Clark's *American Bandstand*, which aired nationally on the ABC network, performing both "Talk to Me, Talk to Me" and "Fever."

That summer, when Darlynn's friend Esther Hawthorne's mother died, Willie arranged for her to fly out to California, where he was performing, so his wife's longtime friend could have a change of scenery. Esther was dazzled by the accommodations–it was the first time she'd ever stayed in a hotel suite. So Darlynn and Esther wouldn't have to sit through all of his shows, Willie designated friends to take them out on the town and show them Los Angeles. He always knew the best places to go.

Eventually, "Talk to Me, Talk to Me" crossed over even more successfully than "Fever" did, reaching No. 20 on *Billboard*'s pop chart–compared to position 25 for "Fever"–and shooting up to the No. 5 spot on the rhythm & blues chart.

Peggy Lee's bass player Max Bennett said he first heard the song "Fever" sometime that spring, when an unknown singer jumped up onstage and sang it at a nightclub in Los Angeles. Sensing that the number was well-suited to Lee's languid, sexy style, he brought it to her attention. Bennett and Lee got the sheet music and put an arranger to work to tailor it for a bluesy white girl from North Dakota.

Bennett must have been familiar with Willie's version, because in a 2009 biography of Lee, Peter Richmond writes that the bass player and Lee wanted to simplify what Willie had done with the song. Richmond describes Willie's version of "Fever" as "laden with horns, gospel voices, electric guitar." Richmond also describes the arrangement on Willie's "Fever" as "over the top," noting that the song begged for "elegant spareness and distillation."

Lee's low-key, sultry voice could convey a rich sadness, and on her early 1940s recordings with Benny Goodman, she shows a facility for the bluesier side of jazz. She also had a well-deserved reputation for a minimalist style that still sounds fresh to this day. But by 1958, her persona as a smoky, smoldering jazz dame had hardened into cliché. The Lee arrangement of "Fever" is stripped down to just upright bass and drums, but it also involves a husky, heavy breathing vocal, massively overdubbed finger snaps and newly written (by Lee), cutesy lyrics about Captain Smith and Pocahontas. Was she "hipping it up with Beatspeak," or laying it on a little thick, like a "square" actor gluing on a goatee to play a beatnik on television? It's clear what the consensus among Willie's peers was, when Lee's record of "Fever" hit the charts and started rocketing to the top.

"Peggy Lee made it famous, but Little Willie John defined it forever," said Ray Charles. "Oh, Peggy Lee! I didn't like it at all," said Grady Gaines of the Upsetters. "We knew who had the best version." There was some real anger behind this grumbling. After years of seeing white pop and jazz artists mine black music for hits and go on to get the big radio airplay (and make the big money) black musicians were fed up. "Peggy Lee couldn't sing like Little Willie John," said trumpeter Danny Moore. "Everybody in the (Hotel) Theresa and all over Harlem were talking about how those white producers who came uptown sneaking around the Apollo Theater recording black material and then you'd hear a white singer on the radio singing the same song. That would put anyone on junk." Etta James never did calm down about Georgia Gibbs' recording of "Dance With Me, Henry," a sanitized-for-middle-America pop version of Etta's song "The Wallflower (Roll With Me, Henry)." Pat Boone went to the bank with a hilariously stiff version of Little Richard's "Tutti Frutti" that betrayed the fact that not only did he not understand the song, he didn't seem to like it all that much either.

According to Willie, at around the same time Lee's version was starting to lift off, sales of his original "Fever" passed the one million sales mark, prompting King to give him a gold record, and a gold Cadillac to go along with it. Faye Pridgon says she laughed when she heard Lee's version, and she claims Willie did too. "That song had gotten a hell of a play in the 'hood long before that girl came along. Willie kept everything comical, and I quite agreed with him. When Pat Boone or whoever covered a song, it was a joke to us. The white people were not necessarily keen on their kids embracing what Willie John was doing, they would prefer one of their own. Hey, so be it, to each his own."

But was is that simple? Was Lee just ripping Willie off? While Gaines dismisses Lee's 1958 rendition of "Fever" as inferior to Willie's, he believes that her cover gave Willie's original version more exposure. "It got big because she was white," Gaines says bluntly. "As far as liking it, I didn't care nothing about her version. But they pushed it. I don't think it hurt Willie John at all, if anything it made him more business. Willie hadn't crossed over too much on the white side, by her doing it, the white side got to know 'Fever'. It didn't hurt him, it probably helped him a lot. I know it did the same thing with Richard when Pat Boone did 'Tutti Frutti'. But at the time, you don't be liking that stuff."

In 1956, artists like Willie—who were hitmakers on black radio—would knock on the door of the pop radio stations, but more often than not, those doors wouldn't open. Little Richard was granted passage, although his ambisexual presentation made everybody more than a little nervous. Chuck Berry—no problem, come on in. Willie got his foot through, but didn't quite make it all the way across the threshold. Willie's vocal on "Fever" doesn't sound X-rated to today's sensibilities, but it was smoldering, dangerous stuff in the mid 1950s. Pop radio wasn't ready to have a black man singing that way, not yet. That sultry sound was more palatable coming from Peggy Lee in those days.

Clarence Avant, Willie's road manager in the late 1950s, explains how segregated radio was then. "Of course Peggy Lee took 'Fever' to a larger audience, but you have to understand something. Back in those days if LaVern Baker or Ruth Brown sang songs, the white artists would come along and take them into the pop area. Until Motown came along, there wasn't much in the pop area (for blacks)."

Billboard liked Lee's rendition. "This chick's phrasing here is a gasser," wrote a giddy reviewer in June 1958. Lee's record of "Fever" hit No. 8 on *Billboard*'s pop charts, an improvement on Willie's performance, which topped out at No. 24. Although to read all reports since then, you'd think she hit the top of the charts and Willie's version languished in obscurity on the rhythm & blues side. Oddly, Lee is even credited for the finger-snapping on "Fever," when that was a straight cop from Willie's version. The cover gave Lee's career a much-needed reboot, as *Billboard* reported in 1959. "This sultry reading of Little Willie John's former rhythm & blues hit. . . brought her back in a big way." It also became her trademark tune, the song that defines her legacy, for better or worse.

In 1956, Lee sold five million copies, while Willie struggled to get over the million-copy mark. Harry Balk believes that proves that if Willie's version had come out later, in a less segregated music environment, and had been more commercially available and more broadly played on pop radio, he would have sold many more copies than he did.

Willie may have seemed feckless, but he thought a lot about the segregation of music and the big business of harvesting black music into white mainstream pop hits. He was particularly incensed that the public had been sold a bill of goods about rock 'n' roll suddenly coming out of nowhere in the 1950s, with Bill Haley and other artists driving the "new" sound. In July, when a *Los Angeles Sentinel* reporter suggested to him that rock 'n' roll and rhythm & blues were the same, Willie erupted. "Rock 'n' roll is not rhythm & blues," Willie insisted. "Every time I hear about that claim, I get mad! Count Basie had been playing rock 'n' roll from 1937 to 1958. White people are just waking up to it. Anything we have they change anyway because we let them do it. It's ours; it belongs to us."

On the other hand, Willie also wanted everybody to buy his music and love him, not just the black community. "I want to sell records to white and colored, and the only way I can is to give them something they want. The only way to do it is to gain their respect. If you don't, they forget you overnight." It had to take some of the wind out of Willie to see Lee's version of "Fever" take off in such a big way. Certainly, for that grueling six-hour session he endured in Cincinnati–finding something sensual in a rough, funky song that he hated–she owed him a sincere thank you at the very least.

In September, *Jet* magazine devoted a whole page of ink to Willie, in a story that proclaimed that there was to be a Hollywood movie of his life. The accompanying photograph shows the singer with Detroit's gospel minister, the worldly Reverend C.L. Franklin of New Bethel Baptist Church, and two other men: Ted Jones and Leon Harrison. Willie is laughing, as usual, and holding a large photo album-type book emblazoned with the words, "The Little Willie John Story." *Jet* reported that the pitch had been submitted to a studio for a "teenage musical," although there is no further mention of a film; the magazine story was probably a photo op meant to hype up interest in such a project. Franklin, a recording artist himself, was comfortable in the entertainment world and familiar with Willie through the fandom of his children Erma, Cecil, Aretha and Carolyn.

Willie's career had turned hot again after "Talk to Me, Talk to Me," so King fired up the machinery to capitalize on his higher profile and released several singles that summer in quick succession; "Let's Rock While the Rockin's Good" backed with "You're a Sweetheart" was released in late June, with "Tell It Like It Is" hitting the stores just two months later.

Willie had high hopes that "You're a Sweetheart" would help break him out of the blues mold. "If I can just get this record to click, I won't have to sing blues any more," he told a reporter that summer. Actually, he wanted to be able to do the smooth crooner thing, while not entirely abandoning his blues fans. Nat King Cole was able to do both—and wear stingy brim hats while he was doing it. "Any time Nat Cole can sing 'Mona Lisa' and come and sing 'Looking Back,' then I know that that's the kind of thing I want to do some day," Willie said. He added: "I will still sing ballads because my soul lies so deep and painful that I have to sing them."

The Apollo billed him as 'the prince of the blues,' but in November Willie received a new tagline when he was advertised at Chicago's Mocambo Club as "The Smallest Man with the Biggest Sound." In the third week of December came his final release of 1958: "No Regrets."

Willie did regret one thing. That same month he got into a scrape in Atlanta; he was charged with making calls on a phony credit card. Willie was released after bonding out, with the promise that he would make good on his long distance charges.

"It's a wonder I didn't jump off a building or commit suicide," Clarence Avant said of the time he spent as road manager for Willie John. "Willie was plain genius when it came to performing, but a pain in the ass. I was so green." Avant was managing Teddy P's Lounge in Newark, New Jersey when owner Teddy Powell booked Willie for a week's engagement. When Powell had to go promote a Sam Cooke show in another city, he left young Clarence in charge, with a warning. "Teddy said, 'Clarence, whatever you do, don't give Willie the money 'til the last night, because he might not show up on Friday.' Willie had that reputation–young, aggressive, but friendly," Clarence said. He, of course, has to qualify that. "He was also the best, kindest guy I ever met in my life."

Sure enough, Willie asked Clarence for some money before the week was up. "I said no!" Clarence said. "Well Saturday he got friendly with me. He was a very friendly guy, especially with the clients, he'd meet them at the bar and whatnot. Everybody just loved him! Then Sunday night, he got *very* friendly, and he asked me, could I work for him?" Clarence said no to Willie, three days in a row–he stood his ground. But Willie wasn't giving up. Clarence didn't get it. "I thought it was a trap because I had turned him down the previous three nights, and Sunday was pay night." Furthermore, he knew nothing about managing a top rhythm & blues act on the road. But Willie kept talking. And Willie was a world-class talker. "I kept saying no because I thought, he's going to get me out there on the road, and he's going to dump me."

Willie left Newark for his next club date, but he kept the pressure up through long-distance phone calls. "He called, and then Darlynn would call me and say 'Clarence, why don't you come down to Philadelphia?' They didn't live in the best neighborhood. But I went down."

Finally Clarence asked his boss, Teddy Powell, what he should do. Powell advised turning the tables on Willie and asking *him* for money. That would prove whether he was serious. Clarence asked for money, and Willie paid up. "I forget what the amount was," Clarence said. "And so I started out with Little Willie John. And what can I tell you, it was a year, *whoo*!"

He may have been a neophyte, but Clarence hit the ground running. On the road with Willie, he quickly discovered what a cruel, punishing schedule the chitlin circuit regulars had to endure. Willie was in demand, and he worked hard. Promoters still didn't think rock 'n' roll and rhythm & blues acts could sell tickets on their own (they were probably right) so they continued the practice of big shows aimed at broke teenagers, sending the acts from city to city for one night engagements. As Clarence describes it, that year was like jumping on a speeding train. "You'd go to Henry Wynn and he'd take you all through the South; Birmingham, Selma, Tennessee, Louisiana, Arkansas, everywhere you can think of. Then there was Don Robey who took you through Texas. Then you'd come out here to San Francisco, play the Fillmore Ballroom, this and that, it was a regular thing. Then you'd go back to the East Coast, play the

Apollo Theater, you'd play Philadelphia, Washington. . . it was a routine. But it worked!"

Managing Willie on the road turned out to be a one-year advanced degree in the entertainment business. "The guy was so far ahead of his time," Clarence marveled. "He was a brilliant guy, to watch him onstage with other acts, whether it was Jackie Wilson or Sam Cooke or Jesse Belvin, or any of the guys around then, Willie was dynamite. He could hold his own." Clarence witnessed the Jackie Wilson psychodramas first hand. "Jackie Wilson was the big star but sometimes Jackie wanted Willie to go on last, because this boy, he'd go on and whine those songs and move around the way he did, and women loved him. He was just unbelievable."

Most of the time, Willie was the headliner. He would get the audience going with "Talk to Me, Talk to Me," "Let Them Talk" and "Fever," but Clarence had a special favorite. "The one I liked was a strange little thing called 'Leave My Kitten Alone'." It was a song that would also capture the imagination of 19 year-old John Lennon, all the way in Liverpool, England.

Clarence had to quit the Willie John carnival after a year. Darlynn John could understand why. "Clarence really, really liked Willie. But he would get very pissed off at him," she said. The financial uncertainty probably was the final straw. Too often, Willie would get to the money first and send it back to his family. Clarence could argue with him, curse him out, but it wouldn't change anything. "One time in Memphis, Tennessee, we needed to pay the lady in the rooming house and I said, 'I'll get the money from Little Willie John.' She laughed. She said 'Little Willie John ain't got no money, because he just tried to borrow some from me!'" Clarence sighed. "You get embarrassed. We didn't have credit cards then! You just had to live day by day with him. But a good heart, a good heart." At least he wasn't green anymore, Willie had lit a fire under him and catapulted him out of Newark. Clarence went on to reach the highest echelons of the music business, managing jazz organist Jimmy Smith, composer Lalo Schifrin and other artists, going on to Los Angeles and launching several record companies, including Sussex in 1971, where he signed Bill Withers. One of the music business' acknowledged godfathers, Clarence served as chairman of the board of Motown Records, and later was called to the board at Polygram Records. But he never stopped talking about Willie. In 2006, *Billboard* featured Clarence in a cover story in honor of his birthday. As always, he told the story of how Willie coaxed him out of Newark and into the music business. "Willie John was slick, but he remained a friend of mine," Clarence said. "He also taught me one thing. Don't believe everything you see, and you better watch your shit."

12

THE HUSTLE CONTRACT

James Brown almost wore himself out telling the story of how he blew Willie John off the stage. He told it in his autobiography, in interviews, to anyone who would listen. There was a lot at stake in the high-testosterone world of male rhythm & blues singers. Every night, on every stage, superiority would have to be proven again. From 1956 to 1960, Willie John was always in play, he was the guy you had to beat.

James and the Famous Flames had been recording for King's Federal Records label since 1956, when they released the song "Please, Please, Please." Syd Nathan wasn't thrilled about the song. He respected a singer like Willie, who never screamed, and enunciated lyrics as crisply as Sinatra, thanks to his Detroit public school music teachers. But Hal Neely personally guaranteed the tune, and it sailed to No. 6 on the rhythm & blues chart. Their next few releases didn't do as well, but in 1958, promoted to King from the "junior" Federal label thanks to Neely's efforts, James and the group burst right out of the gate with the song, "Try Me," which went to No. 1 on the rhythm & blues charts. James' passionate performance on "Try Me" also earned the group a week-long booking at the Apollo Theater starting April 24th, 1959–on the bottom of a bill topped by Willie. The Upsetters were on the show, as well as the comedy act Butterbeans & Susie, Verna White and singer/contortionist (you got a lot for a two dollar ticket at the Apollo) Vi Kemp.

James Brown finally had his chance to go up against the prince of the blues, the guy who tore everybody up. To a proper competitor who thrived on the contest, it didn't get any better than this. Describing his fateful first night on the Apollo stage, James could hardly contain himself. "Little Willie John didn't want us coming on anywhere near him—he knew what we could do—so they had us opening the show," he said in *The Godfather of Soul*. Never mind that it would make no sense for the Apollo neophyte to top the bill over a popular performer like Willie, backed by the high-stepping Upsetters. But let Mr Brown continue. "I came out smoking," James wrote. "The audience went wild. I don't think they'd ever seen a man move that fast. I put them on Little Willie John's case right away."

James pulled out every move he'd developed in his stage act so far, he fell to his knees, cried and pleaded during a song, he had one of the Flames put a coat on his shoulders and lead him off, a precursor of the schtick with the ornate cape that he would refine to an art over the following few years. "Little Willie John couldn't hardly handle it," James crowed. "He said I was using tricks to get over." Yes, indeed he was. James and the Famous Flames kept it up all week, and finally convinced Apollo owner Frank Schiffman to move them into the "co-starring" slot, just before Willie. "He couldn't hardly stand it. He was a balladeer and I ate him alive. He could sing, though. Later I got where I could out-sing him too," James bragged.

It's hard to listen to his 1961 hit "Prisoner of Love" and agree with that last boast. Clearly, he was trying to beat Little Willie John at his own game, proving that he could be a suave, lovesick crooner as well as a dancing, sweating, rhythmic genius. He deploys a fluttering vibrato, singing of romantic anguish in a painfully high part of his range atop a layer of gossamer backing voices. Of course, he can't help but be James, and wail and shriek, screaming *"you... you... you,"* at the end of the track.

There isn't the sense, as there was with Willie, that the voice is being used like a horn, that he was singing as naturally and effortlessly as a bird. James Brown did nothing without sweating, without showing how much effort he was making, proud of his image as the hardest working man in show business. Willie John, on the other hand, made singing seem easy, just like moving one leg in front of the other, just like swatting a fly. "Willie was always, always ready to sing. It was just something that he seemed to love, seemed to be a part of him," said Louise Williams Bishop. She was morning host on Philadelphia's WDAS in the 1950s. Bishop watched him often at the Uptown Theater in Philadelphia and confessed, "I probably had a little crush on him, although he never paid any attention to it." Bishop was usually backstage, where she observed all the performers. "Diana Ross was scared to death," she remembered. "I stood in the wings and held her, and encouraged her to go out there. But Willie, there was never any encouraging. As soon as the spotlight hit him, he came alive."

A December 1959 *Variety* review of an Apollo Theater show featuring both Willie and James restores a corrective balance to Mr Brown's somewhat self-aggrandizing memory. Willie was on the top of the bill again, so if James had indeed eaten him alive in April, it didn't affect the Apollo's billing arrangements. The Drifters were next under Willie on the bill, then the Flames, then Laura Johnson, Stan Kirk, Reuben Phillips Band, followed by a movie screening of *Return of the Fly*.

Variety reported that Willie was not only the "star-singer" of the show that night, but the emcee as well. "…In both capacities (he) attempts valiantly to make something cohesive out of what is otherwise a haphazard collection of acts. Young performer has an easy, winning way and provides show's best moments when he takes over the mike next-to-closing and belts out four numbers ranging from rock 'n' roll to pop to blues. He's an energetic but disciplined performer with a lot of the rhythmic drive that marks Johnnie Ray's delivery, especially in the sweet-tempoed 'Talk to Me' and the bluesy 'Anytime, Anyplace, Anywhere'."

James went on to achieve funk immortality, so it's inevitable that his voice (and version of history) has prevailed, but in 1959 he was no match for Little Willie John. For all his competitive feelings (and Darlynn John believed he was indeed jealous of her husband) James did love Willie. He spoke of him for years with an almost obsessive awe. When he sang "I Lost Someone" at the Apollo in October of 1962, he even riffed on Willie, ad-libbing his crooning, pleading line, *"I need your love, so baaaad"* into the song, immortalized on vinyl on *Live at the Apollo*.

Willie had crossed paths with Sam Cooke as far back as 1950, when Cooke came to Detroit with the Soul Stirrers and played at the same churches as the John family group, the United Five. While Willie's gospel career ended before he hit puberty, Sam stayed on much longer. He didn't make the leap to rhythm & blues until well into his 20s, almost reluctantly, wary of the firestorm of anger he knew would come from his disappointed gospel fans.

Once Sam made his crossover official, he had no problem adjusting. He was gregarious and enjoyed the backstage social whirl as much as Willie did. The two became close, both worldly men who didn't let a girlfriend get in the way of their friendship. Willie felt he could relax with Sam, who treated him fondly, like a mischievous younger brother—six years younger, to be exact. Sam found in Willie an endless source of amusement, and he didn't pass judgment on him the way some people did. People like James Brown. James would chastise Willie for his sometimes questionable behavior, boldly ignoring the fact that he was doing the same things. Because Willie was the alpha dog the first few years they competed, and he considered James his little brother act, it created a complex emotional web of gratitude, resentment and guilt for James. It also helped fuel an ongoing battle of two considerable egos onstage. "James had a preaching bag, a fatherly thing," Faye said. "We were friends but he could be a big hypocrite. He was doing the same things Willie did."

Exactly what things, James' manager and producer at King, Hal Neely, had no hesitation in spelling out: "James Brown, bless his heart, he's been into heavy drugs all his life," said Neely. As for Willie, from drinking and the inevitable backstage pot smoking with other musicians from his teen years on, there were also reports of cocaine use on the road, although heavy drinking seemed to be a bigger problem. Faye snorts at the idea that Willie did anything harder than cocaine, although Neely claimed that he did, and that he sent Willie to rehab several times. At least one friend, Sam Moore, confirms that they sniffed heroin together.

Faye believes that many who talk about drug shenanigans are jealous of Willie. "James had a little bit of a jealousy thing going, too. His was more under control, he would hide behind something like, 'Man you know how I feel about you, you're like a brother to me.' Willie would listen, he was courteous." Willie was always polite, but he would avoid James when he saw his hand in that preaching bag. "I know James loved Willie dearly but Willie didn't spend a lot of time with him, because James was in that chastising mode most of the time," Faye said.

Two months after his April appearance at the Apollo with James Brown, Willie was in New York for a recording session with Henry Glover. Willie had brought an upbeat rocker he wanted to record, a song he'd written with Titus Turner ("All Around the World") and James McDougal. "Leave My Kitten Alone" was, on the surface, a light-hearted pop song with a flare of horns setting a romping pace from the outset. King producer Ray Pennington started out as a country singer but was hired by Syd Nathan as a shipping clerk, then promoted to A&R man–once Syd explained to him what that was. Like most 1950s A&R men, Pennington didn't sign artists so much as produce sessions. He was fascinated by Willie's almost mystical upper range. "He could reach the highest part of his voice, and it's like it went into overdrive, and went on. He could do things with his voice I never heard anyone else do." As a singer himself, Pennington knew what was possible and what seemed beyond human abilities. Because he also had a high tenor, the producer would often record the guide vocals on Willie's songs before he got to the studio.

It's a treat to hear the romantic, lovelorn crooner return to his north end roots, addressing salty remarks to "Mr Dog," advising him of the mayhem that would rain on his canine head if he didn't leave that kitten alone. Willie's vocal, even subverted by a cheesy female "meow" chorus, is more muscular and assured than ever, the essence of male threat. Despite the laugh in his voice, he sounds convincing. It's a virtuoso vocal performance, with Willie singing in his chesty, meatier mid-range, then swooping up effortlessly from his high tenor to what would be falsetto for a lesser mortal. When he makes that vocal run upward, it creates a change in barometric pressure that raises the hair on the back of your neck.

King released "Leave My Kitten Alone" in the third week of June, 1959; it reached No. 13 on the rhythm & blues charts, and No. 60 on the pop charts. With its rolling energy and playful lyrics, it's easy to see how the song appealed to John Lennon and the Beatles. The Beatles were performing "Kitten" in their live set by 1961, if not earlier. Willie's single had been released by Parlophone in Britain, although Lennon was in the habit of picking up American rhythm & blues records brought in by sailors to Liverpool, so it's possible he had the original King 45.

In Mark Lewisohn's *The Beatles on Record*, Paul McCartney mentions Johnny Preston's 1961 cover version of the song, almost a note-for-note copy of Willie's original. But because Lennon sings lead on "Kitten," he most likely chose to do it, and whichever version of the tune prompted that choice is lost in the mists of time. Interestingly, there is a direct emotional link from the comic yet potent masculine warning of "Leave My Kitten Alone," to Lennon's own song,

"Jealous Guy."

A seismic shift was going on at King Records in 1959. Willie's New York producer Henry Glover, the man who harnessed Willie's raw talent and paired him with the right songs and the best arrangements, was leaving Syd Nathan's employ at King Records. Glover had been with King since he quit playing trumpet for Lucky Millinder in the early 1940s. Indirectly, the 1959 payola scandal was to blame.

In the midst of the music industry's collective nervous breakdown over the Congressional hearings on payola—money paid by record companies to radio DJs for airplay—Glover felt that Syd Nathan had thrown him under the bus during his testimony. Syd told investigators that any payola King was involved in was handled out of its New York office. King's New York office was, of course, run by Henry Glover.

Glover promptly quit and went on to work for several other labels, including Roulette. He described his departure as voluntary, but the rumors persisted that he was fired because he'd been caught doling out payola. That rumor was loudly refuted by Hal Neely, who oversaw King's business affairs. "The only two people guilty of payola at King. . . was Syd Nathan and Hal Neely," Neely said. "The other guys were just doing what they were told. They might have passed money, but they didn't unless it was approved. They didn't get the cash until it was approved." Neely added gleefully: "I'm the only record executive they didn't indict for payola, and I'm as guilty as anybody."

His honesty is refreshing, even if it was safely uttered 50 years after the 1959 Inquisition. While only a few took the fall for payola (DJ Alan Freed being one of the most celebrated of the lot) it was no backroom dealing, but an everyday occurrence that oiled the wheels of the music industry. Often it took the benign form of "sponsorship"—a radio station's "Spin of the Day" would be "sponsored by" (meaning paid for by) a record company, without credit of course. Such practices wouldn't make a hit out of a bum song—only rabid, record-buying teenagers could do that—but without it, a record by a new artist might be unjustly relegated to the slush pile. Neely was affably blunt. "In those days, everybody's hand was in the pot."

The problem for artists like Willie was, although King was dispensing payola to DJs just like any other record company (according to Neely) from the mid 1950s into the early 60s, white pop stations were still not adding a lot of rhythm

& blues records–certainly not from core artists like Willie. All the payola in the world was not going to get Hank Ballard and the Midnighters singing double entendres about "working" with Annie played on a pop station. Even a crooner like Little Willie John, with nary a sleazy lyric to his name, had to content himself with small pop victories here and there.

Glover's departure didn't appear to be a devastating blow to Willie, not at first. Willie was already recording many sessions in Cincinnati that didn't involve Glover at all. Ray Pennington started working with Willie in 1958 (Willie's version of Pennington's own song "Heaven All Around Me" was released in 1963) and says that, contrary to the idea that Henry Glover produced most of Willie's sessions, he, Gene Redd and Sonny Thompson were usually the supervising producers in Cincinnati.

For Pennington and the other producers and musicians, Willie was easy. "Very talented. Very talented. All he'd do is sit there and listen. When they give him the paper (with lyrics and arrangement), put him in the isolation (booth), we run it down, and he'd go on and cut it," said drummer Calvin 'Eagle Eye' Shields. "He was jovial, the type of guy who would step on your foot on purpose," Pennington said.

That was the good news. The bad news was that Syd Nathan would usually attend recording sessions if it involved one of his name artists like Willie or James Brown. And of course, Syd and Willie would argue. Even though Syd admired Willie's voice, it was his job to tell him what to do with it.

There would be Willie, sleek in his silk shirt and hat cocked to one side, looking as much like Frank Sinatra (one of his singing and sartorial idols) as possible. Crisply groomed but square-footed, full of north end attitude, he stood up to his sweaty, disheveled boss in the studio. He didn't like this song. He wanted strings on his records. That last request would send Syd into a sputtering, wet rage. "Mr Nathan would be trying to tell Willie how to sing. He always jumped on Willie and told him he wanted to be Sinatra. Mr Nathan would tell him he wasn't singing 'black' enough, only that wasn't the word he would use," Pennington said demurely of his foul-mouthed boss. Willie was no stranger to these kinds of confrontations, he had been around Syd long enough not to take the rough and tumble of those studio rants to heart. "They would always end up all right," Pennington said. "But we'd usually be glad when Mr Nathan left the room, because then we could do it the way we wanted."

Though Syd was rough on Willie, he also had paternal feelings towards him, openly preferring him to some of his other name artists, including James Brown. He could also be generous; Darlynn John remembers a ring with a large diamond that Syd gave Willie to mark the birth of their son Kevin. The ring was somehow lost over the years, but never forgotten.

Still, business was business. The three-year contract Syd had Willie and his other acts sign kept the artists in bondage, because every "loan" they got from Syd–and he was always amenable to loans–would extend the length of the contract. Hal Neely took credit for bringing what he admitted was a "hustle" contract to King Records. Every 90 days the artist had to give King three days of recording time in any city, at the company's option, and if they didn't, the contract was automatically extended for another year.

Neely defended it. "It's a hustle contract, that's true, but you're going to be hustled if you don't." Willie didn't understand Neely's "hustle" contract, that it did not expire with time, but only after he had delivered the stipulated number of sessions–three days of recording, every 90 days. When he didn't record or was unable to record, the liability would pile up. Years later, that would come to trip Willie up.

Despite his tough business tactics–honed after years of riding herd over a roster of volatile, creative country and rhythm & blues musicians in some of the roughest parts of the business–Neely was also fond of the artists he tried so hard to outwit. He was almost as generous in dispensing compliments as he was in pointing out bad behavior. He liked to recount the story of how Willie habitually used the death of a family member as an excuse to ask King for an advance. But death came more than once, for some. "Willie John's mother died three times," Neely said. (Lillie John actually survived until 1999, outliving several of her offspring.) The King executive clearly admired Willie's boldness. And it worked. "I sent it to him," Neely said crisply. "It was his money. Fantastical singer." Despite his close ties with James Brown, Neely declared, almost casually, "Of course, our best singer was Willie John." Naturally, he couldn't resist bragging about it: "I'm the guy who got him, of course."

13

MIAMI

Friends like Bobby Lewis take pains to describe Willie offstage as the effervescent live wire, the heart and soul of the party. "He was really a sweetheart, he loved everybody," Lewis said. "He did not have a prejudicial bone in his body. He would sit and drink and smoke and crack jokes and laugh, that's what he loved. He didn't care who you were, as long as you were decent and treated him with respect." But Willie was also assertive, Lewis recalls. "He was forward! If he wanted to say something he would say it, if he wanted to do something, he would do it."

The doing side of Willie kicked in on a tour stop in Charlotte, North Carolina, in 1960. He and Lewis were part of a package tour with Jackie Wilson, the Four Tops and Baby Washington. Just a few years earlier, the custom was to do a show for whites during the first set, and play for blacks in the late show, but this performance was completely integrated. When the show ended, Willie and the other entertainers were getting onto the bus outside the auditorium when they heard a girl scream. It was coming from a grassy, wooded area across the street. He was easily the smallest man on the bus, "about the size of Sammy Davis Jr," Lewis said, but "He would coldcock you in a minute if you insulted him or made him angry." And on this day, Willie was angry. He jumped off and ran across the street toward the woods. All Lewis and the other musicians could do was chase after him.

"We saw two guys running in one direction, and a couple of other guys running in another direction. White guys." A black girl came stumbling out of the woods, by herself. "We yelled, 'Over here, baby, over here!'" Willie escorted her back to the tour bus and put her on a seat. He had intervened just in time; the men were about to strip the girl of her clothes and assault her. "You know, she might have smiled at them, and they might have walked her over to the grassy knoll," Lewis said. "I can't think that she didn't know what they were going to do. She went with them willingly." But clearly the situation was deteriorating when Willie and company chased the men off.

Once the girl was safe, Willie got off the bus and took off running, to go find the men. Lewis and the others called him back. The concert may have been integrated, but this was still 1960 in the deep South. For a lone black man to run after four or five white guys, no matter what they did, was not a good idea. "I said, 'Willie, get back here you fool!'" Lewis relates. "Willie got back on the bus. We took the girl to a spot where she could walk home. And that was the end of it." Milton Hopkins of the Upsetters had seen Willie bristle if a woman was being disrespected by a man, even if the girl was twice his size. "If you walked in a place and the woman was a foot and a half taller than him, you'd better respect that woman, because he was watching everything. He was that kind of guy."

While Willie had always steered clear of Detroit's street gangs, as Jackie Wilson had, he learned some rough lessons in the north end, and expected to defend himself and any women present. Mertis Sr warned his boys, "Don't start anything, but don't let anyone finish you." Certainly he was as confident as he'd ever been in his personal life; having married what his musician friends termed a "quiet girl," he was enjoying having a settled home and his role as a new father. Whether that contentment played into it, he recorded some breathtaking sides at the end of the 1950s. In December 1959, he was in the studio singing "My Love-Is," a stunning, jazzy number that sounds as contemporary today as the day it was recorded, especially the alternate version, released on Ace's *The King Sessions* 1958–1960, that features just Willie singing over Edwyn Conley's bassline.

In January 1960 King released "Let Them Talk," a soulful ballad recorded at the same June 1959 session in New York that produced "Leave My Kitten Alone." "Let Them Talk" was written by King Chicago A&R man and producer Sonny Thompson, and was a perfect match for Willie's soaring, impassioned voice. Not that others didn't attempt to sing it. Next to "Fever" and "Need Your

Love So Bad," it's one of Willie's most loved and much-covered songs, recorded by George Benson, among others. Willie's version is still much referred to, and got a good reception when it was released, going all the way to No. 11 on the rhythm & blues charts, although it only scraped up to the No. 100 spot on the pop charts.

In June 1960, Willie recorded the sizzling "Heartbreak (It's Hurting Me)." With its piercing, soulful wail, a trio of funky saxophones chugging behind him and an organist seemingly out of his mind, torn between the church and the saloon, the song became an instant sensation on the road, a show-stopper for Willie and the Upsetters.

His 1959 session for "Let Them Talk" had featured strings, which was a great victory by Willie and brother Mertis. King producers, directed by Syd Nathan, resisted putting strings on rhythm & blues sessions, believing that the funky kick of guitar, saxophone and Hammond B-3 was a more appropriate bluesy sound. When Mertis Jr pushed for strings on Willie's sessions between 1958 and 1966, he hit a brick wall of disapproval. "I told Henry Glover, I want to put strings on Willie. He said, 'I don't know, you have to talk to Syd.' I told Syd it was because it'll make it sound more mellow that way. Syd said, 'Well, if they don't like it the way we do it, they won't like it with strings.'" Mertis points to January 1959 and the release of Brook Benton's hit song "It's Just a Matter of Time," with its lavish bed of strings bedded down under his baritone croon, as the turning point. Post-Benton, on the next session, Syd seemed to fold without much persuasion. "Oh yeah, you can use strings!"

Unsurprisingly, Hal Neely had a more cynical view. In the summer of 1960, Willie was in Cincinnati to record "Sleep," a dusty relic from the 1920s originally recorded by Fred Waring's Pennsylvanians, reaching No. 1 on the charts in 1924. Willie was sitting in Neely's Cincinnati office one day, waiting for him. Typically fresh, he was lounging in Neely's chair, wearing his little Sinatra fedora. "He was coming off three or four big records, and he said, 'Hal, I've been thinking. I'd like to use the Cincinnati Symphony on my next record.'" Neely said, "Gee that's a great idea, fine Willie." He picked up the phone and asked to be put through to the director of the symphony. "I said, 'Little Willie John's in my office, and he'd like to record tonight, are you available?'" They were. "So Willie marches out of my office and Syd's, he goes to the studio. He's gone about an hour. He comes back, with his hat in his hand now. 'How many men in the Cincinnati symphony? Mr Neely, who pays for that?' 'Well, you do, Willie.' 'You know, I think I've been a little hasty.'"

But Neely had an idea for a compromise. He called the symphony director back and booked four musicians: three violins (or "fiddles," as he called them) and a viola. And then he overdubbed. There is, in fact, so much overdubbing on "Sleep" that Willie sounds as if he's underwater. He's singing his heart out as usual, and despite a roller rink organ that hijacks the song midway through, it's easy to see how the platter was irresistible to pop consumers in 1960.

Neely agrees with the pundits. "So we did 'Sleep,' and that's the worst record I ever cut in my life, it's screechy and it's bad and they put him on it, they sketched out an arrangement and we overdubbed it about three times, so it sounds like a fiddle section," he said. "It's awful, it's terrible. It went to number one, of course." (Actually, it went to No. 10 on the rhythm & blues chart and No. 13 on pop, but it was a hit, Willie's best performance on the pop charts ever.) Though the song hasn't stood the test of time according to music historians, "Sleep" was considered a hit by the critics of the day. Charles J. Shreiber described "Sleep" in more glowing terms than Neely in his syndicated column "Platter Chatter": "In a week for rock and rollers, Little Willie John reverses the trend by taking Fred Waring's closing theme and giving it a clever rollicking rock beat that has a fresh new sound."

On January 25th, 1960, Darlynn gave birth to Darryl Keith John at the Pennsylvania Hospital in Philadelphia, a little brother for two year-old Kevin. One of that year's presidential candidates, John F. Kennedy, was an icon to African American families, and the Johns were no exception. Willie liked to say that Darlynn was his Jackie Kennedy: slim and chic, soft-spoken and classy. With his parents and numerous siblings at ease in their home on leafy Leslie Street in Detroit, Willie decided it was time for his 'Jackie' and his two sons to have their own place, after shuttling back and forth from his parents' house in Detroit and an apartment in Philadelphia. Darlynn was happy to have Lillie John teach her how to cook Willie's favorite dishes, and when in Philadelphia she enjoyed being close to her family, now she deserved a more settled home. But where?

Willie still had his dreams. He loved California, and had joined the American Federation of Television and Radio Artists' (AFTRA) Los Angeles local, hoping

(**Clockwise from top left**) Darlynn Bonner in Philadelphia in 1953–54, before she met Willie. *Courtesy John Family*. Darlynn Bonner (second from left) with several of her fellow dancers from the Hortense Allen troupe, appearing at the Apollo Theater in 1957. *Courtesy John Family*. Newly married Willie and Darlynn John in a hotel room on the road, circa 1957–58. *Courtesy John Family*. Clineice Stubbs, Darlynn and Willie, Willie's sisters Mildred and Mable, and Levi Stubbs at a Detroit nightclub, circa 1958. *Courtesy John Family*.

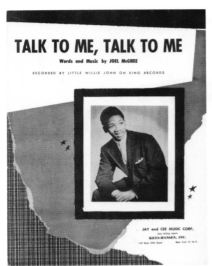

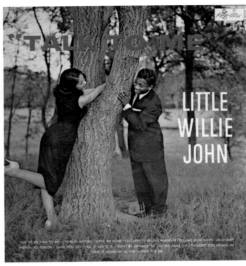

(**Clockwise from top**) After a bit of a hit drought in 1957, Willie came roaring back in early 1958 with "Talk to Me, Talk to Me." *Courtesy Bob Kelly.* King released two albums on Willie in 1958, including *Talk to Me. Courtesy Bob Kelly.* A poster for a Sacramento show in August 1958. *Courtesy Bob Kelly. Mister Little Willie John*, also released in 1958, continued in a pop ballad direction. *Courtesy Bob Kelly.*

Family photo of Willie, Darlynn, William Kevin (2 years old) and Darryl Keith (2 months old) in Philadelphia, circa March 1960. *Courtesy John Family.*

(**Clockwise from top left**) Willie often played at the Rockland Palace in Harlem. On Friday, October 21st, 1960 his friend Sam Cooke was the headliner; Willie and Darlynn bowling, circa 1960–61. *Both courtesy John Family*. Willie and Darlynn at the airport, circa 1961. *Courtesy John Family*. The album *Little Willie John In Action*, released by King in 1960, included "Leave My Kitten Alone," "No Regrets," "Let Them Talk" and his 1955 hit "Need Your Love So Bad." *Courtesy Bob Kelly*.

On July 22nd, 1960 Willie was the headliner on a "midnite" dance at the Roseland Ballroom in Holyoke, Massachusetts. The show really did go from midnight to four am. *Courtesy Bob Kelly.*

(**Clockwise from top left**) "Sleep," released in 1960, was Willie's biggest pop hit; *Come On and Join Little Willie John at a Recording Session*, released in 1962, showcased Willie's virtuosity; *The Sweet, The Hot, The Teenaged Beat* came out in 1961 and was a mixed bag of standards and old hits; *Sure Things*, released in 1961, was packed with hits. *All courtesy Bob Kelly.*

Willie playing horsie in a Chicago hotel room with his toddler sons Kevin and Keith during 1961, while he was engaged at the Regal Theater. *Courtesy Johnson Publishing Company, Inc. All rights reserved.*

(**Clockwise from top left**) Willie and Darlynn in the backyard of the John house in Miami, playing with their sons on the swing set, 1962; Darlynn, Willie and Keith in the backyard of the Miami house, playing volleyball, 1962; Keith and Kevin with Suzie, their housekeeper in Miami, 1962; Willie at the ocean in Miami, 1962; Willie and Darlynn pose with their two sons in Miami, 1962. *All courtesy John Family.*

to get television and film work. But he knew his reserved wife wouldn't settle there permanently. "In California, people were phony," Darlynn complained. "There were a lot of people I just wasn't comfortable around." She came to like many of Willie's showbiz friends, especially Dinah Washington, B.B. King and his wife, Jerry Butler and Lou Rawls—whose hairdresser mother once streaked her hair blonde. But she felt that many of the hangers-on who tagged along with Willie were friendly on the basis of his status, their grins growing wider with the thickness of his wallet.

In Detroit especially, Willie was the big man in town. People were accustomed to his Cadillacs, the way he set up the bar and picked up the tab. Just to look at Willie, all sleekly barbered up and in silk and tweeds, his north end friends thought he must be rolling in dough.

In Florida, they would have a clean slate. Willie couldn't get enough of the ocean, the palm trees and the orange groves. He'd been escaping to Florida since he was 17. Darlynn only vaguely remembered the city from an earlier trip, and when Willie took her there again in late 1960, she thought it was just for a show. "We were on a tour, next thing I know he's taking me to this house," she said. Willie headed for a northwest Miami neighborhood and parked in front of 1090 NW 53rd Street, near the corner of 11th. Built in 1947, the house was a modest, sun-baked one-story stucco structure, a typical Miami house with two bedrooms and what mid-century Americans called a "Florida room," an expansive room on the back of the house with floor to ceiling windows to draw in the sunshine, perfect for relaxing or entertaining. The fenced backyard was thick with flowers, a lemon tree and a rosy, sprawling bougainvillea that took up much of one patio wall in the back. "Do you like it?" Willie asked Darlynn, grinning. "I bought it!"

And he had too, lock, stock and completely furnished in postwar 1950s Miami style, down to the pink flamingo-patterned wallpaper in the living room.

The house may have been small, but Willie hired a housekeeper, Susie, and a butler, Chester, to keep the household humming along for his active young family. There was a little concrete apron in front of the house, as well as a garage where Willie could park his latest Cadillac and store the boys' bicycles. Darlynn only had to open the garage door four or five times for Kevin to get his bike, before the four year-old figured out how to do it himself. Darlynn came outside one day to find the garage door open, and Kevin and bicycle long gone.

Although Willie was still on the road a lot, when he was at home, he was the fix-it man for any problems the boys might encounter. When Kevin's beloved bicycle was stolen, he was inconsolable until Willie walked the boy across 11th Street to the strip mall and bought him a new one. There was a shaded front galley along the front of the house where Willie and Darlynn could sit in lounge chairs and watch the world go by. That is, on the few occasions when Willie was sitting still at all. Fun for Willie always meant living on the edge in one way or another. Neighbors remember seeing Willie's Cadillac flying down the street with Willie, laughing, lying on the hood of the car as a friend raced down the residential road. Lou Devereaux was one of the neighbors who remembered these antics. She lived further down on 53rd, closer to Tenth Avenue. The registered nurse had just given birth to her youngest son, named Keith, just like the Johns' younger boy, when she was invited by Darlynn to come down the street and nurse her new baby at the Johns' house. It was a friendship that would last for years to come.

Willie and Darlynn's house was party central. Lou loved to cook, and would bring her famous barbecued chicken to the house whenever there was a gathering. She's still in awe of the celebrities she met in the Johns' Florida room. There was Willie, glass of Scotch in hand, watching as his wife Darlynn entertained showbiz greats like Sam Cooke, Barbara McNair, Ruth Brown, Sam & Dave, Dinah Washington and Roy Hamilton. Just as often it was a celebrity athlete. Lou met Philadelphia Sixers basketball player Wilt Chamberlain and heavyweight boxer Cassius Clay (later, Muhammad Ali) in the Johns' back room.

Darlynn blossomed in the Southern sun, living among down-to-earth people with actual jobs, even if her Florida room boasted more star power than the cocktail lounge of Miami's Hotel Fontainebleau. "I loved it there because the people were so warm," Darlynn said. "In my background, I never had the warmth and things that I thought other people had, or were supposed to have. I'm comfortable with everyday people—go to work, go to a job—and they were real." It was their first home away from his family, away from her family: just Darlynn, Willie, Kevin and Keith.

Keith, the baby, added a jolt of even more high-octane energy to the household. As soon as he was walking, he and big brother Kevin were exploring up and down 53rd street. Kevin was the boss and leader, while Keith kept everybody laughing. Both were talkative and effervescent, singing in stereo as much as they were chattering–rather like Willie. "They were busy," Lou Deveraux said. She and the neighbors kept a close eye on the two, who were once found smashing outdoor Christmas lights under their feet, just because they liked to hear the pop.

When he was in town, Willie enjoyed going to the fights, partial to a little wager when he went. In the spring of 1961 he, Lloyd Price and Clyde McPhatter got together a 300 dollar "round" pool for the Ingemar Johansen vs Floyd Patterson fight in Miami. Price won the pot, if anyone is counting.

Willie had always loved the water; despite being a city boy he loved fishing in any river, lake or stream he could find around Detroit. Living a few blocks away from the ocean in Miami, Willie was in his element, and he took Darlynn and the boys on many trips to the Caribbean, by sea and air. One year Willie invited James Brown and a party of entertainer friends and made a weekend of it, flying to Bimini to fish, relax and generally carry on. On more than one occasion, when she was out on a boat ride with Willie, Darlynn remembered her husband asking the captain if he could take the wheel of the vessel. To her great consternation, the answer was usually yes, although Willie proved as adept at sailing as any sport he cared to take up.

The happy times started to wind down when Darlynn became seriously ill. She loved Florida, but there was a virus there that clearly didn't like her, and she contracted diphtheria, rare by the 1960s, but not completely eradicated. It was highly contagious, so she was put into isolation at Jackson Memorial. Having a nurse–Lou Deveraux–as a neighbor was a great help. "Lou kept watch over Mom, and kept an eye on us," Kevin said. "My mom says Lou helped her survive."

In 1961, Miami was in full roar after dark. It had been a winter getaway for northerners since the 1920s, and the Mafia moved in soon after that. When Jackie Gleason set up shop and broadcast his weekly CBS-TV show from there in the 1950s, Miami became the hip East Coast party spot for the Rat Pack and the cooler reaches of the entertainment world. On the rhythm & blues side, singers like Dinah Washington were often in residence at the Island Club or at one of Willie's favorites, Sir John's Nightbeat. The Nightbeat was attached to the Sir John Hotel, a high-end outfit catering to black entertainers. Even with the demands of family life, Willie could often be found schmoozing with friends in the clubs, ginning up the laughter with lively repartee.

Willie served as the local rhythm & blues kingpin at the Nightbeat, and from time to time, he was coaxed into doing a show or two. It was in his role as top dog at Sir John's that Willie met Bettye LaVette in 1962. She was only 16, raw and unpolished, and had just recorded her first single, "My Man, He's a Loving Man," on Northern Records. It was a local hit in Detroit, then was picked up by Atlantic and made a modest national splash. When her record started to gain airplay in Miami, Sir John's Nightbeat booked LaVette for an engagement.

There was just one problem. On the way to Miami, she lost her voice. The teenager had only been singing professionally for a few months and the excitement of her early success, and the frequent gigs that went along with it, was wearing her down. When she landed in Miami, LaVette could barely make a sound. "It wasn't that I was drinking or doing drugs, it's because I was up, I wouldn't go to bed, and I was running my mouth," LaVette said. But there she was, on her way to the club, there was no turning back.

She describes the scene: "Everybody's there to see me, my little record is in the top two or three on the little rhythm & blues charts—because back then all they had was black radio." There was a full house, and Little Willie John was seated up front. "Willie John was holding residence then at Sir John's Nightbeat club, he was just calling all the shots." LaVette rasped her way through the first show, but when it was time for the second, she couldn't even whisper the lyrics.

Sensing her distress, Willie left his table and went up onstage. He kissed the teenager and asked the audience to give her a big round of applause. "This girl is from my hometown, and I want you to make her feel welcome," Willie said. He sat down on the edge of the stage and started to sing "Talk to Me, Talk to Me" a cappella, with no accompaniment. LaVette was stunned. Even if her voice should miraculously come back, how could she follow that? "I didn't even know how to sing my own song, much less someone else's. But he just embraced me immediately because I was from Detroit, I was from the north end, like him. We hadn't even met before that."

Did Willie know how he affected people with his voice? LaVette wonders today. Did any singers of his ilk, back then, really understand? "I don't know that they know. I don't think any of us knew how long we would go on, or that when you're 85 or 100, that people might know who you are," LaVette sighed. "I will listen to B.B. King at any time, I will listen to Johnny Hartman at any time, and I will listen to Willie John at any time. This new stuff? Uh uh."

Willie made other friends in Miami as well, it's where he got to know Sam Moore. Moore was singing gospel but also knocking around the clubs, until he met up with Dave Prater at the King of Hearts club in Miami. One night Dave forgot the lyrics to "Doggin' Around" and Sam sang verses at him from the audience. The effect was explosive and the two became Sam & Dave. Sam and Willie just seemed to click. They shared roots in gospel music and both were prone to a certain amount of wildness offstage. By his own admission, Sam drank, partied and did a prodigious amount of drugs. He saw some of Willie's worst behavior, mostly involving drugs and the sort of forward, available women they both encountered in clubs. But he felt he was in no position to point fingers. "Willie John was one of the most brilliant singers you would ever want to come across, bar none," Sam said. "But he had his quirks. I mean, I had them. Jackie Wilson had 'em. David Ruffin had 'em. Sam Cooke had 'em. Marvin Gaye had 'em!. . . I didn't really get into his personal life, because I was doing things myself." Both men also evinced the healthy, technicolor ego of the male rhythm & blues singer. Sam knew when to back off Willie, though; he was not yet the Sam Moore of "Soul Man" and "Hold On (I'm Coming)." If he didn't already know to tread lightly, Jackie Wilson was sometimes there to remind him.

Jackie warned Sam about Willie's competitiveness. Sam recounts a particularly extreme incident that happened at the Nightbeat Club, when a singing contest literally turned the place into a "bucket of blood." The contest was between Willie, Sam and a young singer named Davy 'Dizzy' Jones, who idolized Willie and imitated him in every way. The rules were, Willie would sing something, then either Dizzy or Sam would sing it back in exactly the same way. Sam said: "At the first show, Willie purposely sang those songs in a key you would never want to reach," Sam said, laughing. "Jackie Wilson was sitting in the back of the club. Jackie said to me, 'I know how Willie is, don't try to follow Willie because he'll clean the house with you. Y'all know how to sing, but Willie will *clean the house with you* if you try to follow him.' So I said 'OK.' I sat down." Jones got up, though, and sang after Willie. "Every time he'd match Willie, the house would go crazy," Sam said. "Then Willie took the one song, 'Need Your Love so Bad'. And he's singing it *up there*. When Willie handed it over to Dizzy, I'm not lying, blood started spewing from his mouth. When Dizzy got finished, he had busted his vocal cords."

Fortunately, Charles Williams, Sam's former principal from Booker Washington High School was there with his wife, who was a music teacher. They gathered up Jones and whisked the singer to Jackson Memorial Hospital. "And you know what Willie did? He laughed... hahahahaha," Sam said, laughing himself. And of course, Jackie Wilson had the last word. "What did I tell you?" Jackie demanded of Sam. Sam laughed. "Those two could get into it!"

Darlynn, Willie and the boys were together in the house in Miami on November 22nd, 1963 when word came through the television set that President Kennedy had been assassinated. Kevin remembers that his mother was crying–everybody was crying. Kevin cried, too. For the John boys, Miami would always be the mental image they have of home, where they remember being with their father the most. "Those were the days. . . Mom, Dad, Keith and I together," Kevin said. It wouldn't be the last time the four would be tucked up under the same roof, but it was where they lived together the longest. Despite Darlynn's illness, the memory of life with Willie and the boys in Florida still makes her smile. "It was the most wonderful time in my life," she said softly.

14

END OF AN IDYLL

Although he'd been married for four years and was the father of two boys, at 23 Willie still looked like one of the teenagers who flocked to his shows. Chugging a strawberry shake in a New York coffee shop, he gave an interview in 1961 to his old friend and publicist Masco Young in a column syndicated in the *Pittsburgh Courier* and other black newspapers. "I never hide from the public," Willie said, draining his shake with a straw. "It never pays to try it. The more you try to hide from your fans, the more anxious they are to find you–and they usually do." If he really wanted to get lost, Willie said he knew how to melt into a crowd and disappear, by acting like everybody else.

After 12 years in the music business, the stats on Willie were impressive. He'd sold over seven million records for King and pulled in 100,000 dollars a year. All this and that voice, in a five foot four inch, 126 pound package. Talking to Masco, Willie picks his own favorite songs from his catalog, "Talk to Me, Talk to Me," "Fever," "Sleep" and "Walk Slow."

Intriguingly, he saw the way he and Darlynn were living as progressive, for a show business couple. He believed that by bringing his wife and child on the road, he and Darlynn had started a trend. "A few years ago, you never saw many show people traveling around with their wives and children. Darlynn has been touring the country with me for the entire four years of our marriage." Willie was proud to note that his three year-old son Kevin, referred to in the article as "Little Willie John Jr.," was showing some of his famous dad's singing ability and showmanship, as was one year-old Darryl Keith, but Darlynn wanted nothing more than to have another child, maybe a little girl this time. Willie also announced to Masco that he was forming Kev–Kei Productions (named after his sons) to produce movies, and was shopping around for original scripts "suitable for depicting the Negro's role in American life."

While he loved living in Florida, Willie had no illusions about ongoing racial problems in the South. The often-violent struggle for civil rights seemed to be on his mind more and more as he got older. In the summer of 1961, he held a fundraiser for the NAACP in Tampa, which he said would be the first in a series of benefits raising money for organizations fighting segregation. "As entertainers, we can no longer sit and wait for the Sammy Davises and Harry Belafontes to raise all of the money," Willie said. He urged rock 'n' roll artists who worked frequently in the South (and knew the conditions there) to join the cause.

The Masco interview was in marked contrast to earlier write-ups, when reporters found a carefree, mischievous teenager who was only interested in his next hit song. Although he was not giving up the party life, given the serious tenor of the times—with the battle for civil rights in the South and the increasing role of entertainers like Davis and Belafonte in the advancement of that cause—Willie clearly wanted to be seen as more than just a blues singer. He wanted to make his political views known and speak out on a larger stage than just the chitlin circuit.

Willie's pop success promised to help him gain that broader audience. A story published in *Billboard* in 1961 described a surge in popularity for rhythm & blues and jazz artists. Ren Grevatt singled out Lloyd Price and Little Willie John, "both long associated with the rhythm & blues field, each now have not one but two hits on the (pop) Hot 100... John has 'Cottage for Sale' and 'Heartbreak (It's Hurting Me)'." According to Grevatt, Syd Nathan said that King Records made money with rhythm & blues records, and would continue to release them. "Recently, Nathan's husky voice has been raised to a near-fever pitch. No wonder Nathan's King–Federal axis now enjoys four Hot 100 entries, all of them closely identified with rhythm & blues."

But something was stirring across the North Atlantic, a tsunami of tuneful Brits that would change the landscape of American music forever. Never mind that the British Invasion was based on a slavish devotion to the same rhythm & blues and rockabilly artists it would soon render unfashionable, if not altogether obsolete. As the decade turned from the 1950s to the 60s you could only hear a distant clamor of the nascent guitar army, manned by Rickenbacker 12-strings and reverb-drenched Stratocasters, but it was getting closer by the day.

Motown managed to hold its own during the British Invasion, but rhythm & blues didn't fare as well. The music would have a resurgence from the late 1960s into the early 70s, repurposed as soul music, a brief respite from guitar-based British rock, but for now, things weren't looking too good.

There was no way for Willie to know that a crossover boom in the field of rhythm & blues was coming in the form of a new movement dubbed soul. It was led by so many of the singers who grew up admiring him; Sam & Dave, Aretha Franklin and Johnnie Taylor. And Willie's 1960 hit with "Sleep" had gotten him so much pop airplay that he was poised to finally find mainstream success beyond the usual fan base. If only he could stay focused, and stay alive.

When it came to being busted for marijuana, Hank Ballard and the Midnighters had no peers—they were in their own Hall of Fame. Houston was a town without pity for most rhythm & blues performers, but it was especially perilous for Ballard and his fellow Midnighter Norman Thrasher. The two got on the wrong side of the Houston police when they started "dating" the girlfriends of two local cops. This enraged the lawmen so much that they raided the group's hotel rooms every time the Midnighters set foot in town. Usually their sometime ladyfriends would tip Ballard and Thrasher off when the cops were on their way, so the musicians were able to dispose of anything illegal in good time to meet their visitors. That is, until the time Midnighters guitarist Cal Green was caught with a small amount of marijuana in the pocket of a borrowed coat. Green got three years in Huntsville prison, and Billy Davis replaced him as the Midnighters' guitarist.

Word of what happened to Green spread quickly along the chitlin circuit. The Falcons promised Mack Rice, who was both a singer and the group's manager, that they wouldn't carry any drugs to Houston. "They lied," Rice said. "We came in and (the police) shook everybody's room down. They never found it, but our guitar player Lance hid the weed in the TV, in the slot where you used to put the money in." Lead Falcon Wilson Pickett didn't like that. "Pickett was mad. Boy, he was mad! He said, 'You could have gotten us arrested!'" Marijuana, and marijuana busts, had been rampant in the music business for years. Even the smiling, avuncular Louis Armstrong, beloved by mainstream America, was a frequent user. Cocaine was common in music circles as well, although it seemed comparatively exotic and seedy to mainstream America in the 1950s and early 60s.

Willie was arrested and charged with possession in June 1961 after police found two matchboxes of marijuana in his hotel room in Greensboro, North Carolina. Raiding an entertainer's hotel or dressing room hoping to find drugs was a common police tactic in those days, and both Willie's brother Mertis and Darlynn felt that somebody probably set him up. Clarence Avant wasn't around at the time, so Harry Balk probably heard from Willie that night, one of those after-midnight calls that gave his sometime-manager nightmares.

Billy Davis of the Midnighters laughs. "The (musicians) I knew didn't get it planted on them." He saw it everywhere. "When I first went out on the road I was a kid, 19 years old. I didn't know what marijuana was. I'd see these guys in the group smoking it, Hank and the band, Jackie Wilson, you name them."

Alcohol was easily the most popular backstage intoxicant, and Willie was exposed to it from childhood on, on the rough streets of Detroit's north end, backstage at the talent shows and at the all night singing sessions at the Davison Rec Center. In Detroit, he knew all the best places to drink, and if he ran out of ideas, there were plenty of musician friends who could give him a hot tip, like Joe Weaver for example. Pianist and bandleader Joe, along with Johnnie Bassett, would back up Willie back in their teenaged years, so whenever Willie was back in Detroit it was a fond reunion for the old friends. In one such encounter, Joe was hanging out at the Apex Bar on Oakland with his cousin Benny Benjamin, Motown's top studio drummer, when they happened upon Willie, who was headlining at Phelps Lounge, down the street.

After a few drinks, Willie and his friends walked a couple of blocks east, to a well-known, eminently illegal blind pig where they could drink corn liquor. Joe Hunter of the Funk Brothers, a world-class connoisseur of "cohn likka" as anyone who's seen *Standing in the Shadows of Motown* can attest, always smiled, remembering the place. "Man would give you a glass for 25 cents," he sighed, basking in the memory. Between the corn liquor and musician talk, Willie's showtime at Phelps Lounge came and went, and an irate Eddie Phelps could be heard out on Oakland yelling for him. Joe Weaver laughed himself to tears, telling the story years later.

As for harder drugs, Willie's friends tell conflicting stories. Sam Moore of Sam & Dave said he was first introduced to heroin by Willie. Sam went on to develop a habit, but he insists that was his own doing. "He may have given me my first, but you can't say he's the one who turned me on," Sam says. "I tried it, I didn't like it, and next thing I knew, Willie was gone, he didn't offer me any more." Sam may take the blame, largely, but it still irritates Faye Pridgon, Willie's Apollo Theater girlfriend. "That's a lie," she said. "James Brown's wardrobe mistress turned (Sam) on to it. Willie wasn't even doing drugs back in those days. And heroin was not Willie's drug of choice, he only dabbled here and there." Faye ran into Willie a lot after they'd broken up, and she said Willie would, very rarely, do a "speedball"—a combination of heroin and cocaine—but "nothing to do with needles or a habit." In all fairness, Sam claims it happened later–in the mid 1960s. And King Records' Hal Neely insisted he had sent Willie to rehab a few times.

Whatever the truth of the matter, Willie did get into some scrapes that landed him in court. In Atlanta during 1961, he was charged with racking up almost a thousand dollars in long distance charges on a phony credit card. Another temptation on the road was trying to act the big man with the gun. It happened once when Willie was trying to adopt a hard edge of bravado he felt was necessary in dealing with promoters. Jack Bart, who worked for his father, Willie's booking agent Ben Bart, was exactly Willie's age, 25, in 1962. Jack was dispatched from New York to drive a brand new, four-door white Cadillac to Willie in California, where he was performing. He was to stay with Willie for a week and take care of road manager duties. What happened next, Jack says he won't forget "until the day I die."

Willie and Jack traveled to do a date in Seattle for promoter Charlie Sullivan. Jack had instructions from his father to send a thousand dollars from each of Willie's shows back to New York. It might have been for a general debt, or as payback specifically for the Cadillac, but Jack was under strict orders to send the money. After Willie finished his Seattle show, he came off the stage and found Jack and promoter Sullivan dividing up the money. Jack told Willie, "I've got to take a thousand dollars." After years scrapping for his pay, Willie was in no mood for this, not from a punk kid his own age. Not if he could bark his way out of it. "No, you're not taking any of my money," Willie warned Jack. "So he takes out a pistol and points it at me," Jack said. "Charlie steps between me and Willie and says, 'You don't want to do anything like that, Willie, don't be ridiculous! Put it down.'" Willie lowered the gun. As he did, all the bullets fell out. Jack laughed. "It was a .38 caliber pistol, but he had it loaded with .32 bullets. So he wasn't shooting anybody!"

Nobody said he was Wyatt Earp. Thinking back on it, Jack believes that the cocaine use and drinking that he indulged in out on the road was catching up with Willie. That, and the fact that after more than a decade of rip-offs and hard living on the chitlin circuit, he was probably more than a little fed up. Willie's brother Mertis remembered that he used to get irritated when Mertis sent part of his gig money home. "He wanted to know, 'How much money are you sending home?' Because that was him. Sometimes he would let you do it, and sometimes he wouldn't. He'd say, 'That's my money. That's my money, and I'll do what I want with it.'"

For several years Willie had been on track to the good life. Maybe he wasn't living large in the Palm Springs desert like his hero, Frank Sinatra, but he'd settled down in Florida with Darlynn and was crazy about his two little boys. Friends like Norman Thrasher had seen the change in Willie. Domestic life agreed with him. There seemed to be no limit to what he could do. "When he became a father, he saw his ways different," Thrasher said. "Because he had two of himself. He had himself and he had two people who looked like him, and who were going to be him, and a wife. So he became a different kind of a person. He had more responsibility. He was able to sing better songs, live a better life and present himself to the people of the world as a wonderful person."

To Thrasher, Willie wasn't just a singer. He was *a jazz singer.* Joe Williams was reminded of that one evening in the club on Broadway that Lloyd Price bought and renamed Lloyd Price's Turntable. Williams was singing with Count Basie, Willie's old friend, so Willie and several of the Midnighters went to catch their set. "They called Willie up and invited him to do a couple tunes," Billy Davis said. "He sang and turned the house out." While he was singing, Willie looked over at Joe Williams and grinned. "Willie ate him alive. Joe Williams caught hell coming on after Willie," Davis said, laughing.

In 1962, Willie's longtime opening act, James Brown, was suddenly the toast of the rhythm & blues world. In the fall, James had the genius idea to record his entire Apollo Theater show on an album, *James Brown Live at the Apollo.* His

King bosses had resisted, and James had to bankroll the taping himself, but in doing so, he single-handedly created a new genre: the electrifying, career-defining live album. The old way of doing things that King executives clung to—throwing out 45s one by one, paying the DJs and hoping for a hit—instantly appeared old-fashioned.

As fun-loving as he was, Willie had a temper. Milton Hopkins of the Upsetters observed him for years on and offstage. "The only thing I remember that would set Willie off is when he sensed that you were trying to mess him over. That's the only time that it would really piss him off, and he'd go crazy."

Darlynn didn't see any of that. Always protective, Willie kept his goodtime party buddies away from the family. She would see his face tighten when someone outside of the family tried to pick up Kevin or Keith without asking. Willie would almost growl, Darlynn remembers, when strangers got too close to his sons, but he was always kind and good to her. He did lose his temper with her on one occasion. "We had one fight during the time we were married," Darlynn said. "We were in some nightclub, and I was showing my wedding rings to somebody, somebody I didn't know. I took them off and let her see them and try them on. And he slapped me." She sighed. "It's only now, years later, that I realize the significance. . . because he always wore his ring."

Still, she took the incident seriously. "It wasn't like a big big thing to anybody else, but it was a big thing to me, because my father beat my mother. If anything would break us up, that would break us up." Darlynn left the club and stayed away from Willie for a while, "just to prove a point, that that wasn't going to work," she said. " And he got it! I wasn't going to be with somebody if he was going to hit me. It took me a little time to realize how it happened, to understand his feelings. That was his way of showing how strongly he felt about it."

Thinking back on his star vocalist, guitarist Hopkins' voice softened. "If you look over behind all the bullshit and all the other things that Willie would do and say, I think he was a decent person. That's the way I always felt about him and that's probably the reason why we always got along. I never tried to rub shoulders with him or run in his circles, but I always respected him, and he always respected me. That's the way it was."

While Willie's plans to conquer movies and television hadn't quite taken off, it was a coup when on December 21st, 1962, he appeared briefly on national television, in an episode of *Route 66*, one of the hottest shows on the air. The

CBS-TV anthology series followed the adventures of two searchers driving a Corvette across America. Starring Martin Milner, the episode, "Give the Old Cat a Tender Mouse" had "Tod" (Milner) trying to track down a kooky, bohemian girl (played by Julie Newmar) who he'd encountered some time earlier. In a nightclub scene set in Memphis, Newmar and an actor playing her beau are sitting at a table and Willie can be seen on the bandstand for about 30 seconds. Dressed in a slick band suit with a short jacket, he is clopping claves (percussion sticks) together with great intensity. Willie looks directly into the camera, then off to the side as he continues to play, keeping time with what Kevin John calls the "John head nod."

Apart from *Route 66*, three appearances on Dick Clark's *American Bandstand*, and reportedly, an appearance on the early Jack Paar *Tonight Show*, Willie didn't crack the top level of television variety shows, not on the level that Sam Cooke or Nat 'King' Cole did.

Cooke was about as mainstream as a black pop artist could get, and even for him it was a constant struggle to be booked by the top television shows of his day. Black artists who came out of the big band era like Ella Fitzgerald, Duke Ellington and Sammy Davis Jr were old enough (and arguably, tame enough) to be welcomed into mainstream culture. Not so with the "youngsters," who were mostly confined to Dick Clark's *American Bandstand* or local dance party shows. And it was all too easy to piss Dick off with a suspect attitude or ribald lyrics and be banned from the show, as Hank Ballard found out, when Chubby Checker's version of "The Twist" was aired instead of his original.

"That was one of the things that the artists of that era were plagued with," Jerry Butler said. "There were very few television venues for them to get exposure on. We're talking about only three major networks, and they were not really big on having black artists on, especially from this jungle music that had been ascribed to rhythm & blues. Nat 'King' Cole and Sammy Davis and the Ellingtons and the folks who were the legends of the music industry who happened to be black, they were acceptable but not the new generation kids."

Despite his limited exposure on the small screen, Willie continued to record new tunes in sessions during 1962 that yielded a slew of material pieced out by King over the ensuing years. There was "Until Again My Love," and a topical novelty, "Mister Glenn," (addressing the astronaut John Glenn, whom Willie asks about space girls) in March. He cut "I Wish I Could Cry" in June and

"Half a Love/Without a Friend" in November. Willie's gorgeous take on the country song "Big Blue Diamonds" was put to wax in June of 1962. It was one his brother EJ mentioned years later with great fondness. "My brother could sing anything, we used to hear country on the radio growing up, and he could sing any of that."

King producer Ray Pennington was in the booth when Willie recorded most of these country sides. "We did a whole album of country songs (on Willie) and I assume they were released, I don't remember," he said. "We did two or three pure country sessions on him." "She Thinks I Still Care" was another country lament Willie recorded that Pennington supervised and enjoyed immensely. "He was a real 'up' little guy," Pennington said. "I think he liked me because we were both short. I liked his singing and it was pretty obvious."

Pennington wasn't the only one who liked Willie's crooning on the song. Elvis Presley happened to be listening to George Klein's show on Memphis' WHHM one day in 1962 when Klein played Willie singing "She Thinks I Don't Care." Knocked out, Elvis called the DJ and asked him to bring the record by Graceland after his shift. He did, and Elvis played the song "over and over," according to Klein, who chatted about it with the writer of the song, Dickey Lee, on Sirius XM Radio's Elvis Channel. Lee says he has no idea how his song made its way to Cincinnati and the King studios, but Willie was the first artist to record it, although it's known as a hit for George Jones. Elvis vowed, "The next time I'm in a studio, I'm going to record that song," and he did. The King thought enough of Willie's version that he hung the single in a frame on his wall, where many of his own singles and albums were hung. Today, you can still see Elvis' cherished copy of Little Willie John's "She Thinks I Still Care" hanging on a wall at Graceland.

For a musician, Pennington had lived a sheltered life. He remembered seeing Willie smoke a funny-looking cigarette once, between sessions. "I didn't know what it was," Pennington said. "He was having trouble singing, and it seemed like all of a sudden, he was singing real good." Pennington asked the King studio engineer what Willie was doing. "The engineer informed me. And he said, 'You *can't* be that dumb.' I guess I was!"

Darlynn was always slender, but her bout with diphtheria had left her thin and weak, struggling to keep up with two rambunctious boys while Willie was out on the road. Although he bragged to Masco Young in 1961 that he was forging new ground as an entertainer by taking Darlynn on tour, it was increasingly difficult for his wife to travel with two toddlers, and it became nearly impossible when Kevin started school in 1963. It became obvious that Darlynn and the boys would have to stay in one place, and that place was not Miami. It was a painful decision, but Willie and Darlynn had to bring the curtain down on their expensive Florida interlude. The family let a friend assume the mortgage on their Miami dream home, and they moved back to Philadelphia, to an apartment on Dauphin Street where Darlynn would be close to her sister Marcy and they could save some money.

Willie was on the road more and more, due to mounting debts to King and Universal Attractions from his Cadillacs, his many advances and the money he still sent home to Detroit. Hal Neely admitted cheerfully that King depended upon its artists not really understanding that each advance they got extended the term of their contract. The Dauphin Street apartment was affordable, it was also close to the Uptown Theater on Broad and Dauphin, the Philly stop along the northern route of the chitlin circuit, and the site of many triumphs for Willie.

Darlynn and Willie enrolled Kevin at George Washington Carver elementary school in north Philadelphia, and he used to walk to school with his cousins Valerie, Sharon (who was Kevin's age) and Selena. Keith tagged along when he was old enough to go to kindergarten. Having a father who was a traveling musician was the only "normal" Kevin and Keith knew, but Willie's homecomings were highly anticipated events, and very emotional for the boys. That their dad was playful and loved surprises made his brief visits home even more memorable. Kevin will never forget the day he and his cousins came hurtling out of school for the walk home, to see a familiar, slight figure leaning against a wall, giving them his best grin. "Daddy!" Willie had made an unexpected trip back to Philadelphia and wanted to surprise Kevin, and walk him home. The cousins remember Willie's arm draped around his son's shoulder as they strolled down the street, Kevin chattering excitedly all the way.

In the 1950s and early 60s, there were few entertainers or sports figures Willie had not either encountered or befriended. "Willie knew everybody!" his brother EJ bragged, and it was true, no matter where he went Willie knew half the people in the joint. And almost everybody was glad to see him. There was a notable exception one night in the early 1960s, when in the bustle of a Harlem nightclub on 125th Street, Willie came face to face with the man who would dominate music at the end of the 1960s as much as Willie had in the late 50s. It was as if two distinctly different eras were spinning toward each other, on a collision course toward some sort of musical Armageddon. But it wasn't epic. Instead, it got personal. Jimi Hendrix refused to shake Willie's hand.

The guitarist was still known as Jimmy James back then, and his back was up because Willie happened to be the old flame of his girlfriend, Faye, who was conducting the intended introduction. Neither Willie nor Jimi were performing, they had both come to the club to see Don Gardner and Dee Dee Ford perform their fiery, call-and-response song "I Need Your Lovin," a Top 20 hit in 1962. Jimi "had no reason" for his jealousy, Faye said, although she admits she had bragged about Willie a lot to her sensitive boyfriend. "I was doing this whole Willie praise thing, and (Jimi) didn't take kindly to it at all. Of all the people that he had problems with, in his head, Willie was number one. But it was only in his mind."

Willie encountered a much friendlier reception at another Harlem club, the famed bebop hangout Minton's Playhouse on 118th Street in the Cecil Hotel. He swept in one night with his usual entourage, and caught the eye of young guitarist George Benson, who happened to be a fan. It was just like Willie to know where the hippest jazz clubs were. But he didn't just hang. Willie was recognized by the band, and invited up to sing a song. There Willie, the quintessential blues singer, slayed everybody singing a jazz standard, "Willow, Weep for Me." He bowled over Benson and the sophisticated Minton's crowd. "It was the best rendition of that song I ever heard," Benson said. "He was a great inspiration, a great influence. The way that I approach singing today was largely influenced by Little Willie John."

|15|

NO WAY OUT

Willie was delighted when he heard in the early fall of 1964, that the Beatles had recorded his "Leave my Kitten Alone" at London's Abbey Road studios in August. Kevin remembers his father bubbling over with excitement. After years of recording so many songs written and or controlled by his King bosses, Willie knew it was mostly by writing his own material that he would get any traction in his career. For the Beatles to include one of his songs on one of their bestselling albums meant more than the possibility of fast money. It would put him back into the game.

While the early 1960s were spectacular for the Beatles and the rest of the British Invasion, as well as for Motown and Phil Spector's Wall of Sound, for many of the biggest names from 1950s rhythm & blues, it was as if the curse that befell Robert Johnson was on a time release plan. Tragedy kept on following tragedy.

Jesse Belvin, the crooner whose silky ballad from 1956, "Goodnight, My Love," is one of the all-time classics from that era, died in a horrific, head-on automobile crash near Hope, Arkansas in 1960. He was just 27. It shook Willie up, because he'd just played on a bill with Belvin in Little Rock, and that sort of death on the highway was the great fear of every chitlin circuit performer.

In 1961, Jackie Wilson was shot twice by one girlfriend as he walked into his New York apartment with another (his wife Freda was at home in Detroit). He lost a kidney, but recovered from his injuries—though the same couldn't be said for his ailing career. In 1963, Jackie hit with "Baby Workout," but by

1964 he couldn't get a look into the charts and his career was starting to seem as outdated as his processed 'do.

In December 1963, Willie's good friend Dinah Washington, the queen of the blues, died from an overdose of diet pills in her home on Buena Vista in Detroit, just a stone's throw from the Johns' dream home on Leslie Street.

On Halloween during 1964 Ray Charles was busted at Boston's Logan Airport for holding heroin when it was found on his private plane. Indicted for possession and drug trafficking, Ray faced 20 years in prison, but received a suspended sentence after agreeing to go into rehab.

In 1964, Sam Cooke was making a successful transition through the pre-soul era with "Shake" and "A Change is Gonna Come," but on December 11th, he was shot and killed by a clerk in a fleabag Los Angeles motel. He was just 33.

James Brown proclaimed 1964 a "strange year" in his memoir *The Godfather of Soul.* "A lot of tragedy came to a lot of people I went way back with in the business," he wrote. He included Willie in that group.

Willie's troubles started in the spring, in Fort Myers, Florida, when he was arrested for assaulting a man with a broken bottle in a nightclub. Willie's defense was that someone had thrown a bottle at him onstage, and he threw it back, hitting the man. There was another incident in April when he got into an altercation with a chef who had botched his meal in a restaurant. Darlynn John, explaining the incidents in a letter to the authorities in Washington State, said Willie was being harassed by a Fort Myers club owner who didn't pay him for a gig. After Willie performed at a rival club, the club owner had gone out of his way to cause trouble. "My husband has lots of hecklers and troublemakers to cope with, I know for a fact just how hard he has tried to avoid trouble," Darlynn wrote. Willie jumped bail and left Florida, never to return. But he needn't have left in such a hurry. Trouble was intent on following him.

Willie had started missing dates back in 1962, annoying the Upsetters and drawing notice from the press. In October of 1962, Izzy Rowe reported in his syndicated column that "Little Willie John is headed for serious financial difficulties if he continues to miss contracted dates, his agent is being forced to return deposits." Stanley Robertson noted in the *Los Angeles Sentinel* in July 1964 that Willie had been booked into a prestigious after-hours jazz series at the Adams-West Theatre in Los Angeles, but Lou Rawls had to step in when Willie was "suddenly taken ill."

Willie was caught in a bind. Away from home and Darlynn's calming influence, heavy drinking brought on the epileptic seizures that had plagued him in childhood. His goodtime buddies out on the road weren't about to encourage him to drink less, as that would close the spigot on all the free liquor. Despite the temptations, he had to make his living on the road.

Guitarist Milton Hopkins left the Upsetters in 1963, although the rest of the group carried on playing behind Willie, when he turned up to his gigs, anyway. Because Willie's schedule was becoming more and more erratic, the remaining Upsetters picked up dates backing Sam Cooke, Chuck Jackson and the '5' Royales to stay busy and get paid. Cooke was on a hot streak and giving them the most work between 1963 and 64. It was this period, when Willie and the Upsetters started to work with each other less, that Hopkins believes marks the start of Willie's downward spiral. Without his famous show band, the gigs were smaller and the pay barely covered his tailor's bill. On the surface, Willie was still the urbane, uptown crooner. His suits were fresh, he was neatly turned out and still setting up the house with drinks. But there were fault lines appearing that his old friends could see. His carousing seemed to have a more desperate edge.

Johnnie Bassett was one of the ones to notice the change in Willie. In the 1950s, after years of playing guitar with Joe Weaver and the Bluenotes as the house band for Detroit's Fortune Records, Johnnie went into the Army. He was released from the service in Seattle during the early 1960s, and decided to stay a while, seduced by the lively music scene there. Johnnie found plenty of work backing up acts like Johnny 'Guitar' Watson and Ike and Tina Turner, and he played quite often with young Jimmy James/Jimi Hendrix. Johnnie was one of the last musicians to play behind Willie, ever. He was shocked when he ran into his old friend. "He was in bad shape then," Johnnie said. "We let him sit in and sing a few songs. I was playing with an organ trio, Quincy Jones' brother-in-law Joe Franks' band. As long as we had been together, Willie hardly recognized me."

Johnnie saw the reality behind his old friend's usual bravado when Willie offered to sell him some of his custom-made Harry Kosins suits. Johnnie stands at least six feet tall, Willie was five foot four. Those pants would have barely reached Johnnie's calves. "I said, 'No man, I can't wear your suits, keep 'em," Johnnie recalled. He offered to just give him the money, but Willie insisted on giving Johnnie a suit in exchange for the cash.

It saddened Willie's old friend to see him this way, but he wasn't entirely surprised. "Willie was a defiant person. He got to be in the condition he was because he wouldn't leave the drugs and booze alone." He believes that frustration and anger fueled the drinking. Willie wasn't that way before. "Toward the end of his career he did get angry, because the business treated him so bad," Johnnie said. "People he thought were in his corner, he couldn't count on them, that made him angry. He was angry about King. But he just got out of control. Didn't nobody want to book him because the (talk) that was going around about him. Nobody wanted to handle it."

It didn't matter that Willie had one of the best voices in the business and could still put on a killer show. An outdoor concert at Oakland, California's Frank Youell Field in late September was an example of how bad promotion, lack of publicity and little to no record company support could sink the best talent. The show—featuring a star line-up including Lou Rawls, Willie John and Etta James—was a box office flop, as the *Oakland Tribune* reported. Lack of publicity was blamed for a slim crowd of 600, a chilly breeze warped the tone of the horns and the singers struggled against an inadequate sound system. Rawls was praised for his mournful "St James Infirmary." As for Willie, the critic wrote: "Singer Little Willie John deserved the loud applause he received."

But for Willie and Rawls, giving their all hardly mattered anymore. Willie had been putting on shows like that since he was 14 years old, and what did he have to show for it? A wife and two sons he barely saw while he scraped the barrel for a living in low-rent clubs, and fought King for money, better songs and higher quality sessions.

After jumping bail in Miami, Willie headed for the West Coast, where Mable helped him set up some dates. His sister had asked for her release from Motown Records earlier that year after recording several singles that were too bluesy for the label's teenage audience. She hadn't yet signed with Stax (that would come in 1965 or early 66) so she had time to help out her troubled little brother. She booked him into a series of one-nighters up and down the West Coast to make some fast cash.

One of those bookings was at the Magic Inn in downtown Seattle for six shows over the weekend, Friday October 17th to Saturday the 18th. It was a serious step down from previous engagements in the city—the Magic Inn was a dump. "Imagine the worst place in Detroit," said singer and guitarist Little Bill Englehart, who first met Willie in 1959. Like many young white musicians and fans, he liked to catch the top black acts at the Evergreen Ballroom, south of Seattle. The first time Englehart saw Willie at the Evergreen, the young rocker hustled his way backstage and pressed his new record into Willie's hand. "You'd have thought it was really something, that I gave him a record," Englehart says, laughing at the memory. After that, he would see Willie at least once a year. He even got the Upsetters to teach his band how to do their famous steps. "They were real patient with us, six white guys asking, 'Would you show us those steps?' And they did."

Englehart is still in awe of Willie. "He really had a great voice," said the musician. " I don't know what he'd done before the record thing happened for him, if he sang in church or what. . . His range, and the tone. . . it was kind of nasal, at just the right place. I loved the sound of his voice."

Willie's last show at the Magic Inn ended at 1:30 in the morning on that Sunday, and he and his valet, chauffeur and running buddy Eddie Moore left the club and headed for an even rougher part of town. The music was still going when he arrived at Birdland, the jazz club on 23rd and Madison in Seattle's black neighborhood, the same place where Quincy Jones and Ray Charles both got their start. Willie settled in, tossed back a few cognacs and was invited onstage to sing a few numbers.

It was either at Birdland or another stop, a ratty club called the Black and Tan, where Willie met up with Bill Englehart. "He was drunk," said Englehart. "I had never seen him like that. It was really obnoxious. I walk with a cane, and he came and grabbed my cane. He was walking around with it and I was wondering if he was going to give me that back. He was just making a fool of himself. I really felt horrible." Willie told Englehart that he was going on to a party. A disheartened Englehart refused an offer to join him.

"And then," Englehart said sadly, "he ruined his life."

Bill Englehart saw that Willie was not in a good place that October night, but he doesn't judge. A short story he wrote about Willie, ends with a passage about how Willie had been a big star, but was reduced to working dumps. "Willie didn't take that decline very well." Engelhart wrote. "But would you? Would you?"

It was at a funky establishment called the South End Improvement Club that

Willie and Moore struck up a conversation with two women, Sylvia Banks, 25, and Kay Morgan, 26. While some believed the two women to be professionals, others prefer the term "party girls." In a convivial, boozy haze, the foursome headed for another drinking spot. At some point, a drifter named Kendall Roundtree attached himself to the group.

Nobody was asking anyone for references, but Roundtree had a lengthy rap sheet. He'd been arrested in eight different states for assault, armed robbery, public drunkenness and a laundry list of other offenses. A hulking six foot two and weighing more than 200 pounds, Roundtree had arrived in Seattle that fall and was working as a trashman for a Northern Pacific work gang.

By now it was well into Sunday. Someone suggested continuing the party at Theodore Roosevelt Richardson's illegal party house on 23rd Avenue. And so they did. The details of that epic night-into-day come from an array of almost comically unreliable witnesses. Almost every person in the Richardson house that night made false statements to the police to cover their own tracks, and most changed their stories several times over. One of them even pleaded insanity and took refuge in an asylum. In the end, it's hard to know who, if anyone, can be believed.

The 23rd Avenue house was a small frame structure located in the Central District, the heart of Seattle's black community. Richardson had converted the house into a speakeasy, booming with business on a Sunday, when it was illegal to buy liquor anywhere but a package store. The house was a popular Sunday meeting place for a free-wheeling segment of the black community, and a few adventurous whites. Some of Willie's friends later characterized the revelers in the house that night as gangsters and thugs, but there were some solid citizens present as well, including a well-known black attorney, Jim McIver. According to King County deputy prosecuting attorney Art Swanson, the clientele was: "White, black, you name it–male, female. They were having a good time."

Willie and his entourage arrived at the house at around 2:30 in the afternoon, by taxi cab. Jim McIver and Roundtree immediately got into a heated discussion about Dr Martin Luther King's philosophy of nonviolence. McIver agreed with Dr King, Roundtree thoroughly disagreed. The railroad worker became so agitated that the attorney cut the conversation short and moved to another table to cool down.

There was a small bar setup in the kitchen with three bar stools. Nearby, a breakfast nook offered more seating. Willie and the two women were sitting on the bar stools. When Sylvia Banks left to go to the bathroom, Roundtree came over and sat on her stool. When she returned, Willie suggested it might be polite if Roundtree let the lady have her seat back. Willie's request enraged Roundtree, who had been loud and obnoxious since he'd arrived at the house. "If you want me up, you put me up!" the ex-con snarled. According to Willie, Roundtree also swore and called the women "bitches." Willie said "You're talking crazy," and started to turn away. Mustering all his 200 pounds, Roundtree threw a hard punch at Willie, knocking him off the bar stool and bloodying his mouth.

Owner Richardson grabbed Roundtree and pulled him into the pantry of the kitchen. He talked to him, trying to calm him down. That seemed to work, so Richardson brought him back into the kitchen—but at the sight of Willie, the railroad worker started to attack again. Richardson then put himself in between Roundtree and Willie. Then, he said later, he saw something hit Roundtree on the chest and noticed that he was wounded. Richardson saw Willie holding a steak knife in his hand, as did one other witness. But nobody saw Willie stab the man.

Richardson, with some help from another man in the house, K.P. Smith, tried to walk the wounded man to the front door and out of the house, but Roundtree's legs went out from under him. They let him fall to the floor. Because they didn't see blood on the hulking Roundtree, everybody assumed that he had only suffered a minor blow, and that he was mostly just drunk (later his alcohol level was measured at .33 percent).

Moore helped Willie wash off his face in the bathroom. "He copped a Sunday on me," Willie told the valet, using boxing slang for a knockout punch. He asked Moore to go check on Roundtree. Moore found Richardson trying to heave 200 pounds of dead weight onto the sofa, but Roundtree was mumbling, asking to be left alone. Then he appeared to pass out.

For the following two hours a house full of people, most of them drunk, stumbled around trying to figure out what to do as Roundtree lay in a corner. The fact that they were in an illegal bar, coupled with a deep-seated (not entirely unfounded) distrust of law enforcement in the black community meant nobody wanted to call for help.

Willie said that it was when he was knocked to the floor that he saw and picked up the steak knife. "When it was all over, about ten minutes, I got myself together and in the living room there was a dead man," Willie said. "Well, I called for an ambulance and they called the police. I don't use God's name in vain," Willie added, somewhat inexplicably. "But I didn't do this."

Art Swanson, the prosecutor who tried the case, said there were "all kinds of people" at Richardson's that night who never did come forward and identify themselves. "There were people in the administration of King County there, and when it finally blew up, people ran out the back, there were people running, jumping over fences," he said. "The police never really found out how many people were there." Only seven remained to be questioned.

McIver reportedly tried calling a number of doctors to come treat Roundtree on the sly, but none of them would. Finally, the Shepard Ambulance Company was called. According to the Seattle police report, when the ambulance attendants entered the house, they found Roundtree on the floor just inside the front entrance. They rolled him over, discovered blood on his shirt, and called the police to report a possible homicide.

McIver and Smith had first told the ambulance attendants a tall tale about arriving at the 23rd Avenue house only minutes before Roundtree. When the police arrived, Smith changed his story and admitted he was there, but back in the kitchen during the whole incident.

Eddie Moore, described in the police report as Willie's "business manager," told the cops that he and a group were standing in the front room when Roundtree, who had just arrived, suddenly keeled over in a corner of the room. Figuring he was drunk, they let him lie there for a while. Then, according to Moore, McIver called a doctor, Dr Harry Pass, who advised him to call an ambulance. That blew McIver's yarn about not getting there until later, and the discrepancy was noted in the police report.

Homicide detectives were called to continue an investigation on the scene, while Willie and several of the others were transported to police headquarters. The body was taken to the King County morgue. While they were still downtown, Smith, McIver and Kay Morgan insisted that they hadn't seen a stabbing. But in the cold light of police headquarters Smith confessed to hiding the knife, which was retrieved by police from the backyard.

Willie gave a partial statement. He said he'd taken phenobarbital earlier that day, then drank seven or eight cognacs while bar-hopping. He had an epileptic seizure as soon as he arrived at the 23rd Avenue house, then he remembered nothing.

It was then that Eddie Moore turned on his boss. The valet had not witnessed Willie having a seizure, he said, and he knew what they looked like, he'd seen several during the last few months. Willie would lose control of himself, the valet said. "He falls down, passes out, shakes and froths at the mouth. He knows when one is coming, he doesn't feel well beforehand." Furthermore, Moore said Willie wasn't drunk at Richardson's house, "he was tired." Even worse, Moore now claimed he saw Willie stab Roundtree. Richardson came around to saying the same thing, as did Sylvia Banks, the object of Willie's gentlemanly gesture that had started the fight in the first place.

Willie was booked on suspicion of murder and his clothes and Wittanaeur watch were placed in evidence. The autopsy on Roundtree, performed by pathologist Gayle Wilson, concluded that the knife entered the victim near the collarbone after a downward thrust. It cut through his lung and nicked the aorta.

On Monday the *Seattle Post-Intelligencer* ran a story about the incident, reporting that "William Edward John of Los Angeles" was being held by police, but he hadn't made a statement. That morning Willie was charged with second-degree murder. He pleaded not guilty, posted a 10,000 dollar bond and immediately left town. If all the people who claimed to pay Willie's bail over the years that followed were to gather in a room, it would amount to quite a party. The story has persisted over the years that Sam Cooke and/or James Brown put up bail money; brother Mertis Jr said that he did. The *Philadelphia Tribune* reported in a November 7th story that Willie's manager Clem Williams "and other friends" posted his bail, so it's likely that more than a few people chipped in to spring the down-and-out rhythm & blues legend.

Willie wasted no time; the very night of the day he was sprung, he was onstage singing at a standing room-only gig in a San Francisco nightclub. King Records' Hal Neely (who claimed that he bailed Willie out too) believed that there was some trouble because Willie was not supposed to leave the state. Neely heard about it because Hank Ballard decided to rat out his old Detroit buddy. "Hank called me because they respected me, I think, because I'm honest. He said, 'Mr Neely, I think you'd better know, Willie John is playing the 54 Ballroom this weekend.'" The 54 Ballroom was a large club on Central Avenue in Los Angeles, one of the biggest and most visible places a black entertainer could play in that city. Willie performed at the 54, but according to Neely, he was picked up by a bail bondsman and transported back to Seattle soon afterwards.

Eventually, Willie was allowed to leave the state for work and to visit his family in advance of his January court date. In December, Willie met Darlynn and the boys in Detroit for the holidays. It was here, at Willie's sister Mildred's house on Georgeland, that the news came through of Sam Cooke's murder. Son Kevin remembered seeing Willie lying on his back on the floor, next to the stereo, playing Sam Cooke records over and over. "My father really loved Sam Cooke, as an artist and a friend," Kevin said. "It's one of the few times in my life that I can remember my father being sad, actually crying."

16

THE TRIAL, AND TRIBULATION

Just to put a capper on Willie's year, the Beatles released their new album in December, and John Lennon's feisty version of Willie's "Leave My Kitten Alone" was missing. It wasn't included on either the group's British album, *Beatles for Sale*, or the American version, *Beatles '65*. The song was heavily bootlegged over the years, and the object of much critical praise, compared to the execrable "Mr Moonlight," which did make it onto the disc. "Certainly the most passionate, intense recording ever to stay in the Beatles vaults," Stuart Shea and Robert Rodriguez wrote of "Kitten," in the book *Everything Left to Know About the Beatles*. Having a song on a hit Beatles album wouldn't have solved Willie's legal problems, but it would have been a small bit of solace, a vital reminder of his talent and vast potential to counteract the depressing effects of all those dark reports from a sleazy after-hours drinking party.

There were indications that Willie's last few months of gigging and partying had been wearing thin for even him, and that he might have put the brakes on and avoided tragedy if he were keeping better company. Little Bill Englehart recalled sensing a certain wistfulness when Willie showed the young musician a photo of his family. "It was his boys, and his wife. He talked about his family in a real proud sort of a way. . . . I used to think, I wonder if he just wants to go home."

Art Swanson tried many cases in his time as a King County prosecuting attorney, but he only describes one as "a circus"–the trial of Little Willie John. "I remember more of the details of this case than all the hundreds of cases I did over 40 years," Swanson said. "It was a very, very memorable case for me."

When Willie appeared in court on January 12th, 1965 to face the charge of second-degree murder, Seattle attorney Bill Lanning was at his side. Lanning was the first-call attorney in Seattle for musicians in trouble. He represented Stan Getz in 1954 when the saxophone legend was arrested for robbing a liquor store. Lanning got him out of jail, but Getz skipped town and stiffed him on his fee. Lanning might have been the first call, but by 1965, he was probably not the best one. He was a "good guy," Swanson said, and a friend. But, he was also on his last legs. "He just didn't have the energy for a high energy case." A high impact trial was no problem for prosecutor Swanson, who was only two years out of law school. He did most of his own footwork on the case, interviewing all the witnesses. To his chagrin, Swanson had only circumstantial evidence. There were numerous eyewitnesses, but "nobody saw anything, and nobody heard anything!" Swanson said, laughing. One witness fled to an asylum in Tacoma to avoid being called to testify. But even with those drawbacks, Swanson was prevailing over Lanning.

Willie's trial lasted three days.

Even from the prosecutor's seat, it frustrated Swanson to see Willie's attorney fail to mount a defense that could have saved the singer from jail. Lanning's primary defense was that Willie suffered an epileptic seizure and couldn't remember the events of the evening. Swanson snorts at that. "Kendall Roundtree was a mountain of a man and could have squashed Willie," the former prosecutor said. "Big guy hits the little guy, there's a fight. Self-defense could have given them a wonderful chance at a not-guilty verdict. This guy was breaking loose from the other guys and Willie was trying to defend himself."

Another possible defense, Swanson believes, was that with so many drunk people stumbling around Richardson's house, arguing and interacting with Willie and the victim, all with access to knives in the kitchen, any number of them could have committed the fatal assault.

At one point during her statement, Sylvia Banks told the Seattle cops that she saw Willie stab Roundtree, but in January, at trial, she nervously reversed her account. She hadn't seen that at all, she testified. This confounded the prosecutor, who hollered at her on the stand, to no avail. He did get enough mentions of Banks' earlier accusation into the record, so that the jury knew that she had fingered Willie earlier, but changed her story.

Despite being a criminal defense attorney himself, Jim McIver came off as sullen, thuggish and suspicious on the witness stand. Lanning tried to convince the jury that McIver was a more obvious suspect in Roundtree's murder than Willie, because the two men had an earlier, volatile argument. Lanning actually maintained that McIver committed the crime until the end. No doubt reacting to Lanning's hostility, McIver changed his story several times under cross-examination. Prosecutor Swanson recalled McIver making "three or four, maybe five" different statements to police, then on the stand, his final claim was "I don't know nothin'." that he had been asleep during most of the incident.

Although Swanson thought that Willie had a fairly good shot at being acquitted, there were two things standing in his way: Lanning, and Willie himself.

Willie showed up at court one day with an entourage of boozed-up friends. Lanning advised the judge that Willie was either drunk or having an epileptic seizure. The judge, who had an epileptic child, said he knew that seizures were often mistaken for drunkenness, so he excused Willie from appearing that day. When Willie did take the stand on Monday, January 18th, he was boastful and charismatic, behavior that he had been rewarded for most of his life, but that would win him no favors in the courtroom.

When asked his profession, Willie declared, "Entertainer *unlimited!*" He listed some of his career highlights; performing with Lionel Hampton, writing a couple of million-selling songs, appearing on an episode of *Route 66*. He didn't have to embellish his *curriculum vitae*, but for some reason he did, adding a European tour with Bob Hope that, it's fairly certain, never happened.

That was Lanning's description of Willie's testimony, anyway. Prosecutor Swanson doesn't recall any inappropriate behavior or a detrimental demeanor. But clearly the very middle class, all-white jury–not exactly a jury of Willie's peers, anyway–was not impressed with his career or beguiled with the star power he had come to rely on. Seemingly oblivious to the frosty reception, Willie breezily recounted his version of the events of October 18th. He'd been invited to "Sunday dinner" at Richardson's house. There, Roundtree had smacked him in the mouth, breaking a tooth. He did not stab Roundtree. But he had suffered a seizure that morning and couldn't remember some of the events of the day.

Swanson believes that Lanning should have had a stern talk with Willie, sat him down and impressed upon him the seriousness of the situation. He concedes that sometimes a willful defendant won't listen to his attorney, but Swanson lays the blame for Willie's poor performance on the stand squarely on

Lanning's failure to prepare his witness. "My guess is that Lanning didn't take the time with him, hit him right between the eyes with a ball-peen hammer and tell him how important this is, and get him a script. Tell him what type of things you should do and not do. Because (Willie) was articulate!" He was articulate enough to convince his credulous attorney that he spoke seven languages, and that a gold bracelet he was wearing was a present from actress Ava Gardner. Lanning didn't even seem to catch on when his client sometimes spoke to him in an English accent.

Swanson scoffed, "If I had Little Willie, I would've had him cry, I would've had him look at that jury, I would have looked in his background and elicited stuff that would either make that jury hang up, or (acquit). How can you convict a guy when you have seven eyewitnesses, but none of them saw my guy do it?"

But they did convict him. Not of second-degree murder, but after Lanning's "slipshod" defense of Willie, the jury convicted Willie of manslaughter with a weapon.

When Kim Field interviewed Lanning in the 1990s, the attorney blamed Willie's "arrogant, smart-ass" manner on the witness stand for his conviction. But one of the jurors, Alfred Rousseau dismissed that. He said that Willie's demeanor hadn't really played into their decision and blamed the bad outcome on Lanning, "an ambulance-chaser type." Swanson agreed.

There were other, race-related aspects of the trial that bothered the prosecutor as well. "We had an all-white jury," Swanson said. "There wasn't the kind of racial bias that I saw down South when I was in the Army, but there was an undercurrent of it in the area. At the time, I felt that a black person was probably not going to get the kind of result that maybe a white person would in the same situation."

Although Swanson prosecuted Willie, he liked him. "Usually you come to hate the person you're prosecuting, you believe you're doing society a favor by putting them away. But I liked Willie. He was a gregarious, friendly, talkative little guy." When the two men were sitting out in the hallway waiting for the jury's verdict, they had an affable chat. Swanson has thought about Willie many times over the years.

"Had there been competent counsel aggressively pursuing the case and coming up with a good defense, big guy against little guy, little guy was defending himself, I would have walked that guy out. I would have walked Little Willie out of there. That has always made me feel bad," Swanson said.

In 1965, celebrity news didn't travel around the globe in seconds as it does today. It took several hours for the story of Willie's conviction to be written by wire service reporters and then cabled around the country, inserted into newspapers and distributed the following day. The most detailed stories ran in the black press, but an Associated Press (AP) report turned up in most newspapers. Apparently, it was news when even a "blues singer" whose biggest fame was behind him was convicted of murder.

The AP reported, with a Seattle dateline, that "William Edward (Little Willie) John, 27, Miami Beach, Florida rock 'n' roll blues singer, was convicted here Monday night (18th) of manslaughter. He was charged in the stabbing October 18 of Kendall Roundtree, 34, Seattle, during a party. The 5 foot 3 (sic) 124-pound entertainer had been charged with second-degree murder. A Superior Court jury convicted him on the lesser charge after deliberating more than six hours. John was accused of slaying Roundtree with a steak knife during a Sunday afternoon quarrel in the home of a Seattle man."

Willie's musician friends were shocked. They weren't surprised about the fight, but they couldn't believe the verdict.

"I don't think he should have gotten any time at all," said Milton Hopkins of the Upsetters. He'd seen the scenario many times before. "Same thing, great big old guy talking trash, pushing your woman around. Willie wasn't going to go for that, because an attack on her was the same as attacking him." But this time, Willie was in the wrong place, with a group of shady people who didn't have his best interests at heart. "Them guys that he was hooked in with at that crap game, they were all gangsters and crooks, lifelong criminals," Hopkins said. "Willie had a little (criminal) record too, but nothing like the guys that he was with in that crap game. That guy was 200 pounds, six one, Willie 145 pounds, just barely five feet tall. It was just a bad rap." Hopkins had no doubt that Willie's "slick friends" hooked him up with a lawyer who obviously was not up to the task. Willie's record of minor offenses probably didn't help him, although prosecutor Swanson says it wasn't a huge factor in the outcome of the trial.

Brother Mertis believes the judge wanted to send Willie a wake-up call, after several years of living on the edge. "The judge said, 'I'm taking you off your feet for three years." Strangely enough, Willie's conviction didn't seem to dampen his spirits. Pending sentencing, he posted the 20,000 dollar bond. Mertis Jr says he borrowed against his house to put money up, and Darlynn's policeman brother also pitched in. Willie left the state to fulfill some tour dates and generate some much-needed cash before he was due back in court. A wire service photo shows a jaunty Willie walking through the Sea-Tac airport flanked by a bail bondsman and his manager, Clem Williams. There is a smile on Willie's face, despite the fact that his famous process—in fact, all of his hair—had been shaved off by the jailhouse barber.

His spirits were undoubtedly buoyed by his (temporary) freedom, but he didn't have a lot to be cheerful about. Texas authorities—the bane of Hank Ballard and the Midnighters, and most rhythm & blues performers—had found him in Seattle, thanks to the much-publicized murder rap, and were prosecuting him on a bad check charge. They claimed he'd paid for a charter flight with a 122 dollar and 49 cent check drawn on a bank that didn't exist. He was indicted on the charge in late January 1965.

Attorney Lanning filed for a new trial, but that was denied in early March. He filed an appeal, but claimed he couldn't find Willie to get the 1,500 dollar deposit. It strains credulity today to think that he couldn't track Willie down; at the very least sister Mable had to be easy to find, as she was working as a booking agent in Chicago at the time. Lanning sent letters and cables, several to a bail bondsman in Los Angeles, which were returned stating that Willie was no longer in that city. Lanning then sent a letter to Willie care of the Apollo Theater in New York, advising that if he didn't have the money for an appeal, he needed to return to Seattle so they could file for public funds. He received no response.

In was early May before Willie was tracked down and returned to Seattle by federal marshals. Shortly afterward, Lanning was informed that Willie had decided to relieve him of his duties as his legal counsel and the appeal was dismissed on May 6th for lack of action. Either Willie had given up on the legal system entirely or he was in total denial. He continued to perform and travel, instead of resolving his mounting legal problems. Everybody seemed to feel that he had a good case for appeal. Swanson had already been assigned to other cases, leaving his boss, head prosecutor Thomas A. Stang to oversee sentencing.

The family seemed convinced that Willie's legal problems were being resolved. Sister Mable told *Jet* in late May 1965 that Willie had been sentenced to "three years' probation" and was "free to travel anywhere so long as he reports beforehand to the probation department." The John family was happy about the resolution, she said. In reality, Willie's days of wandering around the country were numbered. He was brought back to Seattle in late August, taken into custody by the King County Sheriff's Department, and remained there until January 1966.

If he still evinced cheerfulness, even in jail, with the hammer of the law about to crash down, it's probably because all Willie could think about that fall was the impending fulfillment of one of his most cherished professional goals. Not even prison could stop him—he would record again, and this time, with the best record company in the world—Sinatra's label.

17

A DREAM DEFERRED

He may have been back in stir, but Willie had reason to be optimistic: his career was about to go into overdrive. He was going to be a Capitol recording artist. For the kid from Cardboard Valley who patterned his haberdashery and crisp enunciation on Frank Sinatra to be signed to the label by Voyle Gilmore, Sinatra's producer, was the ultimate high. In 1965, Gilmore was Capitol's director of A&R, but back in the early 1950s he was the producer in charge during Sinatra's breathtaking run of Capitol albums, "Come Fly With Me," "Only the Lonely," and others that came to define his career.

When the Capitol contract came up, Willie didn't give King Records a second's thought, assuming time had expired on that obligation. "When I made the deal (with Capitol) Willie had told me that his contracts were up with King and to do it," Mable said. "I made that deal for a 10,000 dollar advance. Long time ago, that was a lot of money. But that was what the attorney was asking for." It's not known whether the attorney who needed the money was Lanning, dunning Willie for previous services, or a new attorney.

These mundane legal details didn't interest Willie much; what was more important is that he was finally going to record in Studio A at Capitol, backed by the famed Wrecking Crew, the cream of the crop of Los Angeles studio musicians. There would be no Hal Neely tricking him out of a string session, no Syd Nathan screaming at him to stop singing like Sinatra, there Willie would receive the respect and support he deserved.

At Capitol, David Axelrod was the obvious in-house choice to produce Willie. Axelrod, who grew up in Los Angeles hanging around Central Avenue, soaking up gin and jazz, had turned his wayward life around to become a hot producer at Capitol during the 1960s. He'd somehow made a bestselling album with television sensation David McCallum, teaming up with producer and arranger H.B. Barnum. Next Axelrod took charge of Lou Rawls, a rare signing for Capitol, which as a company was late to nurture black talent.

Being a fan of almost exclusively black music himself, Axelrod had been urging Capitol to bring on more black talent in the wake of Rawls' success, even launching a black music division—though he insists that he wasn't actually the one behind Willie's signing. One day Axelrod was buzzed by Voyle Gilmore's secretary and asked to come up to the A&R chief's office. When he got there, he found Willie John sitting back on a chair, chatting companionably with Gilmore, who introduced Axelrod to his new project. He was put in charge of Willie's sessions, set to start in February 1966. Willie was granted parole to go to Los Angeles to record in February, thanks to the vigorous maneuvering of Gilmore, Mable and others.

Axelrod has often said that Rawls wasn't pleased about Willie's signing to Capitol, and was even less pleased that his producer would be involved with Wilie's projects. But at 77, his memory of some of the minor details of events 40 years in the past might not be entirely accurate. For example, Axelrod insists that Willie's sessions took place in 1965, despite what the Capitol logs say (February, 1966) and that he produced Willie before Lou's great success, which is why Lou was jealous. The producer also says that Rawls and Willie didn't know each other when, in fact, the two singers were good friends. Darlynn John recalls seeing Lou on many occasions, and Rawls' mother, who worked in the beauty salon in a Los Angeles hotel where the Johns would stay, styled Darlynn's hair from time to time. Nevertheless, it is possible that Rawls was feeling a little territorial, even being friendly with Willie. It's also possible that Axelrod was over-stating the singer's possessiveness, or misremembering the intensity of the emotions expressed.

However Rawls felt about it, Axelrod and Willie went over a list of possible songs. Once they'd hammered the songlist out to their mutual satisfaction, Axelrod tapped his favorite collaborator, producer and arranger, H.B. Barnum, to put together the musical charts for Willie and the session band. Barnum had worked with Axelrod on all the Rawls sessions; he was also from Detroit and knew Willie, though he'd never worked with him before.

"There were guys with those high voices like Willie John, Jimmy Scott, Frankie Lymon, but Willie had his life in his voice," Barnum said. "When he sang the blues, he *sang the blues,* you had no doubt that he was living what he was singing." Barnum has worked arranging charts and producing for countless vocalists over the years; for Capitol, Motown and Aretha Franklin, for whom he still serves as arranger. Looking back over all that talent, he rates Willie and Aretha as the two best singers he ever heard, gifted with both technical ability and a fiery, spiritual feeling that can't be manufactured or learned. "In my world, of that era, between Aretha and Little Willie John, there were no other singers," Barnum said. "Even today! Little Willie John, he and Aretha had the ability, they were each like a horn player. Plus they had the mechanics to do anything they wanted to do. Willie could sing jazz, scat, anything he wanted to do. He just had a tremendous voice."

Although fans of Willie's music are used to hearing him sing a certain way on his hit King recordings, Barnum says it's important to realize that didn't define him—it wasn't all he was capable of doing. "We'd sit sometimes and he would do things with his voice and I'd just be amazed, that he'd have such control. He'd do it for fun, then laugh about it. He'd say, 'You didn't know I could do that, huh? Hahaha!' He was just so, so great."

The sessions went well. "We had a damn good time recording," Axelrod said. "But it was very strange. The sessions had to start at midnight. So we went from 12 to three in the morning. That's the way he liked to record. Of course it was double pay for the musicians." "Then again," Axelrod laughed, "he wasn't paying." (Actually, the Capitol logs show that Willie only did one night session, on February 19th. The other two sessions were on February 24th, one in the morning and one in the afternoon.)

After years of being nickled and dimed at King, Willie was in the lap of luxury at Capitol, and they spared no expense. Among the many Los Angeles musicians on the sessions were guitarists Jeff Kaplan, Arthur Wright and Les Buie, bassists Jimmy Bond and Carol Kaye, drummer Earl Palmer, vibraphonist Gary Coleman, and a horn section that included Tony Terran and Freddie Hill on trumpet, Clifford Scott and Jim Horn on saxophone. On top of that was a string section, including six violins, two violas, a cello and a harp. And this time, Willie didn't have to pay for it.

"They never bothered me, I could use as many or as few men as I wanted to,"

Axelrod said. "They didn't know who I was using anyway. Capitol was great. Capitol was the greatest label there was." The producer enjoyed working with his new charge. "Do you know, it was impossible not to like Willie, just because he was Willie. He was one of the nicest guys you could ever meet. I never saw him get angry. When he came into the Tower, he was beautiful. We'd sit and talk in my office, we could talk for two hours, drinking scotch." The Capitol sessions were technically unfinished. Willie was recorded singing with the musicians, as Axelrod and Barnum liked to do. But then they would bring the singer back in, record the voice and slice the later vocal in. "That's what we had planned to do," Barnum said. But one day Willie was hanging out with him at the house, the next day he was gone. They never did get to overdub those vocals.

Willie's sons have listened to the Capitol sessions many times over the years. While some fans prefer his funkier, rhythm & blues King Records recordings to the heavily orchestrated Axelrod treatment, his sons disagree. Kevin John loves that his father finally got the A-list treatment he had always longed for, the Sinatra experience that he had been dressing for over decades. Sensitive to the nuances of his father's voice, Kevin believed he sounded deliriously happy. "He *was* happy," said Axelrod. "He got a good advance! And he was feeling great. He really thought he was going to win that appeal." The appeal that never was.

Willie's Capitol sessions went so well, producer Axelrod was convinced the record would sell. "That album came out terrific," Axelrod said. "I really think it would have sold. And then Lou would have been a problem." They never got a chance to find out. Syd Nathan and Hal Neely got wind of the sessions, and set King Records' lawyers onto Capitol.

Willie's new label was already reluctant to release an album by an artist who would be behind bars soon and unavailable to promote a new record. The legal sabre-rattling from King Records was the last straw. Capitol put the 11 masters on the shelf, deep in its legendary vaults, where they would languish for decades.

In 1967, Voyle Gilmore reported to the Washington Department of Corrections that Capitol considered the 8,000 dollars the company had advanced Willie for the 11 unreleased masters unrecoupable because of "legal entanglements." Gilmore also wrote a letter to the parole board on Willie's behalf, remarking that as an entertainer, Willie was able to make good money and the executive was sure he could resume a profitable career.

If it seems odd that the label had signed and recorded Willie without making sure he was contractually free, producer Axelrod points out that in that era, A&R directors like Gilmore had absolute authority to sign artists and set up recording sessions. There were usually no questions asked, until it was too late, of course.

Still aglow from the February Capitol sessions, and with no inkling that the release was doomed, Willie returned back east to play some dates Mable had booked for him in Detroit, Toledo and New York.

With his legal problems hitting a fever pitch and the prospect of prison looming, Willie was eager to do one last show in Detroit. After a March 31st to April 4th engagement at the Pal-A-Drome nightclub in Toledo, Mable booked him into the Phelps Lounge in Detroit for a week's stand, from April 15th to the 24th. The contract shows that he was expected to perform from ten pm until two am each night, with a seven pm Sunday matinee, for a pretty good payday (in 1966) of a thousand dollars for the week. Mable was wired a hundred dollar deposit that she arranged for Mother Dear to pick up in Detroit.

Eddie Phelps, owner of Phelps Lounge, took an interest in Willie's legal troubles, at least temporarily. A cryptic item referring to Phelps as a sort of Mr Big in Detroit appeared in Ziggy Johnson's May 7th column in the *Chicago Defender.* "Eddie Phelps of Phelps Lounge can be listed as a performer's benefactor," Johnson wrote. "Little Willie John will attest to this. Sorta reminds one of Atlantic City's 'Daddy Lou' Barnes, who our town's Mike Guinyord calls 'Poppa Joe.'" Phelps might have been one of the most powerful men on the music scene in Detroit, but he wasn't able to stop the inevitable when it came to Willie John, or even slow it down.

Willie also played the Apollo one last time. He couldn't have known it at the time, but it was to be his final appearance at the site of some of his greatest triumphs. Sugar Ray Robinson and all of Willie's New York friends came to see him that night. One of those friends came to collect on a favor. While Willie was in jail in Seattle in the fall of 1965, he'd written to his friend, baseball player Jim 'Mudcat' Grant of the Minnesota Twins, who was playing in the World Series. Willie told Grant that the Twins had to win the first game in the Series. A carton of cigarettes was riding on it. The Twins won the game (although they lost the Series to the Dodgers) and Willie won his bet, so at the end of the show, he invited a giddy Grant to come onstage at the Apollo to take a bow.

The Phelps Lounge show was almost like a triumphant homecoming. Willie pulled his sons onstage to do their duo act. The boys sang Jackie Wilson's "Baby Workout," Sam Cooke's version of "Frankie and Johnny," and Sam & Dave's "Hold On (I'm Coming)," with Kevin singing the lower, Dave Prater parts and Keith taking Sam Moore's high tenor leads. Willie was having the time of his life.

The John boys were no strangers to performance. From the age of two on, Kevin was apt to belt out his father's song "Talk to Me, Talk to Me," to the delight of the family and friends like Dinah Washington. 'The queen' would always ask the fledgling performer to sing when she visited the Johns in Miami. The boys didn't have to be encouraged to sing (and in Keith's case, dance) by their proud father, although Willie would often rehearse Keith repeatedly in the proper way to execute a slide onstage.

After the Phelps run was over and the applause faded, Willie was forced to return to Seattle into the custody of the King County Sheriff's Department on May 10th. On May 25th, he was transferred to the Washington Corrections Center. In July of that year he began serving a sentence of eight to 20 years in prison, with a minimum sentence of seven and a half years. After sentencing, he was transferred to Washington State Penitentiary in Walla Walla. From all accounts, it took time for news of the sentencing to trickle back to Detroit and the family. Mable was busy with her career, Darlynn had been kept in the dark about the pending sentencing and just about everybody thought an appeal was automatic and in the works.

Darlynn was so traumatized by her husband's incarceration that she buried her feelings over the years, and finds it painful to call back memories. She did work diligently at the time to provide prison authorities with information about Willie, his family life, medical and emotional issues, and anything else they needed, as he was processed into custody—writing in polite, schoolgirl-precise script.

In interviews with prison officials, Willie admitted that he had a drinking problem. Darlynn confirmed that, but insisted that her husband was "about to lick this problem" before he'd gotten into trouble in Seattle. When Willie showed up for a department of corrections pre-prison physical, he was "glassy-eyed" and appeared intoxicated. If Darlynn was aware of the extent of the problem, the boys were not. Kevin insists he never saw his father drunk.

Prison records indicate that Willie was recommended for alcoholic treatment. He also reported that he'd suffered from epilepsy since he was 13, and regularly took carbitrol, a combination of a sedative (carbromal) and a barbiturate (pentobarbital). Carbitrol did help to control Willie's seizures, but because it was a barbiturate it was also easy to abuse. Willie admitted that drinking worsened his seizures, and when he mixed alcohol with the carbitrol or took more than one pill a day, things could go downhill fast. The drug has a number of other side effects too, including aggressive or violent behavior.

Prison psychologists observed that Willie was intelligent and highly sociable, but also "hyperactive," and prone to grandiose statements. He bragged about how much money he made as an entertainer, pegging his yearly salary at 100,000 dollars. Darlynn later revealed that it was half that amount. With Willie in prison, money was tight, and Darlynn was going to have to go back to work to support their two young sons.

Willie listed his hobbies as golf, tennis, dominoes and reading the Bible. He included cooking, and entertaining his children among his favorite activities. While he admitted he socialized with women on the road, he insisted that he was true to his marital vows. Willie described Darlynn as understanding, and "a constant source of pleasure to him." Darlynn didn't pretend that her husband had not done wrong in recent years. But she told prison authorities that Willie was also an excellent provider, a "wonderful" father ("They worship him," she said of their sons) and she felt that Willie had been properly chastened by his troubles in Seattle. She intended to stick with her husband, she said. "Being with his parents and the children and I seemed to have a good effect on him when we were all together at Christmas," she wrote. "I know this tragedy has had a very sobering effect on him." He often said that he'd like to become a minister. "He was brought up in a very religious home, so this would only be second nature for him," Darlynn reported that when she talked to Willie, he always expressed regret and worried about Kevin and Keith hearing about his problems.

Willie's friends and family discovered that he was a prolific correspondent. He wrote many letters to Darlynn and his sons, often advising Kevin and Keith on aspects of the music business. He encouraged them to write music, not just sing and perform it, suggesting they form a publishing company and call it Kev–Kei. Willie tried to maintain a strong presence in his children's life, offering advice and encouragement. Kevin was learning how to play guitar, so Willie sent him an article about jazz guitarist Wes Montgomery as inspiration. "There was no way that I would ever be a Wes," Kevin said, laughing, but he treasured the clippings.

Willie also exchanged letters with James Brown, Syd Nathan and Hal Neely, and he wrote to his Capitol producer David Axelrod. But that was a one-way communication. He wrote to me every two months or so," Axelrod remembered. "He was just talking to me about how he wished the record would come out, and how much he liked working with me, kind of thing." The producer didn't answer Willie's letters. "He knew I was never going to answer him. To write a letter to someone in prison, you have to fill out a form that's as thick as a phone book. They want to know too much. None of their business. So I didn't fill it out."

|18|

TRAGEDY

Willie's prison term started out smoothly in the summer of 1966. He took classes, working toward a high school degree, and served on the prison's entertainment committee. Then the melancholy news came in the fall that Willie's father, Mertis Sr, had died in Detroit on November 3rd, Mable's birthday. Mertis had been ailing for some time, and his son's trial and imprisonment had grieved him terribly.

As 1967 pressed on, problems started to crop up in Willie's second year of imprisonment. There were enough of them, authorities believed, to delay his chance for parole. Many of the incidents were related to his epilepsy. Although the prison knew he suffered from seizures, and Darlynn had told them he was particularly prone to them while sleeping, there were several times when Willie was disciplined for being asleep and not hearing the call to stand in his cell for the count of prisoners. He explained that he was sometimes unable to wake up because of his condition, but that excuse was dismissed. A hearty eater all his life, Willie was even punished for taking an extra "hamburger steak" at dinner one night, a scene that recalls Dickens' Oliver Twist asking for more porridge in the poorhouse. Because there had been more of these petty incidents in 1967 than the previous year, the parole board decided to delay action and "look at him again in a year." He was scheduled to come up before the board again in July 1968.

Willie continued to write long, effusive letters, especially to Darlynn and the boys. A letter he wrote home in January is particularly poignant, expressing a surprisingly ebullient spirit and high hopes for the future. Willie wrote that he could find no hate in his heart for anyone, not even the majority of people he'd encountered in life who were only there for what they could get from him. He admitted that prison had put the brakes on an alarming lifestyle.

"At the pace I was going, I would no doubt be in the same place as Nat, Dinah, Sam Cooke or Otis," Willie wrote. "I have accepted my vacation as an answer to someone's prayers. Just tonight I asked God, was my purpose for experiencing this incident to let me and my family live, be successful and love—love? A voice within me said, 'Yes.'" Willie thanked God for his second chance, and said he saw clearly, heard well, sang better and had only four things on his mind: religion, his family (Darlynn and the boys), freedom and business. He professes his love for Darlynn, Kevin and Keith, tells his wife he'll never forsake her again and that he will always tell her the truth, no matter what. Of course, rascal that he was, he asks that she not inquire about the past. Willie had not been a faithful husband, Darlynn knew that, but she was convinced of his sincerity in promising to do better. The kind of company Willie was keeping on that night in Seattle was not lost on her, and she says that another woman in Los Angeles, known to Mable, had struck up a friendship with Willie and continued to write to him in prison. But as Darlynn insisted to prison authorities, to Willie's relatives and everybody else, she had forgiven her husband and she intended to stick with him.

Willie continued, "I am glad to know you get a kick out of our sons... I will never let you be sad... As long as there is peace with you, love, I'll be home so don't worry. By now I guess you've got the things I sent. Tell my sons to write me." Willie also asks his wife to tell Mable to have everybody who was anybody write letters on his behalf to the parole board and provides the address to the Washington State Board of Parole. "I go before the board again in July. Flood them with letters from everyone who knows where I am."

Willie was getting some ink in the press on the outside thanks to an old friend, soul singer Joe Tex. In a half serious, half comical crusade, Tex was denouncing James Brown for calling himself "Soul Brother No. 1." Tex explained his beef to the *Chicago Defender*.

"The title of 'Soul Brother No. 1' rightfully belongs to a guy named Little Willie John," Tex said. "I really don't know where James Brown gets the idea he is the king! Some of us have very short memories." Apart from calling James out publicly, Tex sent telegrams to 11 radio stations challenging him to a "Battle of the Year for the Title of Soul Brother No. 1"—insisting, if there were any doubt, that he was serious. "The big problem, of course, is getting James Brown to respond," Tex said. "He may feel that Little Willie John is a thing of the past, and no longer really eligible for the title. But I presumptuously think that no one can top Little Willie and when he returns to the music scene, he'll prove it!" Tex went on to say that if he won the title of Soul Brother No. 1, he was going to present it to Willie when he got out of prison.

James claimed the rivalry between him and Tex was humorous, the sort of public display of macho bravado that had been going on for a decade between all the young turks of the rhythm & blues world. And maybe he was right. Maybe it was mostly posturing, but there was a frisson of real animus. Tex was riding around in a tour bus emblazoned with a banner that said "Soul Brother No. 1," which particularly annoyed James, who told him to cut it out. But Tex clearly wanted to draw attention to Willie, even though he'd been out of the public eye and off the stage for two years.

Despite the upbeat tone of Willie's letters, Darlynn was hearing disturbing reports about his treatment in prison. James Brown visited Willie several times, and was one of many who helped pony up money for Willie's bail. One visit in the spring of 1968 revealed his old Apollo Theater sparring partner in terrible shape. "I was shocked to see how this once robust entertainer had become wheelchair bound, hacking and sniffing with pneumonia that he had picked up in his cold prison cell. I vowed that I would get him out again, but he just shook his head," James wrote. Willie told him that the only way he'd get out of prison was "horizontally."

It's a far cry from Willie's insistent instructions in January for everybody to write letters to the parole board on his behalf. It's possible James was being overly-dramatic, but it's also possible that at some point, prompted by his treatment in prison, Willie simply gave up. One of his fellow inmates wrote letters to Darlynn after he got out. "It was someone who had written a couple of letters and told me about a couple of things that happened," Darlynn said. "He said that Willie was neglected, that he wasn't getting proper medical attention."

Darlynn passed on the letters to Mable in Chicago, who gave them to civil rights activist Reverend Jesse Jackson, also based in Chicago. "(Jackson) knew Willie, and he had said he knew he was going to look into it," Darlynn said. At the time, Jackson was national director for Operation Breadbasket of Martin

Luther King's Southern Christian Leadership Conference. As a close friend and associate of the civil rights leader, he was on the balcony of the Lorraine Motel in Memphis on April 4th, 1968, when King was shot and killed, so for much of that month Jackson was busy with King's funeral, and the ensuing fallout and civil unrest.

On April 30th, Jackson did write a letter to the Washington State Parole Board on Willie's behalf. He spoke of how Willie's music spread cheer, but that his music also reflected the "corrosive sorrow" of the black community. Jackson mentioned a gospel concert planned, at which Willie would make a second debut. He pointed out that Willie acknowledged the mistake he made and the debt he needed to pay to society, but that now he needed to return to the concert stage. The letters from Willie's fellow prisoners that were passed on to Jackson, were, unfortunately, never returned to Darlynn.

Many others from Willie's life and career wrote letters on his behalf to the parole board. Robert (a.k.a. Bobby) Schiffman of the Apollo Theater wrote that he'd known Willie since he was 15, and saw him develop into an "internationally known headline attraction." He described Willie as a "wonderful, soft-spoken, quiet and reserved" gentleman and opined that he could only have been guilty of an act of violence under extreme provocation. Houston music titan Don Robey, who owned Duke and Peacock Records and ran the Bronze Peacock nightclub, wrote saying that he had presented some of Willie's first national appearances. Robey praised his great talent and that "boyish, witty" personality, asking that Willie be granted his freedom.

It had to be a blow when Willie got the news, in March 1968, that Syd Nathan had died in Cincinnati. This was his King Records boss, the man who oversaw his biggest years of stardom and remained one of his biggest fans, boasting to the end that he was a better singer than James Brown and other rhythm & blues braggarts. Although Syd and Hal Neely blocked Willie's Capitol record from being released, Syd and Willie still corresponded as the old record man's health failed. Neely visited Willie in prison and tried to help get him out, by his account. Willie was probably worth more money to Neely out of prison than in, but that couldn't have been the only reason he went out of his way. King Records might have been a dysfunctional family, but as James Brown often pointed out, it was a family just the same, and Syd Nathan was the short, wheezing, eternally irate father figure.

Sometime in late 1966 Darlynn and the boys moved from Philadelphia to Detroit in order to be closer to Willie's family. It made it easier for Willie to visit the entire clan when he was out on parole. By then, the dream home on Leslie was long gone. Willie had bought the house in 1957 and made the monthly payments on it, but turned the responsibility over at some point, reasoning that the house was full of adults. Most of his grown siblings were working, and he had his own mortgage and family to worry about in Miami.

"Willie just gave, gave, gave," Darlynn said. "It was never enough."

By early 1968, Willie's mother Lillie and brothers Raymond, Toronto, Haywood, EJ and sister Delores with her family, were all living in an apartment building on Clarendon in Detroit. Darlynn, Kevin and Keith moved into a basement apartment in the same building. Mable was living in Chicago and recording for Memphis' famed Stax Records. She had a top ten rhythm & blues hit with the mournful, sexy Isaac Hayes–David Porter-penned "Your Good Thing (Is About to End)" in the summer of 1966, just as Willie received his sentence.

Delores and Darlynn were good friends, often spending the days together. One day in late May they were in the lower level of the apartments when Kevin remembers hearing an unearthly wail coming from the room where the women were. A Western Union telegram had arrived from Walla Walla, Washington. Darlynn and Delores were huddled in a mass, crying and wailing so loudly that Kevin knew that, whatever the news was, it had something to do with his father.

Willie was dead.

Kevin remembers his grandmother and aunt wailing, and his mother repeating the phrase, in between sobs, "Such a terrible place, such a terrible place…"

Willie John died at 7:40 am on May 26th, 1968 in the Washington State Penitentiary hospital. The cause of death listed in the prison medical examiner's report and on his death certificate was "massive acute myocardial infarction," or heart attack. Also cited was a recent thrombosis (blockage) of the left coronary artery, with a recorded onset of only a few days.

Just four months previously, Willie had been writing to Darlynn saying that he was in good health. For a man just six months past his 30th birthday with no apparent history of heart disease, to suddenly die of a heart attack was startling– and suspicious. The death certificate indicates that an autopsy was performed, and that those findings "were considered in determining cause of death," but in

96 pages of documents relating to Willie from the Washington State Department of Corrections, there is no copy of any such autopsy report.

When Willie died, the family was told that he had been admitted to the prison hospital earlier in May with pneumonia. James Brown also reported that Willie was suffering from pneumonia in prison. Curiously, there is no record remaining of his treatment in this respect, only notes about his epilepsy, and the sudden onset of a heart attack in May 1968.

Conspiracy theories started circulating almost immediately, among his peers in the music business, and especially in the black community. Musician Little Bill Englehart was friends with a man, Denny O'Brian, who was in prison with Willie. "Denny said that they killed him," Englehart says. "I don't know that for a fact. But from what he told me, Willie was friendly with the guards, and I guess some people took that wrong. I don't know if he was saying anything he shouldn't say… but Denny said that they killed him." O'Brian can't be pressed on the claim today; he died about ten years ago, according to Englehart.

Former King Count prosecuting attorney Art Swanson, who successfully prosecuted Willie, also believes that he died as a result of a violent attack in prison. "I don't think there's any question that he was assaulted in prison and that he died because of congestive lung failure, because of fluid in the lungs, which occurs because of a fall," Swanson said. "Willie pops off, he had a big mouth, and they don't take that sort of thing. I'm sure that he got into a fight and somebody killed him."

Though Willie had been out of the public eye for two years, his sudden death sent waves of loss through Detroit, saddened by the passing of the city's first great rhythm & blues star. The heartbreaking circumstances around his death, his relative youth and tremendous talent made him the talk of the music business, in Detroit and elsewhere.

His body was conveyed from the Colonial Funeral Home in Walla Walla, Washington and flown to the Motor City, the site of his early boyish adventures and triumphs. Mack Rice accompanied Willie's sister Mildred and several others to Detroit Metropolitan Airport to meet the Delta Airlines jet that brought Willie home. He was taken to the Cantrell Funeral home on Mack, on Detroit's east side. Between June 8th and 9th, hundreds of Detroiters flocked to Cantrell to get one last glimpse of Little Willie John, lying in repose in his bronze casket.

Willie was famous again, in death, once more the crooner who tore the charts up with "Fever," the boy with the golden voice that nobody could beat. On Monday, June 10th, a crowd of 3,000 gathered at the New Bethel Baptist Church for his funeral. Mourners packed the pews of the 2,500-seat church, spilling out onto the sidewalk and street. Many in the crowd were music fans straining to get a glimpse of some of the stars expected to arrive to pay homage to their friend.

The air in the old church was thick with spring humidity, the packed-in humanity and the heavy scent of floral tributes sent by Motown, Atlantic Records, Stax, King Records, Universal Attractions, the Four Tops, Berry Gordy Jr and Smokey Robinson. There was the inevitable large floral musical note set near Willie, emblazoned with the word "Fever."

Willie's cousin Dorothy Mae Thompson bought Kevin and Keith (aged ten and eight, respectively) Nehru jackets to wear to their father's funeral. The surviving photos show the boys looking understandably stunned.

Johnnie Taylor sang "When the Saints Go Marching In," and organist Edward Robinson played "Precious Lord," sung by Reverend C.L. Moore. The pallbearers were a virtual who's who of the rhythm & blues world, most from Stax-Volt or Atlantic Records. Sam Moore and Dave Prater of Sam & Dave; Johnnie 'Who's Making Love' Taylor, Joe 'Skinny Legs and All' Tex and Eddie 'Knock on Wood' Floyd bore their friend's casket into the church.

The service was conducted by the Reverend C.L. Franklin, Aretha's father, and Willie's long-ago friend. Reverend Franklin told the assembled that it was not his intention to conduct a service that was sorrowful, but one that would be appropriate to Willie's "spirited disposition." According to the *Michigan Chronicle*, Franklin's son Cecil spoke, as well as King Records executive Gene Redd, who had produced many of Willie's Cincinnati sessions. "Willie must be remembered for his talent, which was a source of enjoyment for a great deal of people throughout the nation," Redd said.

Kevin John remembers seeing Diana Ross of the Supremes and Berry Gordy Jr among the throngs paying their respects at his grandmother Lillie's house after the funeral. Gordy had come a long way from his scuffling days in the 1950s, hustling songs to Willie and Jackie Wilson. Kevin noticed what only a ten year-old would, that the glamorous Ross was quiet while everybody else talked, singing softly to herself the Crispian St Peters' pop song from two years earlier, "I'm a Pied Piper."

The symbolism of the sleek, successful soul stars from Motown, Stax and Atlantic coming to pay tribute to a great, fallen star of the previous decade, a singer they had imitated and idolized, was not lost on many. From bespoke suits, Cadillacs, gold records and a palm tree-shaded home in Miami, it had all ended for Willie with abuse in a prison cell. The *Chronicle* described it as a "tragic homecoming" for 30 year-old Willie, "the first of the current genre of pop singers to bring recognition to Detroit as a breeding ground for exceptional talent." Willie had burst out of Detroit and onto the national stage through sheer will and guts, a decade before there was a platform like Motown. He and his brothers ran his Cadillacs ragged over the two-lane highways of the segregated South, scraping a living out at a dollar and a half auditorium shows. The glamorous Motown stars in attendance had gotten a taste of just how hard things could be when they played Motortown Revue tours in the South during the 1960s, but it was an unforgiving world Willie had been navigating since he was a teenager in the mid 1950s.

Willie and others paved the way for the great pop successes of Motown and those that came after, and particularly for the soul explosion that launched Sam & Dave, Taylor and so many of the Stax and Atlantic artists. The explosive combination of a voice with the fire and intensity of gospel, driven by the instrumental intensity of rhythm & blues, was always there in Willie's music. Now, packaged as "soul," it was crossing over and selling millions to avid baby boomers whose culture wasn't as segregated as their parents' generation.

When asked if he thought Willie would have done well if he could have cut loose from King and gotten onto white-hot Stax in the 1960s, Sam Moore doesn't hesitate with an enthusiastic "yes." "He would have been amazing! After all, they had Johnnie Taylor, a singer in the same vein, they had Sam & Dave. With the right material, which at the time they were writing, (Willie) could have done wonders. He could have done wonders."

DETROIT

L ate in the summer of 1968, there was a knock on the door of Darlynn John's upstairs flat in Detroit. It was a special delivery package. The return address: Capitol Records, Los Angeles. With the boys' help, she opened it to reveal a record. Somebody at Capitol had taken it upon themselves to send Willie's family an unmastered dub recording of his unreleased sessions, the last music Willie had ever recorded. Kevin played the dub until the grooves were worn out. It served as therapy for the lonely ten year-old to hear his father's voice again. "Since my father was gone, this was the only way that I could feel near him," Kevin said.

Several other dubs of those sessions made their way to Capitol staffers, musicians, family and friends. Over the years many dreadful, muddy bootlegs of Willie's dream album were bought, sold and traded, thrown together from one or another of the cold wax dubs that had managed to trickle out. For years, when the family wrote letters to Capitol or called asking about a legitimate release of the tapes, archives staffers insisted that the tracks couldn't be found. Kevin John never gave up, and in 2006, in response to yet another one of his queries, Capitol told him that not only did they have the tapes, but they all had been preserved in digital form. Overjoyed, he tried to raise the money to master and license a release of his father's last recordings.

Willie's music hadn't provided Darlynn John and her sons much financial security over the years. Kevin and Keith had long ago been launched successfully in life, but they'd hoped that the Capitol sessions would expose fans to Willie's first new music in decades and that their mother might benefit from the proceeds of that renewed popularity. But Ace/Kent Records in Britain, tipped off by a former Capitol archives employee, beat the Johns to the punch. "Nineteen Sixty-Six–The David Axelrod and HB Barnum Sessions" (named for the producer and arranger of the sessions) was licensed from Capitol and released by the British label in 2008, only available in America as an import. Kevin was so pleased that a new generation of fans would get the chance to hear what he considers his father's best work, remastered and in digital form, that he didn't have the heart to be anything but thrilled about the Ace release.

Willie's voice sounds decidedly more mature than it did on his early King singles, for some listeners it stands as a riper, lush sound. Kevin believes that his father was cannier about the way he used his remarkable instrument during those Capitol sessions. And the arrangements H.B. Barnum wrote for the songs fit this more sophisticated style. "The wonderful string and horn arrangements just seemed to caress and bring out the best in his voice. Almost 40 years later, I get chills down my spine, listening."

For Darlynn and Keith, the sound of Willie's voice was a painful reminder of their loss. For years, Keith couldn't listen to his father's music. Over time it became easier, and today he is as active an advocate for his father's legacy as his older brother Kevin. But, for Darlynn, it's a different story. Whenever her sons would bring her a new collection of Willie's music, she would thank them profusely, all smiles, but then tuck it away on a shelf. "I hear some of it was released overseas," Darlynn said, of the "Nineteen Sixty-Six" sessions. "I can't listen to any of it, myself. I listen (to his music) when other people play it, but otherwise I put them all together, on a shelf. I don't listen to them because. . . I just miss him. All these years later."

In the summer of 1968, Willie's mother Lillie, along with her children Raymond, Haywood, Toronto and Mildred (with her son) moved to a house on Steel Street, off Chicago Boulevard. EJ had his own slick bachelor pad, complete with white leather sofa, on Ewald Circle. Brother Mertis Jr lived on the west side, where he operated a barbershop and a record store, Mert's Records on Chene. Mable was long gone from Detroit, traveling with Ray Charles as his head Raelette. Darlynn and the boys had moved from Clarendon to an upstairs flat on Ilene Street, a floor above Willie's sister Delores and her family. It was an emotional time for the boys. While they followed the Detroit Tigers' run to the World

Series that summer with the rest of the city, the loss of their father and the frenzy of his funeral weighed heavily on their spirits.

On the November 3rd, 1968, friends and family put on a concert in Willie's honor at the Veterans Memorial building in downtown Detroit. Many of Willie's friends flew in to perform, including Sam & Dave, Joe Tex, Lee 'Workin' in a Coal Mine' Dorsey and Little Milton, who had memorably recorded Willie's first hit as "Grits Ain't Groceries" in 1969. Also performing that day were sister Mable John, Johnnie Mae Matthews, Renae Jackson and the man who had married Willie and Darlynn in 1957, Reverend Clinton Levert. Kevin and Keith also performed, doing the duo act that had always tickled their father. Top Detroit DJs 'Frantic' Ernie Durham, Martha Jean 'the Queen' Steinberg, Joe Howard and Lee Garrett of WJLB helped preside over the show. Sam Moore described the evening as "very emotional," and there is no doubt that it was.

Mable had a tribute booklet printed up that included a biography of Willie's life, with photos of him throughout the years, and tribute ads from his funeral taken out by King Records, Atlantic, Capitol, Stax-Volt, James Brown, Harry Balk ("With sincere thoughts for a wonderful association") Hal Neely, Sam & Dave, Ray Charles, 'Frantic' Ernie Durham and others. His sister even reproduced Willie's ninth grade report card from the fall 1953 term at Pershing High School. The report card showed that Willie earned the top grade, an A, in three subjects: World History, ROTC and Choir, and a B plus in both General Math and Literature. "The saying has been for years that black boys and girls go into show business because of little ability to do anything else, or a low IQ," Mable wrote. "Just take a look at one of his Pershing High School report cards. He could have just as easily chosen any profession he desired, but he was a born entertainer."

That same night, across town at the Grande Ballroom, the Jeff Beck Group was performing with a young unknown named Rod Stewart on vocals, playing songs from their new album "Truth" for a packed audience of drug-soaked hippie kids. It might have been in a different galaxy. Stewart had stitched a style together from bits and pieces of American rhythm & blues, mostly singers who had copped style and form from Willie. But it didn't matter, the pop world had moved on from Willie years ago.

Nothing about Willie's death in prison made sense, but Darlynn didn't have the time or money to have it investigated. She didn't have the wherewithal to question why Willie's royalty checks were so skimpy either, when she even got them. Thinking about the last few years of Willie's life was so painful for Darlynn, that for years she couldn't even say the word "prison," or refer to what happened to her husband. She needed to reserve what energy she had left to support and watch over two active young boys during the turbulent post-riot years in Detroit. Working part-time in her brother-in-law Mertis' record store wouldn't begin to pay the rent, so Darlynn went to work as a bank teller for Michigan National Bank. She stayed there for decades, until she retired in 2000.

As a full-time working mom, it was all Darlynn could do to keep track of the boys. She often found herself chasing Keith with "the belt." Keith knew that if he ran into his room and slid under his bed as far as he could, his gentle, soft-spoken mother could still reach him and whack him. "She couldn't reach me with the switch, though," he said gleefully, referring to the branch she'd make him snip from a tree in the yard. Darlynn agrees. "The switches didn't work under the bed."

For Kevin, quieter (relatively speaking) and studious, 1968 was the dividing line between life with his father, and life without. Without was much harder. Just a few years earlier, their dad had been Detroit music royalty, but after Willie's death, his sons were left floating without their father's influence. They were plagued by cruel playground taunts such as "your dad was a jailbird," and worse. Both sons felt protective of Darlynn. "She had a hard time," Kevin said. "It's bothered me that all of her life, she's had to focus on us. It's kind of hard for me even now to think about that."

Charlie Collins loved Little Willie John. If he had to pick his favorite Little Willie John song, it would be the choice of so many—"Talk to Me, Talk to Me." Collins was living in New York in 1957 and 58 when a musician friend took him backstage at Small's Paradise Club in Harlem. There he introduced him to a slight, dapper man. "This is Little Willie John," the friend said. Collins couldn't believe it, looking at the singer with a "You're *kidding*!" He wasn't kidding. Willie called out a characteristically upbeat "Hi, Charlie!" For the next few minutes, Collins mostly listened as Willie and the other performers laughed and talked. "I didn't want to impose, he was busy and famous," Collins recalled. When he got home, he told his wife how excited he was to shake Willie's hand and talk to him. "That was my first time meeting one of the John guys," Collins said.

Ironically enough, Collins was an agent for the Federal Narcotics Bureau, a precursor of the federal Drug Enforcement Agency, in New York. When a friend at the agency went to work as head of security for Motown Records, he asked if Collins would like to come to Detroit to work for the label. Collins agreed. Later he went to work directly for Stevie Wonder as his security manager. Collin had just arrived back home in Detroit one day in 1978, when he heard singing and playing coming from his basement; someone was pounding away at the Wurlitzer piano Stevie had given him. "Who is that?" Collins asked. His wife Peaches said there were two boys downstairs, visiting their daughter Tracy.

Collins went flying down the stairs to hear more. His daughter introduced him to Keith John, 18, and Kevin John, aged 20, the sons of his musical idol. He was stunned. When he learned that the Johns had no piano at home, Collins was incredulous. Little Willie John's sons had to have a piano. He called his boss up and told him he was going to give them the Wurlitzer. "Steve, you gotta hear these two kids. They are *bad,* they are Little Willie John's kids and they can sing and play. I'm gonna give them this piano that you gave me." But Stevie had written a special song on the Wurlitzer ("Til You Come Back to Me," for Aretha Franklin) and he wanted his security manager to keep it. "But they've gotta have a piano, they're talented!" Collins pleaded. And that's how it came to be that Stevie Wonder bought a piano for two young men he had never met. But the singer had been a staunch fan of Little Willie John's as a boy, "Talk to Me, Talk to Me" had been his favorite song too.

Like their father, both Kevin and Keith had always found refuge and pleasure in music. Their mother loved to listen to them. While Keith sang in the high part of his father's vocal range and Kevin took the huskier lower end, Darlynn could hear her husband in each of their voices, sometimes at unexpected moments.

Early on, in 1973, the boys entered a talent show at Ecorse High School sponsored by Washington Bullets basketball star Archie Clark, an alumnus. The John brothers won with their rendition of the Jackson 5's "I'll Be There." Clark visited the Johns soon after, and even played basketball with the boys, but the promised record contract with his "Archie Clark Productions" never did materialize. There were other opportunities. Val, the girl whose mother fed Willie John when he briefly ran away from home, was married to Obie Benson of the Four Tops and working as a writer and producer of musicals. She and Motown star Kim Weston took an interest in Willie's sons, and got them booked on local Detroit television shows billed as the John Brothers, including an appearance on comedian Soupy Sales' annual charity telethon. The brothers also sang and danced in lead roles in *Little Red*, a show written and directed by Val Benson, where the Little Red Riding Hood fable was recast into a musical set in "the hood."

In 1973, before either John boy had graduated from Cooley High in Detroit, they were recording at Electric Ladyland in New York with producer Jack Taylor of Rojac and Tayster Records. Taylor had success producing Big Maybelle (including her 1968 tribute to Martin Luther King, "Heaven Will Welcome You, Dr King") but there was a bit of a culture clash between him and the Johns. The producer was an older man (although he would later go into hip-hop), had health issues, and the brothers were skeptical of some of the business dealings swirling around him. At any rate, it didn't pan out into a release.

Kevin graduated from Cooley in 1976, and Keith followed in 1979. That year, the two finally met their piano benefactor, Stevie Wonder, at a concert, but they had a firm offer of a management deal from Ike Perkins and a production deal from old family friend and Philly soul legend Bunny Sigler, so they set off for Philadelphia. After doing background vocals on sessions for 'Uncle' Bunny for the group Instant Funk, the brothers recorded their own single, "Try to Walk a Mile in My Shoes" ("I Just Wanna Be Free") under his direction. This time their record came out, released by RCA in 1980. By then Kevin was 22, and Keith was 20.

The single did well in Detroit, getting good airplay on WCHB and WJLB, and selling in the thousands. After RCA didn't promote the single, Kevin and Keith asked to be let out of their contract. A year later, when they were recording with another producer, Stevie Wonder flew the brothers out to Los Angeles. They spent the next several years, on and off, recording all sorts of music for him, including their own version of Willie's "Talk to Me, Talk to Me."

Despite years of sessions, Wonder never finished the John Brothers album, but in 1984 Keith John started performing live with him, the only male vocalist to do so. Kevin, married with two sons of his own, gave up a full-time music career to work for a computer company and pursue his spiritual interests in Detroit. Wonder did write and produce a song for Keith, the melting, gorgeous ballad "I Can Only Be Me" that appeared on the soundtrack of the 1988 Spike Lee film *School Daze*. Intriguingly, the late Eva Cassidy, whose music reached a wide audience only after her death, recorded Willie's "Fever" and "Need Your Love So Bad," and she also recorded a version of Keith's "I Can Only Be Me." Did she purposely record music by father and son? In the end, we'll never really know, but ironically, her favorite singer was Stevie Wonder, a human musical link between Willie and Keith.

LEGACY

Willie wasn't entirely forgotten in the 1980s and 90s, although it sometimes seemed that way. Interest in classic rhythm & blues would surge every so often, and Willie's music was periodically re-released on best-of packages by King (now Gusto) and Rhino records.

Willie's music, with the deep emotional fabric and unique texture of his voice, was a natural choice for mood-setting on the big screen. "Fever" was featured in the Matt Dillon's *Big Town* (1986) and several other films. In 1996, director John Sayles chose two less obvious songs of Willie's for his movie *Lone Star*. Willie's tear-soaked, bluesy ballad "You Hurt Me" plays in the background in a scene in *Lone Star* that takes place in a juke joint as the corrupt sheriff (Kris Kristofferson) bullies a young bartender. Then he can be heard crooning the stripped-down, jazzy "My Love Is" during the film's romantic climax, when the sheriff finally realizes that he's still in love with his high school sweetheart. Willie is singing with no dialogue getting in the way; just as he half-sings, half-talks the ending line "My love is the deep blue sea," the music fades out and the two lovers speak. Sayles is a real fan. "You just don't hear enough of him today, he's one of my favorite singers," the director said. "'My Love Is' was a song that never got to be the big hit that 'Fever' did, but it had this great haunting quality to it, it's very romantic. It was a great era for singers."

Willie's face and the tragic story of his final years in Seattle were splashed across the cover of *The Village Voice*'s music supplement in 1990. The lengthy article, written by Kim Field, described Willie's rise to fame and rapid fall, with detailed reporting on the Seattle incident. Field, a musician himself, had first encountered Willie's music when he was a college student in New York years earlier, following harp player Paul Ascher around, trying to soak up everything the former Muddy Waters sideman knew. "Paul Ascher was the first white guy in Muddy's band," Field explained. "Playing harp for Muddy Waters is like playing tenor for Count Basie. I just followed him around like a puppy dog for a couple of years as he tried to give me quasi-lessons."

When Ascher invited him to his house, Field was beside himself. It was still difficult to find obscure blues albums then, and he was sure there would be stacks of vintage blues vinyl at Ascher's pad. When he got there, sure enough, there were piles of great blues and rhythm & blues records, but the discs were strewn around the floor, without covers. Ascher played some of them, but the records were so scratchy, Field could hardly hear the music. "One of the records was a King album by Little Willie John," Field said. "I remember (Ascher) picking it up and saying, 'This probably won't play.'"

But there was a larger lesson that the young musician took home that day. Muddy Waters, Ascher told him, and "all the heavy blues cats" were fans of Little Willie John. Field tucked away Willie's name for future research. A few years later, he returned to his hometown of Seattle. Field was playing a dive bar one night when he encountered a man who had served time in the state prison with Willie. Intrigued by the stories the man told, Field started seeking out Willie's records. "I was just completely blown away," Field said. "The guy was just insanely talented. And the whole thing was when Willie was what, aged 17 to 24? Seven to eight years? He was probably just coming into his voice in some ways, we'll never know."

Some time in the 1980s, Kevin and Keith John heard that their father was being considered for induction into the Rock and Roll Hall of Fame. The brothers talked to friends and did press interviews, hoping to get a groundswell of support to push the induction through. Like so many things in Willie's life, it wasn't easy. In all, Willie was nominated eight times to the Rock and Roll Hall of Fame. Finally, on the eighth nomination, he made it through to the Hall of Fame's Class of 1996, along with Pink Floyd, David Bowie, the Velvet Underground, Gladys Knight and the Shirelles. It's as if, for one last time, the same blazing energy that launched 16 year-old Willie out of Detroit's north end could not be denied.

Gladys Knight was an Atlanta teenager when she performed with Willie on the chitlin circuit in the late 1950s. She was and is a big fan. "'Grits Ain't Groceries,' are you kidding me?" she said with a laugh. As far as Willie's wild streak, she insists on putting it in context. "A lot of us were young in the business. When you got in the business you were in the adult world, but you were still a kid, you were still young. So you did a lot of stupid things that you wouldn't have done if you were the mature person you eventually had to become." Knight sighed, "He had a real nice family."

Keith John remembers the day in 1995 when he got the news that his father would be honored by the Rock Hall. He was with his boss, Stevie Wonder at the time. Music critics often snort at the Rock Hall's many omissions and some of their more mystifying choices, but it is an honor that the artists' families deeply appreciate and is always front-loaded into the first paragraph of a musician's obituary. When Keith shared the good news, Stevie had an idea. What if *he* inducted Willie into the Rock and Roll Hall of Fame? What if he gave the speech? And what if Keith sang "Fever" with Stevie on backing vocals and piano? Of course. He didn't know, but the Hall of Fame had been trying to contact Stevie and get him to participate in the induction ceremonies for some time, without success, so nobody had to be convinced.

The next issue was, which two family members would accept the honor on Willie's behalf at the Waldorf-Astoria in New York? The Rock and Roll Hall of Fame only gives each inductee two paid-for tickets to the dinner. Darlynn wanted both of her sons to attend the ceremony and accept the honor for their father, but Kevin insisted that his mother go with Keith and Stevie. Kevin was content to go to Cleveland and take part in the lavish VIP festivities at the museum with his wife Cathy and their sons Kevin II, then 13, and Keith, nine.

So it was that on a bitterly cold late January day, Kevin put in a full shift at work, then drove his family and a few friends from Detroit to Cleveland. It was even colder when they arrived at the wind-whipped I.M. Pei-designed museum looming over Lake Erie. But watching Stevie Wonder and his brother pay homage to his father on a large screen in the comfort of a museum screening room, Kevin felt he had the best view.

In New York, Darlynn John arrived at the hotel feeling under the weather. Keith suggested that she rest while he and Stevie went to the ballroom for a quick run-through of the evening's program. Keith ran over his speech, which he had written together with Kevin. "I was never prouder of my dad than on that night," Kevin said. His own young sons were finally seeing Willie, the grandfather they never knew, celebrated publicly by some of the giants of the business.

Because there were no film clips of Willie available, during the video presentation, photos of him flashed on the screen as his music played. Then the audience heard the rumbling baritone voice of Johnny Otis, the Greek–American bandleader, songwriter and King Records talent scout who had discovered Willie at the Paradise Theater—a year ahead of Harry Balk and a few others. Otis gave a quick capsule summary of Little Willie John's career for those in the audience who might need it. "When I met him, and found him, Little Willie John may have been only 13 and a little guy, but he had a great big talent," Otis said. "Little Willie John created 'Fever,' and then Peggy Lee and many other people, in the wake of his great record, made their versions. But the definitive version is Little Willie John's." After the video presentation ended, Keith then belted out "Fever" for all he was worth, accompanied by Stevie on the piano.

Afterward, Darlynn stood nervously on the podium with Keith, who couldn't stop smiling. Stevie Wonder spoke next. "As a little boy I grew up listening to the music of Little Willie John, and I used to hear stories of how he would play at the Fox Theatre and turn it out," Stevie said. He recalled sitting on the floor of his Detroit house when he was little, listening to Willie's songs on the radio and never imagining that he would know Willie's family one day and become an artist himself. Stevie spoke of "the joy of being the one to induct a great talent, someone who inspired me, into the Rock and Roll Hall of Fame, and also to have the pleasure of presenting these awards to the wife and also to the son of a great talent." Stevie laughingly added, indicating Keith to the crowd of industry big shots, "Get him a record contract."

Keith accepted on behalf of the family, and rattled off some of the musicians inspired by Willie; George Benson, Donny Hathaway, Jeffrey Osborne, Levi Stubbs of the Four Tops, ". . . and the Big Cheese right here," he laughed, nudging Stevie Wonder. "Our family is very excited about this award because now people who didn't know him previously will get to know the impact he had on music and the music industry," Keith said. He added that he and his brother were "purely ecstatic" for their mother, who had been "floating on air since she learned my dad would be acknowledged for this well-deserved, we believe, spot

(**Clockwise from top left**) Willie with Darlynn, who wears the de rigueur mink even in the balmy Florida weather, circa 1962–63; Willie and Darlynn glammed up to go to a function at the Hotel Fontainebleau, Miami, 1962; Willie and Darlynn lounge in a hotel room out on the road, circa 1962–63; Willie and Darlynn with Willie's sister Mildred and brother Raymond John, circa 1963; Darlynn with Willie's mother Lillie John, 1962–63. *All courtesy John Family.*

(Top) Willie at Detroit's Henry the Hatter, circa 1963. **(Below)** Darlynn (second from left) pictured with Willie's sister Mable John, his mother Lillie and his friend, singer Johnnie Taylor, 1963–64. *Both courtesy John Family.*

(**Top**) Willie with tenor saxophone player Grady Gaines (in center) and his ferocious backing band the Upsetters. *Courtesy Grady Gaines.* (**Below**) Willie with his mother and a gang of his siblings during one of his gigs at a Detroit club, either Phelps Lounge or the 20 Grand. Left to right, Mildred, her boyfriend Vance, Willie (standing), Donald Smith (Delores' then-husband), mother Lillie, Delores, Ernest and Raymond. 1963–64. *Courtesy John Family.*

(**Clockwise from top**) In the Washington State penitentiary, Willie wrote many letters, especially to his two sons, and to his wife Darlynn. *Courtesy John Family*. Photo of the house on 23rd in Seattle, then run as an illegal, after-hours party spot. *Courtesy Kim Field*. Schoolboys Keith and Kevin John, circa 1966. *Courtesy John Family*. When Willie was released from prison in 1966, sister Mable booked several engagements for him, including one at the Apollo Theater and one at Phelps Lounge. *Courtesy Timothy Caldwell collection*.

(**Clockwise from top**) Willie's funeral in June 1968. Pallbearers, left to right, Chit Chat Club Manager Henson West, singer Johnnie Taylor (with sunglasses), Dave Prater (behind Taylor), Sam Moore (with sunglasses) and Joe Tex (looking to the left). *Courtesy the* Michigan Chronicle. John Brothers promotional shot from their years working with Stevie Wonder, circa 1983–84. *Courtesy John Family.* Mable John with her nephews, Keith John at left, Kevin John at right, at their father's funeral, June 1968. *Courtesy the* Michigan Chronicle.

(**Top**) Stevie Wonder, Darlynn John and Keith John backstage at the Waldorf Astoria, at the Rock and Roll Hall of Fame induction ceremony for Willie, January 17th, 1996. *Courtesy John Family.* (**Below**) Family friends TC and Kacina Shane (right) accompanied Kevin John and his family to watch Willie's induction into the Rock and Roll Hall of Fame. To the left of the Shanes is Willie's grandson Kevin II, Kevin John, his wife Cathy, and in front, Willie's grandson Keith. *Courtesy John Family.*

(**Top**) Willie's sons Kevin, left and Keith, right, with their beloved Uncle Ernest in Detroit, in 2005. *Courtesy John Family.* (**Below**) Darlynn John, Kevin John, Willie's longtime manager Harry Balk, and Keith John, in April 2006 at a restaurant in Oak Park, just north of Detroit. *Courtesy John Family.*

(**Top**) Val Benson, Darlynn John and Clineice Stubbs at the Stubbs home in Detroit in 2006. *Courtesy Clineice Stubbs.* (**Below**) Kevin John, his wife Cathy, Darlynn John and Keith John surround Willie's old friend from the Hotel Theresa days, Little Jimmy Scott, backstage after Jimmy's show at the Detroit Institute of Arts in 2007. *Courtesy John Family.*

in music history. She just wants to say…" And then, Darlynn's soft voice was finally heard: "I just want to say thank you very much, and I am very happy and very, very pleased."

Later, Stevie and Keith sang with Joan Osborne. Keith chatted with Ahmet Ertegun, Mariah Carey, Gerald and Eddie Levert; enjoyed a brief mutual flirt with Natalie Merchant and talked contracts with at least one record magnate, anyway.

To friends and family, Willie was so full of life that faded black and white images in old scrapbooks only capture a shadow of his exuberant personality. Asked to choose his favorite song of Willie's, his old friend B.B. King groans. "That's sort of like asking me what I like better, ice cream or cake." He thought for a minute. "There's 'Home at Last' and that one, 'Talk to Me,' 'Let them Talk' … all of these are favorites of mine." King sang part of another song of Willie's he loved to hear, "Now You Know": "*Now you know how it feels…* It's about a person that has never been hurt, but hurts everybody else."

Hearing a record of Willie singing the jazz standard "The Very Thought of You" sent Sam Moore into a nostalgic reverie about his friend recently. "It's not about Mable, it's not about (Willie's) brothers, it's about Willie," Sam said. "I learned a lot from that little guy! I did! How to step on a stage, how to perform, set up a song, how to carry yourself. And Willie could walk on a stage—well he always wanted to be Sinatra anyway, with his little stingy-brim hat, cocked on the side—he'd walk on the stage with his collar open and the tie hanging, and he could stand there and oh, to see him! I would stand in the wings and watch." Sam even dressed like Willie. There are photos of Sam & Dave wearing identical little "stingy brim" hats on the back of one of their albums. "Oh *man*, how this little guy, this giant of a guy could stand there and just mesmerize you with that voice. *Where did that voice come from*?" Sam bellowed, warming up into a church-filling howl, like a Southern preacher. "That was a *God*-given idea. He was a *God*-given talent! They called him a *blues* singer, they called him a *jazz* singer, but to me, Willie was just a singer that could sing *the telephone book*!"

For years after Willie's death, his friend, singer Jimmy Scott still talked about him to anyone who would listen. This was the man whose voice made Willie sob to Joe Hunter, "This guy can beat me singing." Jimmy thought the world of Willie as well. "He was a stone genius," Jimmy said. "It was just one of those things. He got mixed up with the wrong people, and you can't get everything when you want it. But other than that, he was a good little cat." Willie's influence as a soul muse percolates through several generations of singers. "He's one of the four or five most important writers and singers and stylists, in my book," said Boz Scaggs. "He was right up with Ray (Charles), Sam Cooke, he's up there with the greats."

Within the family, his sons often asked their uncles about Willie's temperament, described as doomed and violent in so many mawkish online biographies. "Let me tell you, so you'll always remember," Mertis Jr told Kevin. "He wanted to make people laugh. He'd do things to make you laugh, to make you happy. . . as far as a short fuse, *uh uh.*" In 2006, Ernest John sat in a restaurant near his Detroit apartment and talked about his long-dead older brother. With his short, wiry build and feisty demeanor, EJ looked eerily like old photos of Willie. Normally soft-spoken, on the subject of his brother, Ernest became very animated. "Not many people that's gone as long as my brother has, and they call his name all the time," EJ said. "People call me Little Willie John's brother. And I say, 'That is not my name!' I say, 'My name is EJ.' But I'm awfully proud of him. He took me all around the country with him."

Willie's transcendent music and the tragedy of his abbreviated life has made him a compelling, almost mythic figure to songwriters. In Robbie Robertson's 1987 song "Somewhere Down the Lazy River" he sings of *"lying in the back seat, listening to Little Willie John."* Folk and blues singer Tom Russell wrote a song, "Blue Wing," that touches on another person who's passed into folklore, the prisoner at Washington State who shared a cell with the great singer. Russell sings:

He had a blue wing tattooed on his shoulder
Well it might have been a bluebird I don't know
But he gets stone drunk and talks about Alaska
The salmon boats and 45 below
He said he got that blue wing up in Walla Walla
And his cellmate there was Little Willie John
And Willie he was once a great blues singer
And Wing and Willie wrote them up a song.
Said it's dark in here; can't see the sky

But I look at this blue wing and I close my eyes
Gonna fly away beyond these walls
Up above the clouds where the rain don't fall
On a poor man's dreams.

Russell explained that the song was fiction, that he never met such a prisoner, but he did get to know someone who was close to Little Willie John, Otis Blackwell, the co-writer of "Fever," in the mid 1980s. Russell heard many stories from Blackwell, "and that must have seeped into the song," he said.

The passage of years can't diminish what's left–recordings of a voice bursting with life, expressing the deepest pain and, on the turn of a dime, a joyful swagger. Blessed with an uncommonly supple vocal instrument, Willie sang every note as if his life depended on it, with the same passion that he lived his brief life. Nobody had a name for it in the spring of 1955, but what 17 year-old Willie did in a recording studio in New York with "All Around the World" had the sort of piercing, gospel-born intensity that came to be codified in the 1960s as soul music. That passion captured the hearts of all who saw him in the funky theaters of the chitlin circuit, but his influence also radiated out over the years thanks to fans like Marvin Gaye, James Brown, B.B. King, Stevie Wonder and Aretha Franklin. His life may have ended, but his music endures.

A leaden gray sky, the kind that hangs over Detroit for days on end in the winter, will sometimes remind Darlynn John of her long-lost young husband. "If the sun wasn't shining and it was dreary, Willie could change the day," she said. "That's what attracted me to him. He could change the day." If he had only survived those last 60 days until his July 1968 parole hearing, "We would have had a beautiful life, we would have known each other better," Darlynn said wistfully. "I can't remember a time, even now, when I don't miss him. But I will see him again."

SELECTED BIBLIOGRAPHY

INTERVIEWS BY SUSAN WHITALL WITH THE FOLLOWING PEOPLE:

Arthur Swanson
B.B. King
Bettye LaVette
Billy Davis
Bobby Lewis
Bobby Taylor
Charles Connor
Clarence Avant
Cora Robinson
Darlynn John
Dave Usher
David Axelrod
Ed Bierman
Esther Hawthorne
Gladys Knight
Grady Gaines
H.B. Barnum
Jerry Butler
Jimmy Scott
Joe Hunter
John Sayles
Johnnie Bassett
Kim Field
Lattimore Brown
Lithofayne Pridgon
Little Bill Englehart
Little Richard
Lou Devereaux
Mable John
Mack Rice
Mickey Baker
Milton Hopkins
Norman Thrasher
Phil Townsend
Sam Moore
Solomon Burke
Stanley Lee
William Colden
Wilson Pickett

INTERVIEWS BY SUSAN WHITALL & KEVIN JOHN WITH THE FOLLOWING PEOPLE:

Ernest John
Harry Balk
Levi and Clineice Stubbs
Mertis John
Raymond John
Valaida Benson

INTERVIEWS BY KEVIN JOHN WITH THE FOLLOWING PEOPLE:

George Benson
Jeffrey Osborne

BOOKS:

Bjorn, Lars and Jim Gallert. *Before Motown: A History of Jazz in Detroit 1920–1960.* Michigan: University of Michigan Press, 2001.

Butler, Jerry and Earl Smith. *Only The Strong Survive: Memoirs of a Soul Survivor.* Indiana: Indiana University Press, 2004.

Fox, Jon Hartley. *King of the Queen City.* Illinois: University of Illinois Press, 2009.

Fox, Ted. *Showtime at the Apollo: The Story of Harlem's World Famous Theater.* New York: Mill Road Enterprises, 2003.

John, Mertis. *My Life and Experiences in the Entertainment World.* Detroit: Meda Publishing, 2001.

Chapter 1: Mama was a Genius

(*"After the war, in 1950, there were 300,506 blacks in the city."*) Source: U.S. Department of Commerce, Bureau of the Census, United States Census of Population, 1910–1970.

(*"My earliest ambition was to be another Paul Robeson…"*) Young, A.S. 'Doc'. "Little Willie John, 5-4 Ballroom Star, Once Wanted to be a Caruso." *Los Angeles Sentinel* (Los Angeles, CA) July 24, 1958.

Chapter 2: No Blues in this House

(*"All the bad people lived on the east side."*) Gordy, Berry. *To Be Loved, The Music, The Magic, The Memories of Motown.* New York: Warner Books, 1994.
(*"Hide the neckbones, here comes Willie John…"*) Otis, Johnny. *Red Beans & Rice and Other Rock 'n' Roll Recipes.* Petaluma CA: Pomegranate, 1997.

Chapter 3: Willie is discovered...Again

(*Johnny Otis' thoughts on discovering Willie John at the Paradise.*) Interview with Johnny Otis by John Morthland in *Creem*, November 1971.

Chapter 4: A Surprisingly Well-Poised Boy

Author Unknown. "Detroit Boy Dares N.Y. Show World." *Detroit Times*, December 8th, 1953.

Author Unknown. "Detroit Boy Takes Part in Christmas Song Derby." *Detroit News*, December 29th, 1953.

Chapter 5: The Dirty Boogie

(*"I wasn't making much money..."*) Young, Masco. "The Tribune Sips a Shake with Little Willie John," *Philadelphia Tribune*, April 4th, 1961.

(*Henry Glover information*) Interviews Glover did with Steve Tracy, in Jon Hartley Fox, *King of the Queen City*. Chicago: University of Illinois Press, 2009. (Anyone writing about King Records owes a huge debt to Tracy, who did an extensive interview with Henry Glover in "King of the Blues." *Blues Unlimited,* vol 87–89, 1971–72.)

(*Mertis... noticed right away that Willie's voice had changed."*) Mertis John. *My Life and Experiences in the Entertainment World.* Detroit: Meda Publishing, 2001.

(*Description of Willie looking grown up*) Joe 'Ziggy' Johnson. "Zig Zag with Ziggy Johnson," *Chicago Defender,* October 29th, 1955.

(*Hal Neely's claim that he discovered Willie*) from the 2002 interview he did with Brian Powers of the Cincinnati Public Library and Jeff Yawley. Used with permission.

Chapter 6: Walk Slow

("He sang with the pain and real-life experience of an adult...") Etta James and David Ritz. *Rage to Survive: The Etta James Story.* New York: Villard Books, 1995.

("Willie John was the artist of all artists...") Steve Tracy, Fox, Jon Hartley. *King of the Queen City.* Champaign: University of Illinois Press, 2009.

("That family was like the Jacksons!") from an unpublished audio interview conducted with King musician Calvin 'Eagle Eye' Shields by Brian Powers of the Cincinnati Public Library and Jeff Yawley. Used with permission.

Chapter 7: Fever

(Otis Blackwell's account of the writing of "Fever.") Editorial, *Time Barrier Express Magazine,* July 1979.

(Joe Tex's claim that he wrote "Fever.") Cliff White. "Bumps 'n' Bruises in Mississippi: On Tour with Joe Tex." *New Musical Express,* May 14th, 1977. Joe McEwen. "Joe Tex: The Soul of an Underdog." *The Boston Phoenix,* May 21st, 1977.

Chapter 8: Success

(Account of Willie at "My Nerves" recording session) Editorial, Rock and Roll Stars, 1956. Retrieved from rocksbackpages.com.

(Details of April attack on Nat King Cole in Birmingham, Alabama) Gary S. Sprayberry. "Interrupted Melody: The 1956 Attack on Nat King Cole." *Alabama Heritage,* Winter 2004.

(Details of Big Rhythm and Blues Show '56 being curtailed after racial tensions in the South) Rick Coleman. *Blue Monday: Fats Domino and the Lost Dawn of Rock 'n' Roll,* Cambridge, MA: Da Capo Press, 2006.

(Audiotape of Bob Dylan at a 1980 concert in San Francisco talking about seeing Little Willie John back in the 1950s, in Detroit) courtesy Paul Tillman.

("I'm the king of the rock and rollers...") Wynonie Harris. *Cleveland Call & Post,* November 3rd, 1956.

Chapter 9: Talk to Me

(If you do have a tight-knit family...") Susan Whitall. *Women of Motown.* New York: Avon Books, 1999.

Chapter 10: A Valuable Science

(Charles Connor's account of the Upsetters' act and Willie's onstage antics) from Charles Connor's unpublished memoir written with Leslie, *Keep A-Knockin',* held in the Archives of African American Music and Culture. Indiana: Indiana University.

Chapter 11: The Prince of the Blues

("Peggy Lee made it famous, but Little Willie John defined it forever" –Ray Charles) from David Ritz liner notes to Ray Charles. *Rare Genius: The Undiscovered Masters.* Concord Group, CRE-32196-02.

("Peggy Lee couldn't sing like Little Willie John") Sondra K. Wilson. *Meet Me at the Theresa, the Story of Harlem's Most Famous Hotel.* New York: Atria Books, 2004.

(Harry Balk's opinion that Willie's version of "Fever" would have sold many more millions if he had access to the same market Peggy Lee did.) Kim Heron. "Sound Moves from Father to Sons." *Detroit Free Press,* November 30th, 1980.

(Willie complaining, "Rock 'n' roll is not rhythm & blues!") A.S. "Doc" Young. "Little Willie John, 5–4 Ballroom Star, Once Wanted to be Caruso." *Los Angeles Sentinel,* July 24th, 1958.

(Willie's high hopes for "You're a Sweetheart") A.S. "Doc" Young. "Little Willie John, 5–4 Ballroom Star, Once Wanted to be Caruso." *Los Angeles Sentinel,* July 24th, 1958.

Chapter 12: The Hustle Contract

("Little Willie John didn't want us coming anywhere near him...") James Brown with Bruce Tucker. *The Godfather of Soul.* New York: Macmillan Publishers, 1986.

(Hal Neely anecdotes) Unpublished interview of Hal Neely by Brian Powers and Jeff Yawley, 2002.

("Young performer has an easy, winning way...") Editorial, "Review of Apollo Theater Show." *Variety,* December 16th, 1959.

("When he was in town, Willie enjoyed going to the fights") Major Robinson. "New York Beat." *Jet,* March 1961.

Chapter 13: Miami

(Hal Neeley's account of the "Sleep" recording session) Unpublished audio interview conducted by Brian Powers of the Cincinnati Public Library and Jeff Yawley, 2002.

Chapter 14: End of an Idyll

(Interview with Willie) Masco Young, "The Tribune Sips a 'Shake' with Little Willie John." *Philadelphia Tribune,* April 4th, 1961.

Chapter 15: No Way Out

(Witness accounts of the October 18th, 1964 incident) from an unredacted copy of the police report obtained from Seattle police, 1964.

(Darlynn John's comments on Willie John) Darlynn John to Washington State Department of Corrections, 1965. Washington State corrections file on William Edward John.

Kim Field. "Rock & Roll Quarterly: Fever & Fate: The Strange Story of Little Willie John." *Village Voice 35*, March 27th, 1990.

Chapter 16: The Trial, and Tribulation

(Agreement to perform at the Phelps Lounge) signed by Mable John on behalf of Little Willie John, March 21st,1966. Courtesy Timothy Caldwell Collection.

(Agreement to perform at the Pal-I-Drome) signed by Mable John on behalf of Little Willie John, March 21st, 1966. Courtesy Timothy Caldwell Collection.

(Mable John to Phelps Lounge, telegram) April 10th, 1966. Courtesy of Timothy Caldwell Collection.

(Attorney Bill Lanning blaming Willie's "smart-ass attitude") Kim Field. "Rock & Roll Quarterly: Fever & Fate: The Strange Story of Little Willie John." *Village Voice 35*, March 27th, 1990.

Chapter 17: A Dream Deferred

(Details of Capitol sessions) Liner notes by Tony Rounce for Little Willie John. *Nineteen Sixty-Six: The David Axelrod and HB Barnum Sessions*, 2008.

(Willie's admission of his drinking problem) Details of Willie's incarceration from Washington State Department of Corrections documents.

("I have accepted my vacation as an answer to someone's prayers") Willie John to Darlynn John, letter, January 7th, 1968.

(James Brown's recollections of seeing Willie in a wheelchair, suffering from pneumonia) James Brown. *I Feel Good: A Memoir of a Life of Soul.* New York: New American Library, 2005.

(Interview with Joe Tex about his feud with James Brown) Lee Ivory. *Chicago Defender*, March 13, 1968.

Chapter 19: Detroit

Rita Griffin. "Tragic Homecoming: Thousands Attend Rites for Little Willie John." *Michigan Chronicle*, June 15th, 1968.

Chapter 20: Legacy

Stevie Wonder and Keith John. "Rock and Roll Hall of Fame Induction Speech," from videotape provided to the John family by the Rock and Roll Hall of Fame, January 17th, 1996.

LYRICS:

"Blue Wing." Words and music by Tom Russell. Copyright © 1990 End of the Trail Music (ASCAP)/Administered by Bug Music. All rights reserved. Used by permission. Reprinted by permission of Hal Leonard Corporation.

"Fever." Words and music by John Davenport and Eddie Cooley. Copyright © 1956 by Fort Knox Music, Inc. and Bug Music-Trio Music Company. Copyright renewed. International copyright secured. All rights reserved. Used by permission. Reprinted by permission of Hal Leonard Corporation and Fort Knox Music, Inc.

"The Hucklebuck." Words by Roy Alfred, music by Andy Gibson. Copyright © 1948, 1949 by Bienstock Publishing Company, Jerry Leiber Music, Mike Stoller Music, Bug Music-Quartet Music and Seven Eight Nine Music Assoc. Copyright renewed. International copyright secured. All rights reserved. Used by permission. Reprinted by permission of Hal Leonard Corporation and Bienstock Publishing Company.

"Talk To Me, Talk to Me." Words and music by Joe Seneca. Copyright © 1958 by Fort Knox Music, Inc. and Trio Music Company. Copyright renewed. International copyright secured. All rights reserved. Used by permission. Reprinted by permission of Hal Leonard Corporation and Fort Knox Music, Inc.

"Walk Slow." Words and music by William E. John and Darlynn John. Copyright © 1961 by Fort Knox Music, Inc. and Bug Music-Trio Music Company. Copyright renewed. International copyright secured. All rights reserved. Used by permission. Reprinted by permission of Hal Leonard Corporation and Fort Knox Music, Inc.

"Nobody Knows You When You're Down and Out." Words and music by Jimmy Cox, 1923. All efforts were made to trace a copyright holder; if you are own the rights in this work, please contact Titan and we would be glad to place the appropriate credit in any future printing of this title.

LITTLE WILLIE JOHN

SELECTED DISCOGRAPHY

CATALOG NUMBER	SONG TITLE & RELEASE DATE

SINGLES

PRE-KING

Little Willie John, Two Lads and a Lass. **Prize 6900**	**"Mommy, What Happened To Our Christmas Tree/Jingle Bells"** December, 1953.
Little Willie John with Paul Williams. **Rama 167**	**"Ring a Ling Ling"** 1955.

KING SINGLES

Little Willie John. **King 4818**	**"All Around The World / Don't Leave Me Dear"** July 1955. (Top Billboard position: No. 5 R&B).
Little Willie John. **King 4841**	**"Need Your Love So Bad"** November, 1955, (Billboard: No. 5 R&B); **"Home At Last"** Little Willie John, November 1955. (Billboard: No. 6 R&B).
Little Willie John. **King 4893**	**"Are You Ever Coming Back / I'm Stickin' With You Baby"** March, 1956.
Little Willie John. **King 4935**	**"Fever / Letter From My Darling"** April 1956 (Top Billboard positions: No. 1 R&B, No. 24 Pop).
Little Willie John. **King 4960**	**"Do Something For Me / Suffering With The Blues"** August 1956.
Little Willie John. **King 4989**	**"I've Been Around / Suffering With The Blues"** 1956.
Little Willie John. **King 5003**	**"Will The Sun Shine Tomorrow / A Little Bit Of Loving"** 1956.
Little Willie John. **King 5023**	**"Love, Life And Money / You Got To Get Up Early In The Morning"** 1957.
Little Willie John. **King 5045**	**"I've Got To Go Cry / Look What You've Done To Me"** 1957.
Little Willie John. **King 5066**	**"Young Girl / If I Thought You Needed Me"** 1957.
Little Willie John. **King 5083**	**"Uh Uh Baby / Summer Date"** 1957.
Little Willie John. **King 5091**	**"Person To Person / Until You Do"** 1957.
Little Willie John. **King 5108**	**"Talk To Me, Talk To Me / Spasms"** January 1958. (No. 20 Pop).

Little Willie John.
King 5142

"Let's Rock While The Rockin's Good / You're A Sweetheart"
1958.

Little Willie John.
King 5147

"Tell It Like It Is / Don't Be Ashamed To Call My Name"
1958.

Little Willie John.
King 5154

"All My Love Belongs To You / Why Don't You Haul Off And Love Me" 1958.

Little Willie John.
King 5170

"No Regrets / I'll Carry Your Love Wherever I Go"
1959.

Little Willie John.
King 5179

"Made For Me / Do More In Life"
1959.

Little Willie John.
King 5219

"Leave My Kitten Alone / Let Nobody Love You"
1959.

Little Willie John.
King 5274

"Let Them Talk / Right There"
October 1959.

Little Willie John.
King 5318

"Loving Care / My Love Is"
1960.

Little Willie John.
King 5342

"I'm Shakin' / Cottage For Sale"
1960.

Little Willie John.
King 5356

"Heartbreak (It's Hurtin' Me) / Do You Love Me"
May 1960.

Little Willie John.
King 5394

"Sleep / There's A Difference"
September 1960. (Billboard: No. 10 R&B, No. 13 Pop).

Little Willie John.
King 5428

"Walk Slow / You Hurt Me"
December 1960.

Little Willie John.
King 5452

"Leave My Kitten Alone / I'll Never Go Back On My Word"
1961.

Little Willie John.
King 5458

"I'm Sorry / The Very Thought Of You"
1961.

Little Willie John.
King 5503

"(I've Got) Spring Fever / Flamingo"
1961.

Little Willie John.
King 5516

"Take My Love (I Want To Give It All To You) / Now You Know"
1961.

Little Willie John.
King 5539

"Need Your Love So Bad / Drive Me Home"
1961.

Little Willie John.
King 5577

"There Is Someone In This World For Me / Autumn Leaves"
1961.

Little Willie John.
King 5591

"Fever / Bo-Da-Ley Dino-Ley"
1962.

Little Willie John.
King 5602

"The Masquerade Is Over / Katanga"
1962.

Little Willie John.
King 5628

"Until Again My Love / Mister Glenn"
1962.

Little Willie John. **King 5641**	**"Every Beat Of My Heart / I Wish I Could Cry"** 1962.
Little Willie John. **King 5667**	**"She Thinks I Still Care / Come Back To Me"** 1962.
Little Willie John. **King 5681**	**"Doll Face / Big Blue Diamonds"** 1962.
Little Willie John. **King 5694**	**"Without A Friend / Half A Love"** 1962.
Little Willie John. **King 5717**	**"Don't Play With Love / Heaven All Around Me"** 1963.
Little Willie John. **King 5744**	**"My Baby's In Love With Another Guy* / Come On Sugar"** 1963.
Little Willie John. **King 5799**	**"Let Them Talk / Talk To Me"** 1963.
Little Willie John. **King 5818**	**"So Lovely / Inside Information"** 1963.
Little Willie John. **King 5823**	**"Person To Person / I'm Shakin'"** 1963.
Little Willie John. **King 5850**	**"Bill Bailey / My Love Will Never Change"** 1964.
Little Willie John. **King 5870**	**"Rock Love / It Only Hurts For A Little While"** 1964.
Little Willie John. **King 5886**	**"All Around The World / All My Love Belongs To You"** 1964.
Little Willie John. **King 5949**	**"Do Something For Me / Don't You Know I'm In Love"** 1964.
Little Willie John. **King 6003**	**"Talk To Me / Take My Love"** 1965.
Little Willie John. **King 6170**	**"Fever / Let Them Talk"** 1968.
Little Willie John. **King 6302**	**"All Around The World / Need Your Love So Bad"** 1970.

KING ALBUMS

Little Willie John. **King 564**	*Fever* 1956. (Nurse with thermometer cover)
Little Willie John. **King 564**	*Fever* 1957. (white cover)
Little Willie John. **King 596**	*Talk To Me* 1958.
Little Willie John. **King 603**	*Mister Little Willie John* 1958.

Little Willie John. **King 691**	*Little Willie John In Action* 1960.
Little Willie John. **King 739**	*Sure Things* 1961.
Little Willie John. **King 767**	*The Sweet, The Hot, The Teenage Beat* 1961.
Little Willie John. **King 802**	*Come On And Join Little Willie John At A Recording Session* 1962.
Little Willie John. **King 895**	*These Are My Favorite Songs* 1964.
Little Willie John. **King 949**	*Little Willie John Sings All Originals* 1966 (Mono).
Little Willie John. **King Ks-949**	*Little Willie John Sings All Originals* 1966 (Stereo).
Little Willie John. **King Ks-1081**	*Free At Last* 1970.

NON-KING ALBUMS

Kent CDKEND305, *Nineteen Sixty-Six: The David Axelrod and HB Barnum Sessions.* Recorded in 1966 (for Capitol) Released in 2008 by Ace/Kent. Tracks: "Country Girl" a.k.a. "Home at Last" (Take 8), "Suffering with the Blues "(Take 4), "I had a Dream" a.k.a. "Just a Dream" (Take 7), "Never Let Me Go" (Take 4), "If I Loved You" (Take 2), "(I Need) Someone "(Take 12), "Welcome to the Club" (Take 8), "Early in the Morning" (Take 8), "In The Dark" (Take 1), "Crying Over You" (Take 2), "You Are My Sunshine" (Take 3), "Country Girl" a.k.a. "Home at Last" (Alternate Take), "Suffering with the Blues" (Alt Take), "I Had a Dream" a.k.a. "Just a Dream" (Alt Take), "Endless Sleep, Never Let Me Go" (Alt Take), "Welcome to the Club" (Alt Take), "Early in the Morning" (Alt Take), "In The Dark" (Alt Take), "Crying Over You" (Alt Take).

NATIONAL TELEVISION APPEARANCES

American Bandstand **May 6th, 1958**. Sings "Talk To Me, Talk To Me." and "Fever."

American Bandstand **Jan. 23rd, 1959**. Sings "You're a Sweetheart."

American Bandstand **Sept. 28th, 1960**. Sings "Sleep."

Route 66 **"Give the Old Cat a Tender Mouse" CBS-TV** episode, aired Dec. 21st, 1962.

Sources:

Whitburn, Joel. *The Billboard Book of Top 40 Hits*. New York: Watson-Guptill Publications, 2000.

Ruppli, Michel. *The King Labels: A Discography*. Connecticut: Greenwood Publishing, 1985.

Author's research

SPECIAL ACKNOWLEDGMENTS

Thank you to Darlynn John, Keith John, Ernest John, Mable John, Mertis John Jr and Raymond John, who shared memories of Willie generously.

To the staff of the Azalia Hackley Music Library at the Detroit Public Library's main branch, which is a great source of information on Willie John. Brian Powers, a librarian at the Cincinnati Public Library and King Records historian provided vital information and sources.

To radio friends David Washington of Pontiac, Michigan's WPON-AM, Pat St John of Sirius/XM Radio, Ann Delisi of Detroit Public Radio WDET-FM and Harvey Holiday of Philadelphia's WOGL.com, who talked up Willie's story, played his music and helped with sources.

Thank you to Stephen Hawkins of King/Gusto Records, who dug into the King archives for photos. To author and musician Kim Field, who wrote the 1990 *Village Voice* article on Willie's trial, shed light on various aspects of the incident in Seattle, and was kind enough to take a photo of the house in Seattle.

Arthur Swanson, the Seattle prosecutor who tried the case against Willie. Art has had many years to ponder Willie's case, and his thoughtful, compassionate take on his troubles were profoundly helpful.

Thank you to Willie's friends B.B. King, Clineice and Levi Stubbs, Jerry Butler, Sam and Joyce Moore, Norman Thrasher, Lou Deveraux, Jimmy and Jeanie Scott, Clarence Avant, Sir Mack Rice, who all shared their stories. To George Benson, who called all the way from New Zealand on the night of a concert, just to talk about Willie. To Grady Gaines, Charles Connor and Milton Hopkins, the surviving Upsetters, who are all great storytellers, and were generous with their time (and in Grady's case with their photos).

Thank you to Allan Slutsky, Steve Shepard and Cathy John, who read an early draft and gave useful suggestions, and Tom Nanzig, who helped unearth vintage newspaper stories. To Susan's *Detroit News* editors Rita Holt and Felecia Henderson for their patience, and to Bob Kelly of Titan Books, who allowed access to his wonderful cache of Willie posters and ephemera. To Dave Marsh for his usual acerbic kindness and advice, and to Susan's family, the Whitall/Witherow clan, who were supportive as always. Thanks to agent David Dunton, who got it from the start, and to editors Katy Wild, Lizzie Bennett and Nadine Monem, who smoothed the way to publication.

—Susan Whitall and Kevin John

AVAILABLE NOW

MATT MONRO: THE SINGER'S SINGER
by Michele Monro

The story of one of Britain's most iconic singers, following Matt Monro's life from his poverty-stricken upbringing in war-torn Britain to his steady rise to fame that saw the singer battling the highs and lows of the entertainment industry to become one of Britain's best-loved entertainers.

Including never-before-seen photography, exclusive correspondence between Matt and some of the biggest names in the music business and a rich array of personal anecdotes, this is the first comprehensive look at the life of the man his peers dubbed 'the Singer's Singer', the irreplaceable Matt Monro.

ISBN: 9781848566187

Paperback edition coming soon

AVAILABLE NOW

BOB MARLEY AND THE GOLDEN AGE OF REGGAE

1975–1976 THE PHOTOGRAPHS OF KIM GOTTLIEB-WALKER

During 1975 and 1976, renowned underground photographer Kim Gottlieb, and her husband, Island's publicity head Jeff Walker, documented what is now widely recognized as the Golden Age of reggae. Over two years of historic trips to Jamaica and exclusive meetings in Los Angeles, Kim took iconic photographs of the artists who would go on to define the genre and captivate a generation, including Peter Tosh, Bunny Wailer, Toots Hibbert, and, of course, Bob Marley himself.

Kim's photographs include never-before-seen performance shots, candid behind-the-scenes footage of Bob's home in Jamaica, and exclusive records of key moments in reggae history. With a foreword by acclaimed rock journalist and director Cameron Crowe.

ISBN: 9781848566187

AVAILABLE NOW

THE COMPLETE DUSTY SPRINGFIELD

Foreword by Petula Clark

Drawing on meticulous archive research and interviews with Dusty's friend
and collaborators, this book details every song in Dusty's entire catalogue. This
revised edition includes new chapters on the Lana Sisters and the Springfields,
expanded entries on Dusty's solo tracks and an in-depth analysis of Dusty's live
work for TV and radio.

ISBN: 9780857681409

COMING SOON

THE COMPLETE DAVID BOWIE

Critically acclaimed in its previous editions and now extensively revised, expanded and updated, The Complete David Bowie is widely recognized as a foremost source of analysis and information on every facet of Bowie's career. The A-Z of songs and the day-by-day dateline are the most complete ever published. From the 11-year-old's skiffle performance at the 18th Bromley Scouts' Summer Camp in 1958, to the 62-year-old's cameo appearance in Bandslam in 2009 and beyond, *The Complete David Bowie* discusses and dissects every last move in the rock star's most fascinating career.

ISBN: 9780857682901

Coming Soon from Titan Books

The Beatles on Television (New Edition)
ISBN: 9780857685711

Bob Dylan: Alias Anything You Please
ISBN: 9780857685568

The Complete Abba (40th Anniversary Edition)
ISBN: 9780857687241

The Complete Kylie (25th Anniversary Edition)
ISBN: 9780857687258

Dave Grohl: Nothing to Lose (4th Edition)
ISBN: 9780857685971

I Was A Teenage Sex Pistol
ISBN: 9780857687463

The Jimi Hendrix Experience
ISBN: 9780857685551

The Kings of Leon: Sex on Fire (New Edition)
ISBN: 9780857687173

Led Zeppelin
ISBN: 9780857685964

Panic on the Streets: The Smiths and Morrissey Location Guide
ISBN: 9780857685773

Pink Floyd (New Edition)
ISBN: 9780857686640

Queen: The Complete Works
ISBN: 9780857685513

The Who
ISBN: 9780857686633